Development in Practice Readers

Series Editor : Deborah Eade

Development with Women

Introduced by

Dorienne Rowan-Campbell

RAWAT PUBLICATIONS

Jaipur • New Delhi • Bangalore • Mumbai

ISBN 81-7033-948-0

Indian Reprint, 2006

Published by
Prem Rawat for **Rawat Publications**
Satyam Apts., Sector 3, Jawahar Nagar, Jaipur - 302 004 (India)
Phone: 0141 265 1748 / 7006 Fax: 0141 265 1748
E-mail : info@rawatbooks.com
Website: rawatbooks.com

Delhi Office
4858/24, Ansari Road, Daryaganj, New Delhi 110 002
Phone: 011-23263290

Printed at Chaman Enterprises, New Delhi

Contents

Preface

Deborah Eade

It has long been argued by various UN agencies that the critical determinant of women's socioeconomic status is education, and that 'education, education, and more education' (as UK Prime Minister Tony Blair put it) is the key to achieving social development by improving the wellbeing of girls and women and thus promoting gender equity.[1] The statistical link between high female educational levels and a reduction in female fertility has also served to bring on board those aid agencies for whom gender justice is not a necessary goal in itself. However, the fact that twice as many women as men in the world would be unable to read a simple newspaper article demonstrates that for many millions of girls the right to education — and to 'free universal primary education' as enshrined in the Universal Declaration of Human Rights (UDHR) — is a long way from realisation.

Even if all girls and boys did have an equal chance of going to school, criticisms of the formal education system abound and are most trenchantly expressed in the work of the late Brazilian educationalist, Paulo Freire. Leaving aside questions about universal access, and about the quality of formal education and its questionable links with upward social mobility, it is important to go beyond simple headcounts and ask what factors most influence children's academic performance; and how far educational opportunities for girls actually translate into well-paid, satisfying jobs and a more rewarding and fulfilling adult life.

The experience of the industrialised countries, where formal education is compulsory for 10 years and a high percentage of students remain in full-time education for 15 to 20 years, has some useful lessons to offer; lessons that are highly relevant to social activists and organisations in a wider range of fields, who want to articulate a vision of development that is truly shaped by those whom the prevailing paradigm ignores, oppresses, exploits, or marginalises. Given that most people living in poverty are women and girls, this is necessarily a vision of development which places feminism at its core.

In the late 1970s, feminist educationalists in the UK were focusing attention on whether mixed or single-sex schooling better served girls' interests. Of particular concern at the time was the drop-off in girls' educational performance at secondary school, particularly in mathematics and the sciences. By then, it was no longer acceptable simply to attribute this to 'biology' (the argument that girls reach intellectual maturity sooner than boys, but that boys then overtake them in adolescence since men are, by nature, intellectually superior to women) ; other causes had to be identified. Sex-differentiated data on educational attainment were then scarce, and an understanding of gender as a social category had not yet passed into popular consciousness, far less into attitudes of the formal establishment.[2] A great deal of pioneering work was to be done in order to challenge the conventional view that since society is made up of two complementary sexes, schools should reflect this, irrespective of the fact that girls' academic performance at single-sex schools was consistently higher than at mixed schools, while the opposite held for boys.[3]

The period saw numerous reviews of educational materials which revealed that the degree of sexism (and, indeed, racism and class discrimination) in textbooks on every subject, from infant school to university, was even more marked than in the real world (Spender 1982:61). Empirical research linked the differentiated performance of girls and boys to the sex and, more critically, to the attitudes of their teachers — boys did better in the science subjects that were traditionally taught by men, though girls performed just as well in these subjects if they were taught by women or in an all-female environment. In the context of this Reader, however, some of the most interesting studies concern the practices and perceptions of dedicated teachers (and the perceptions of their pupils) who wanted to practise gender-fairness in the classroom. Dale Spender of the Institute of Education at London University, for instance, tape-recorded a large number of her own and others' classes. She found that even when the teachers' explicit aim was to divide their time equally between male and female pupils, this was never achieved:

> At the end of the lesson I have felt that I managed to achieve that goal — sometimes I have even thought I have gone too far and have spent *more* time with the girls than the boys.

> But the tapes have proved otherwise. Out of ten taped lessons (in secondary school and college) the maximum time I spent interacting with girls was 42 per cent and on average 38 per cent, and the minimum time with boys 58 per cent. It is nothing short of a substantial shock to appreciate the discrepancy between what I *thought* I was doing and what I actually *was* doing. (Spender 1982:56, emphasis in original)

More telling still is the fact that the boys shared the same perceptions:

> 'She always asks the girls all the questions' said one boy in a classroom where 34 per cent of the teacher's time had been allocated to girls. 'She doesn't like boys and just listens to the girls' said another boy where boys had interacted with the teacher for 63 per cent of the time; and these are among some of the more 'polite' protests. (ibid.:57)

As Spender bleakly comments: 'Because we take it so much for granted that boys are more important and deserve more of our time and attention, giving the girls 35 per cent of our time can feel as though we are being unfair to the boys' (ibid.:56). In other words, schools reproduce the prevailing values of society more often than they challenge them. Some of the main mechanisms by which boys would command attention included collectively and individually engaging in unruly and disruptive behaviour whenever a girl was speaking, or whenever a 'girlish' ('sissy') subject was the topic of discussion. In this way, they would both set the agenda — football was a legitimate and serious topic, reproductive health was not — and force the girls (and the teacher) into silent compliance.

> The implication is that *both* male and female pupils experience the classroom as a place where boys are the focus of activity and attention — particularly in the forms of interaction which are initiated by the teacher — while girls are placed on the margins of classroom life. (Stanworth 1981:34)

This was found to affect how students rated their own ability and performance, with boys characteristically having inflated self-images *especially* in relation to girls, whereas the reverse was true of their female peers:

> In the 19 cases out of 24 where pupils' rankings were different from those of their teachers, all of the girls underestimated their rank; all but one of the boys overestimated theirs. Furthermore, two-thirds of these errors involve only classmates of the other sex — that is, girls down-grading themselves relative to boys, boys up-grading themselves relative to girls. (ibid.:40)

Clearly, in an all-female environment, girls would not be forced into either competing with boys on male terms (i.e. becoming a surrogate male) or being a negative reference group for boys (i.e. assuming a 'typical' feminine role). On the other hand, the chance for girls and boys to learn mutual respect, and to challenge damaging gender stereotypes, would be very much reduced. One proposed solution was to teach subjects associated with strong gender stereotypes in same-sex groups, but to have mixed classes in subjects that are perceived as more gender-neutral; in other words, to recognise that the power dynamics at play in mixed settings are generally disadvantageous to females and to be committed to dismantling these gender-based impediments. But this solution would require greater resources in the form of additional teachers, classrooms, administrative workload, and so on; resources that were seldom forthcoming as state schools have increasingly had to raise their own funds for books and other basics. The parallels with what Dorienne Rowan-Campbell describes in the context of individual development projects — in the allocation of funds, in programme design, in the articulation of policies, in setting development priorities, in agencies' organisational structures, in individual development workers' behaviour — are staring us in the face.

In so many situations, and in so many ways, however tenuous is women's grasp of rights that are supposedly universal, already this is felt to be too much — an 'imbalance' in the natural order of things, something to be redressed. Again, this is borne out in the context of current debates on education in the UK. While female representation in the upper echelons of most professions remains disproportionately low (and the percentage of women in low-paid, low-status, part-time or temporary jobs disproportionately high), girls' academic performance has been generally improving over the past ten to15 years across all disciplines, right through to university level. It is odd that, in a meritocratic society, men's actual and potential average earnings should continue to outpace women's by some 30 per cent. Still more remarkable, as girls' performance improves after centuries of enforced underachievement, protests are voiced about 'male social exclusion', and the spectre of 'maternal deprivation' rears its head once again as it did in the 1950s.[4] Rather than considering proposals to re-orient the education system better to meet the needs and potentials of *all* of tomorrow's citizens (which would mean a real transformation of the economic base of society, and thus a new division of work between the sexes, particularly in relation to the unpaid reproductive labour that women generally perform), the focus has been on compensatory investment in boys's schooling and on rectifying the 'unfair advantage' supposedly enjoyed by girls. Patriarchy, after all, sees women's empowerment in terms of winners and losers.

What does all this tell us about how we can achieve gender justice? First, it reinforces Dorienne Rowan-Campbell's argument that learning to work in and with mixed-sex groups does not mean that women and men don't also need to work in a same-sex environment on issues concerning gender identity; and that such environments can be a valuable way to develop a critical consensus. Within development organisations, this suggests that gender mainstreaming and gender specialisation are complementary, not mutually exclusive, strategies. Second, it emphasises that despite certain gains, women continue to be prevented from realising their full potential because of patriarchal structures and institutions which constrain them, and because of prejudices about their proper station in life. The essays in this Reader attest to the many ways — from psycho-social pressure to sheer brute force — in which women are told when they are transgressing the accepted norm. Third, it demonstrates that good intentions are not enough to make our own behaviour consistent with the goal of gender justice. Gender trainers, development professionals, social activists — in short, change agents — are highly motivated people. But, like the teachers who wanted to be gender-fair in their classrooms, there is often a large gap between what we as individuals and in agencies aim to do and genuinely believe we are doing, and what we are actually doing. We constantly need to seek critical feedback, and to collaborate with others in finding new ways to close the gap.

Working for gender equity, for development with women as well as with men, is not something that can be compartmentalised. It is not an issue one chooses to sign up for on one day but not on another; it cannot be divorced from political action. It has to be a way of life, and it cannot be done alone.

Notes

1 Oxfam International's education campaign falls squarely within this gender equity tradition, while also articulating an argument frequently advanced by UNICEF, namely that the single most important contribution to improving the life-chances of infants and children is to educate the girls who will become mothers. See <www.oxfam.org.uk> for details.

2 Ann Oakley's ground-breaking work *Sex, Gender and Society* was first published in 1972, and had been reprinted five times by 1980. However, it was not until her work on issues such as motherhood and housework began to appear in popular as well as academic form that her ideas gained widespread currency.

3 See R. R. Dale's influential three-volume work, *Mixed or Single-Sex School?*, London: Routledge, 1969; 1971; and 1974. He maintained that girls' depressed academic performance in mixed schools was of less importance than the 'social advantages' of being educated alongside boys — 'advantages' that would translate into lower status and lower-paid work opportunities in adult life.

4 In *Maternal Deprivation Reassessed*, Harmondsworth: Penguin Books, 1972, Michael Rutter argued against the blanket and ideologically motivated assumptions about what was then — and is still — viewed as the 'problem' of working mothers, and called instead for a focus on what, in any given circumstance, actually constituted 'bad' childcare.

References

Spender, Dale (1982) *Invisible Women: The Schooling Scandal*, London: Writers and Readers Publishing Cooperative.

Stanworth, Michelle (1981) *Gender and Schooling: A Study of Sexual Divisions in the Classroom*, London: Women's Research and Resources Centre Publications.

Development with women

Dorienne Rowan-Campbell

I would like to feel that when history counts the votes as to which of the 'isms' has had the most impact on twentieth century lives, feminism will be judged as the most important human movement. By feminism I mean that women's movement which speaks to the most profound yet basic of changes in the roles, the rights, and the relations which govern connections, commerce, and intimacy between women and men. This movement offers a vision of equality in society, equity in partnership, and freedom from gender stereotyping — freeing each person to pursue the roles best suited to their needs and talents. The movement has been dynamic because the struggle for change takes place not on the world's battlefields but at home and in the most intimate space, the human heart. Feminism has had the potential to touch every man, woman, and child because its basic tenets remain relevant whatever the conditions under which people live, regardless of the dictates of totalitarianism, globalism, communism, or capitalism, or whether they suffer racism, ageism, or sexism.

In the middle of this century the women's movement, largely quiescent in public consciousness since the Suffragettes, staged a comeback. In true twentieth-century style, feminism — North American and European feminism — became a media event. While coverage tended to emphasise radicalism, describing women as 'libbers' and thus perhaps alienating many women and men, there was an unprecedented exposure and level of public debate of feminist issues and concerns. This debate moved the matter of women's equality beyond domestic boundaries to the global stage; again at a remarkable level, inspiring the First World Conference for Women held in Mexico 1974. After four UN

World Conferences and one year devoted to women, the world seems to agree that women should have equality and equity and that gender issues are of some importance.

Why, then, are these changes that the world appears to agree are necessary so slow in coming? Why, all around the globe, are women still working longer hours and earning less than men? Why haven't laws which allow discrimination against women been changed and their implementation ensured? Why are so many women still illiterate? Why are so many women still chattels of their spouse and his family? Why is violence against women and children, particularly young girls, so prevalent? The third millennium approaches, yet practitioners still struggle to bring to development work a consciousness of gender issues that will change lives — and hearts — and bring about a world where women and men equally determine how to enhance their own lives and their communities and societies.

Sadly, history is likely to judge that although feminism had the potential for tremendous reach, its scope was never fully realised in the twentieth century. Perhaps we are still too close to judge accurately either our shortcomings or our successes. This essay reflects on the segregation and isolation which confront those who seek to breach the ramparts of male hegemony and bring down the walls of gender inequality. It examines the strategies of the women's movement as applied to development work with women (primarily gender training and mainstreaming) and assesses the barriers to change which have been erected to counter its challenge to patriarchy. It also looks forward to some of the areas of positive change, and to the urgent need to anchor these early in the next millennium.

Male hegemony corrupts development initiatives which are designed to make a positive difference in women's lives and, by extension, the lives of their families and their men. This is especially visible in the way development has been directed towards and channelled through women, particularly with the concept of income generation, in the handling of violence against women and domestic violence, and in the question of participatory approaches for sustainable development. Particularly disheartening is the manner in which men tend to avoid attending to or participating in discussion of issues that relate primarily to the concerns of women. Development with women has therefore largely been development for women by women with women; and therein lies some of the seeds of its under-achievement.

The Adinkra symbol Sankofa, a stylised bird moving forward yet ever looking backward, reminds us that it is impossible to understand the present without being aware of and understanding the past. To understand the present situation let us glance over our shoulders at the end of the seventeenth century in Europe, when the structures of male dominance begin to be institutionalised and gender discrimination codified. We then need to consider the emergence of the international development enterprise and, lastly, the role and impact of global corporations.

Sankofa

'Nature', wrote Dr Samuel Johnson, 'has given women so much power that the law has very wisely given them little'. His aphorism might be said to sum up the thinking of his age.

> [D]uring the seventeenth and eighteenth centuries western society began to find solutions to the problems of organisation brought by the changes that occurred in technology, agriculture, industry, commerce.... Discrimination against women as opposed to prejudice against women and injustice dealt women by particular legal practices became part of the new structures that emerged, and as these new structures emerged and as they affected the lives of more and more people in more an more ways, so discrimination against women became more and more widespread, more and more accepted and more and more difficult to combat... The late eighteenth century and early nineteenth century see the construction of a particular culture through western society, and this results in new and particularly damaging levels of discrimination against women. (Griffiths 1976:99)

Gender discrimination thus became codified and accepted as justified. Women slowly became minors too incompetent to manage their own finances; they lost their medieval rights to work as *femmes soles* (Clark 1968). This happened at a point in history which was to have a dramatic impact on the countries now called 'developing'.

The seventeenth and eighteenth century European societies began the transformation from agrarian to industrialised economies,which changed the nature of work. It became a separate activity, moved from the home into a defined 'workplace'. As this occurred, the familial relationships which had hitherto existed between apprentice, journeyman, and master or mistress and servant, began to erode. A distinction began to be drawn between domestic and economic functions (Griffiths 1976), and more and more the male shouldered the economic functions, while the female remained to deal with the domestic. These values, attitudes, and institutions were transferred to other societies through the colonisation process, which lasted into the twentieth century. All colonial powers took with them and applied to their colonial holdings that western model of organisation which overtly discriminated against women.

Examples abound of the collision and collusion between the existing gender prejudices and discrimination and those imposed by the colonial powers. Barbara Rogers (1980) has noted how the colonial structures deprived women in Africa of their usufructural rights, in much the same way as the Enclosure Acts in Europe deprived the peasantry of access to village commons. This separated women from access to and control over their means of production.

A more basic separation also occurred: the isolation of groups of women from that greater 'community' of women. Colonial structures used class and race to separate women from each other. By placing strictures on association across race and class lines, colonial rule enforced distances between mistress and servant, between merchant's wife and soldier's wife, between locals and expatriates. Women who shared a common condition and experience could not join together to explore the possibility of fighting for change. Further, under the guise of being protected by men, women in fact were used to maintain male hegemony. And maintain it they did: not only by failing to challenge inequality or sustaining male privilege through their supportive reproductive role, but also by making colonialism economically viable. Catherine Hall documents the vast sums of money invested in colonial ventures which men gained access to through middle-class marriage as a wife's property became the property of the husband upon marriage, to do with as he wished [Hall 1996].

Developing countries internalised colonial norms of sex discrimination and for the most part situated them as the proper order of things as they became independent of the coloniser. Layered above this remained whatever local traditional forms of prejudice had already existed. Traditional expressions of female power and authority had already virtually vanished.

The next wave of support for male domination came in the form of the 'missionaries'. Both the religious and the development missionaries carried with them clear ideas about the role and status of women and, consciously or not, applied these tenets in their work. International development emerged as a discipline and industry of its own, and many caring, well-meaning, and committed workers nonetheless conveyed their version of what it was appropriate for women to do, and a vision of what 'developed' women should be like, without any reference to the women themselves and their local situation.

Directions in development thinking and practice are branded as much by personalities and prejudices as by concepts and ideals. USAID, in analysing their staff complement over time, discovered that the early aid workers were overwhelmingly from the southern US states. It emerged that development work, although not highly paid, was attractive to southerners who earned less than their counterparts in the north. Analysis also revealed that most of these southerners were male, white, and had less education and experience than those recruited from the northern states.[1] One might question their impact on how development was delivered. Given that they had been brought up in a society that openly articulated disparaging views on the relationship between race, sex, and intellectual capacity, how effectively were they able to interact with people from the 'developing' world? What were their expectations of the potential of non-white races and of women to benefit from development opportunities? It is clear that the 'who' of development — the people and personalities involved — is as important as the work carried out, and just as critical as the 'why' — the principles that guide it.

Both women and men, even those who volunteered to work in far-off countries in order to share their fortune of birth and education, still carried with them embedded prejudices about the role and place of women. In the early days of voluntarism through CUSO (Canadian University Service Overseas), VSO (Voluntary Service Overseas, part of the British government's volunteer programme), and the US Peace Corps, there is no indication that the issue of non-discriminatory development with women was discussed even in preliminary briefing and orientation. Volunteers carried the meaning if not the overt message of discrimination; most failed to challenge existing bias and stereotypes.

Although many attempts at change are being introduced, most development organisations, even NGOs, are still rather patriarchal structures. The scale of hierarchical intensity increases from NGO through bilateral to multilateral agencies, rising to an apex in the World Bank and the IMF. Correspondence from the World Bank's external gender consultative group reveals the slow rate of response to issues raised by them; the IMF appears to be entirely silent on gender issues:

> Men are aware, although they may not think about this consciously, that everything lies in appearance, and so will fight for appearances and forget or ignore realities. ... This situation is endemic in all patriarchal institutions. (French 1985: 305)

Development organisations have become adept at dealing with women in development and gender issues. In this Reader, Sara Longwe shares with us the insights gained from her repeated visits to Snowdida about the blocking strategies employed to prevent gender policies or actions which might facilitate women's empowerment. The current set of strategies is borrowed from the management ethos of global corporations: true to a concern for appearance, these involve maximising political correctness, going through the right motions, the right pronouncements, and then returning to 'business as usual' in the certainty that little will dislocate corporate reality.

Gender and diversity training and the management of change are a growth industry with consultants invited to perform in many major companies as well as in development agencies. The failure of diversity training to change, for example, the racist and sexist reward structure exposed in a legal suit brought by employees of Texaco Corporation in the USA — a company with apparently open and affirmative recruitment and promotion policies — raises questions as to whether such training was really ever intended to change attitudes.

An examination of the way in which gender training is applied in development organisations would raise similar questions. There are always some staff who are committed, interested and who want to see change. Many attend because cognisance of gender issues is said to be a required work skill to be employed routinely. Development agencies and the UN have made a large investment in training. Most organisations, however — and there are exceptions — fail to follow up the training by developing structures which require accountability on gender issues. There are few penalties for failing to undertake a gender impact assessment, for failing to identify gender issues in log-frame analysis, or for failing, during the planning process, to include indicators through which action on relevant gender issues might be evaluated. In this regard, the attitude of the development sector differs little from that of major corporations.

A 1990 poll of chief executive officers (CEOs) from Fortune 1000 companies revealed that '80 per cent acknowledged that sex discrimination impedes female employees progress but less than 1 per cent regarded remedying sex discrimination as a goal their personnel department should pursue' (Faludi 1991:xiii). Many of these companies are multinationals which export these same attitudes and the values that underpin them in influencing business, government, and the labour force in the developing countries where they operate. Many multinationals operate in free trade or protected zones where work billed as opportunities for women, who represent the majority of their employees, oppresses them in conditions as much to be deplored as those in the early days of Europe's industrial revolution. The women have little option but to take the work offered on the terms offered. With the economic downturn in Asia, young women and job-seeking immigrants face a different challenge, a labour market 'fast degenerating into a sea of lawlessness and corruption. Inhumane sweatshops, people-smuggling scams, forced prostitution and indentured servitude are fast becoming the new emblems of Asia's hard times'. (*Newsweek* 1998)

There have recently been exposés in the USA of large multinational garment producers who exploit the US immigrant population in factories which equal the appalling work conditions hitherto prevalent in developing countries. These corporations thus continue their exploitation of unskilled and semi-skilled female labour. They do so without a concern for developing promotion and career opportunities for capable women, all the while maintaining a veneer of solicitude for those affected by sex and gender discrimination. The values espoused by these global corporations set a standard — a minimum standard — for attention to gender concerns by appearing to act on the management of change as if gender issues mattered, while in fact doing little to affect the status quo. Their political correctness seems to have inspired many followers in the development world: corporate image is becoming more important than corporate reality.

Effects in the field

Participatory methods

Male resistance and continued male hegemony affect the way that practitioners who work with women can implement development options. A body of learning and literature on participatory methods has evolved from the experience of working with women's groups, of rotating leadership responsibilities, of sharing skills, information and knowledge, and of cooperative activities.

Female work and management styles are often characterised as being highly participatory, complementary, and cooperative, styles until quite recently discounted in the management literature. In fact, men are generally not encouraged to adopt participatory approaches to work, management, or relationships. What patriarchal institutions tolerate, expect, and reward is 'different forms of obedience' — such as conformity and uniformity — all inspired and maintained by fear (French 1985:308-315). It should therefore not be surprising that while participatory development is widely accepted as a concept, it exists only minimally in development practice, both in fieldwork and in the institutional arrangements of development agencies. A few organisations such as Proshika in Bangladesh strive to make their programmes highly participatory and gender-balanced but for most, participation seems to be viewed as the 'soft side' of development which takes too much time to initiate relative to the outcomes. When agencies do take this path there are often problems. All too often the methodology 'silences spontaneous demands and elicits, at least, a re-packaging within the vocabulary of participation' (Jackson, in Eade 1997).

The UN family appeared to place a high value on NGO collaboration and participation in the debates and international conferences of the 1990s. Yet recently, the very NGOs which had contributed so effectively at UNCED in Rio, Cairo, Copenhagen, and Beijing, and created such a close partnership with the UN agencies, found themselves exiled from any real participation at the follow-up to the International Conference on Population and Development ('Cairo Plus Five') at the UN General Assembly. Further, a number of countries, including the Vatican, sought to renegotiate the gender-aware language and empowering statements on reproductive rights that represented a break-through for the women's movement when they were agreed in Cairo. With Copenhagen and the 'Beijing Plus Five' assessment meetings scheduled for the year 2000, NGOs are noticeably concerned at this *volte face*.[2]

If participation is associated with female ways of operating, is it perhaps this element of the feminine that agencies find so difficult to accommodate? True participation, after all, involves the development agent voluntarily giving up power over design, direction, and priorities and sharing accountability for project outcomes or, in the case of the UN, for conference outcomes and directions.

A further impediment to the wider introduction of participatory development approaches lies in the current operational structures of multi- and bilateral development agencies. More and more agencies are hiring consultants to do the work of development thinking and implementation for them. Agency staff now function as development managers; costing, accountability, and results are the bottom line. Although they espouse the language of participation, these managers often find participatory development very difficult to deal with. The executing agencies and the consultants link directly with the field, but the agency managers operate from a distance, their development experience mediated by the consultants. If a project is truly participatory, the agency manager responsible for it loses even more control, because decisions and activities are now legitimately field-driven and the outcomes, management structures, and timing that had been conceived of for the project might all be overturned by a people-based plan.

Income generation

While development strategies have sought to bolster women's economic opportunities they have long addressed the question in a unique way. The answer, it appeared, lay in income generation. Income generation is the feminised diminutive of employment in much the same way as occupations are named to diminish the role women play when they perform them: there are shepherds and shepherdesses, stewards and stewardesses; men are chefs, but women are cooks.

The thinking behind income generation indicates that project planners situate women in their domestic setting and identify earnings as allied to this role. While this might have been an appropriate entry strategy to counteract male resistance to women's self-actualisation through independent earnings, women never seem to graduate from these programmes. Still on offer from the 1950s to the end of the century are kitchen gardens, sewing, embroidery, chicken rearing... it is rather like developing an educational programme which for ever traps adults in kindergarten. Even where new avenues for earning are identified, such as the owning and running of restaurants in Bangladesh (see Mahmuda Rahman Khan's essay in this Reader), the close association with women's traditional, accepted household roles feeds the stereotype of what women can and should do, and as such may be limiting. These projects must be as much about finding sustainable solutions to employment as they are about women's empowerment, and about changing society's acceptance of a narrow set of roles for women. In their current form, income-generation projects may restrict women by giving them very limited access to economic opportunities, few possibilities for growth, and little choice. It is perhaps not unexpected that there are many reports, repeated across cultures, of instances where income generation is taken over by men once it does become real economic activity. The money and ideas are stolen, and the women left to limp along as before.

Violence

One of the concerns that unites women all over the world is violence. Women have lived with male violence against them for centuries and turned it in on themselves, blaming themselves for its occurrence, wounded and ashamed. Raising the issue in public debate was seen as so politically charged that the first two World Conferences for Women dealt with the issue under the heading 'Peace': peace in the home. This allowed for rhetoric but not for real change. Over the years the accumulation of research and the testimony of an ever-increasing number of support groups, crisis centres, and shelters have made the personal public, and laid the shameful open. Yet this does not appear to have caused the problem to diminish. Whether the new openness menas that more violent crimes against women are reported, or whether there is an actual increase, the extent of the violence is numbing. Early strategies that suggested that women's autonomy would lead to a decrease in violence against women are called into question. Policies of 'zero tolerance', which do exist in some countries, have supported women, and have led to men being jailed, but have not yet brought about a change in society's tolerance of this abuse.

Violence against women is a critical tool in the maintenance of male hegemony; it is the means by which the patriarchal requirements of conformity and obedience are extended to women and enforced. In hierarchies, men may obey through fear of losing jobs, status, or power; women are made to fear violence. As violence is inextricably linked with male hegemony, only ending that hegemony is going to reduce violence and persuade citizens that it is an issue for societal concern rather than an isolated private problem. It is also crucial to reduce women's complicity in the violence against them, by rejecting the socialisation which allows women to pretend that to be beaten is to be cared about, and the asymmetrical relations of power which require the bartering of self for money and protection. Most important, change will never happen without the partnership of men.

Re-examining approaches to participation, income generation, and reducing violence against women may hold a key to rethinking how to make development with women more productive, inclusive, and effective in the twenty-first century. These issues do not exist in a vacuum. They are part of the mix of approaches that practitioners have adopted in the past 50 years, and should be seen in the context of two of the most important strategies employed to enhance development with women: gender mainstreaming and gender training.

Mainstreaming and gender training

Mainstreaming refers to the systematic application of a gender-aware vision to corporate activities, government and agency policies, and to the introduction of routine management procedures to ensure implementation. Mainstreaming arose in response to the isolationist strategies which marginalised those responsible for women's concerns in government and agencies, compromising their capacity and reducing their reach. Mainstreaming poses a challenge to the operation of patriarchy, its intent being that women's perspectives, knowledge, capacity, and difference become part of the mainstream of development options and national life, thus changing both.

Analyses of gender mainstreaming in governments identify a number of barriers. Prime among them is a lack of understanding by policy makers of the strategy itself and of the role of focal units on gender issues. In the Caribbean in the early 1980s, the permanent secretaries responsible for women's focal units admitted that they did not have a very clear idea of their role, mission, capacity, or how they could be managed and supported. In preparation for Beijing 15 years later, the same questions were asked, and senior policy makers *still* did not understand the role of focal units or appreciate the need for mainstreaming. Zero progress?

Although mainstreaming is discussed in all development organisations, not enough effort has been made to ensure responsibility and accountability at several levels. Best practice suggests that a variety of change agents at numerous levels and with different roles both inside and outside the organisation are needed to anchor changes. Change agents at the executive level are critical to the introduction of change, but so too are those at the operational level who maintain the changes on a daily basis, giving life and expression to policy. Equally important are the outsiders, the consultants who work with the organisation bringing expertise and external validation to corporate efforts. In the case of change strategies such as gender mainstreaming, the media, researchers, writers, and the academic community, all keep the issues alive. Without this interaction between internal and external agents, and without a critical mass of staff who maintain change within the organisation, it is difficult for change to take root (Kantor 1983). Experience also shows that gender mainstreaming quickly becomes merely an activity, and one that is repetitive. An effort to mainstream is made, situations and personalities change, there is a hiatus, and the whole process begins again. Many of the organisations begin an attempt at mainstreaming with commitment from senior levels, and with the establishment of a small focal unit with responsibility for initiating the process. Little structure is put in place. Often the individuals designated as links to the units with responsibility are given this task in addition to whatever else they do, and most usually, they are women. Then directions change and gender issues become a second- or third-rank priority, and the focal unit is exposed as too weak to challenge this reduced commitment. Because the issues have belonged to a small group of people and because mainstreaming efforts have never been entrenched in the system, it is all too easy to derail gender initiatives or to cause them to under-perform. The system also reinforces the minimalist approach to gender mainstreaming by paying most of its gender consultants less than those who work in other fields.

Within the UN agencies, a new pattern has been emerging: that of rotating leadership on gender issues. Various agencies have taken the lead, then slipped back only to be succeeded by another. In this way, the system can always point to what is being done somewhere — preferably somewhere else. In the early 1990s, UNICEF took a lead with a strongly articulated policy and clear guidelines for action from its Board. A programme to support this was developed and gained fairly wide acceptance. Within three years, however, priorities shifted as leadership changed and gender issues were no longer on the front burner. UNDP has now taken up the mantle of leadership. It has strong policy mandates, financial allocation strategies to ensure mainstreaming, additional staff, and has issued statements about accountability and the need for closely monitoring the initiative.

One of the flaws of a mainstreaming strategy as it is currently employed is its almost exclusive focus on the structures of power and on changing institutions. What is left out is any attempt to influence the organisation's ideology and consistently challenge the ideology of patriarchy. It is the converse of the feminist movement which mainly challenged patriarchal ideology, rather than its structure. A more synergistic link between mainstreaming and gender training would deliver an emphasis on structural change and change in attitudes and ideology.

Gender training is the most powerful tool in the storehouse of change activities. It is only through training and sensitising both women and men that the personal can be made the political. But the training often has not gone as far as is required to truly anchor change, and it has not been used as effectively as it might be to address ideology. Too often, it is weighted towards achieving competence rather than commitment.

Further, although the lessons on best practice exist, practitioners still have difficulty in ensuring that gender training is tailored to current realities in each society, community, and situation. Every society has gender concerns which are immediate and important; the task is to identify them and to incorporate them into the syllabus design. The inability to apply lessons learned as widely as might be desired relates to who controls the organisations and the resources. Patriarchy is not likely to invest extensively in a medium directed at its own demise. Hence, much of the really creative and effective gender training is funded by small organisations which are less concerned about maintaining male hegemony. Many of them are in fact women's development organisations.

In the long term, gender training must move beyond sensitisation and awareness — not only towards developing competence and skills in recognising and dealing with gender issues in the workplace, but also towards transferring these skills to the personal level. The heart has been difficult to reach. Let me give an example. A high-level seminar on male gender roles in the family was going smoothly with little disagreement. A segment which dealt with television and its impact on children and on gender socialisation used an exercise in which all participants watched a music video. The men were asked to express their gut reactions to the video, and the women were asked to predict what the men would feel and say. When the groups' views were compared, there was anger. The men felt that the women demeaned them by making assumptions about what men think and react to; the women suspected that the men were being dishonest about their reactions and only expressing what they thought would be acceptable. The session ran an hour and a half over time, but offered both men and women an opportunity to express concerns, attitudes, and assumptions which they had not aired in the other sessions, moving the seminar a little way beyond political correctness.

The challenge for practitioners is to find creative and effective ways of revealing the attitudes held by both women and men and to create a safe arena for both expressing and addressing them. Most gender training in development organisations is actively discouraged from venturing into this field, the argument being that staff will be uncomfortable and that they really need skills and knowledge, not basic attitudinal change. If attitudes are to change, however, organisations need to open their doors to challenging and perhaps uncomfortable forms of gender training and sensitisation.

While making people aware of how gender affects their lives, their development programmes, the outcomes of their activities, is indeed important, the message and the medium often become confused. Too many programmes designated as gender training are almost entirely women-focused and do not reach male participants. A training colleague once confided that she had had a difficult time in Western Samoa where she was undertaking a gender training programme. She had looked at the situation of women and their inequality, which the men present did not receive well. At the time, Western Samoa had an extremely high incidence of young male suicide, largely attributed to changes in society in which young men no longer won their spurs through deeds of valour and found no satisfying alternative for self-realisation. By contrast, women had clear social roles which were less affected by changing lifestyles. In addition, women in the village were responsible for a clean environment, for pure water, and thus attracted the attention of the development agencies and became involved in small projects. An opportunity was missed. If the issue of male suicide had been part of the training programme, perhaps the males might have paid more attention.

Gender training and mainstreaming need to be linked in a more holistic way so that gender training is seen as capacity-building in its widest sense. It is not merely a short mandatory course; indeed, it becomes the primary tool for achieving mainstreaming, in the sense of an organisation's capacity to understand, analyse, and implement conditions that create a gender-friendly workplace — in itself a dismantling of male hegemony. Gender analysis and gender training should be addressing basic organisational and personal change. Gender training needs to become more process- and experience-oriented without losing the skill-based elements so necessary for project development and management. Mainstreaming should lead to a total change in workplace values, so that decisions are more widely shared, childcare and parent leave are important, families and relationships count, and respect for a diversity of voices and views is enshrined.

Subversive strategies

Perhaps the millennium is the moment to begin actively to subvert some of the strategies used against women's empowerment and to turn these in on themselves.

In the 1970s and beyond, many development agencies had an avoidance strategy for women and development issues. They hid behind excuses such as 'development deals with people, not with men or women' or 'we only look at people'. It is unlikely that there has been a gender training programme held where someone did not ask, 'what about development for men?' These concerns must be creatively acted upon.

Gender analysis has allowed us to examine the gendered realities of 'the people'. However, we need to revisit those statements and make certain that we are indeed looking at the human dimension, at the men and women behind the gender issues. Gender analysis lets us separate men and women in order to understand their concerns, but we must do more to reintegrate the two, in order to act positively on what we have understood. Despite the many men who now work on gender issues and the many mixed training teams, all too often the issues which affect women most specifically get picked out and dealt with; but men's roles, the asymmetry in power relations, and the patriarchy trap for men are little attended to. If this does not change, gender training will continue to argue the case for women and fail to engage men as partners, as change agents, and as converts. In practice, development with women will remain development without men, and it will be less effective because of it — a conundrum, as it is male hegemony which unpicks the gains made by women and challenges incursions into male privilege.

Why not begin to work with men's groups? Women found that working together as women, at least for a time, strengthened their capacity to understand and articulate their situation. Men need to be able to do the same. Establishing men's groups does not mean following the 'my mother failed me' school of male sensitivity or the construction of the male mystique, but a genuine search at the roots of male gender socialisation and a concern for liberation from patriarchy.

But first there is the question of establishing trust. The experience of the women's movement throughout the centuries and specifically in the past 30 years, demonstrates that the time of greatest danger to making gains is not when women have achieved full equality but when the possibility increases that they might do so (Faludi 1991). The past 15 years have demonstrated that men have been very wary of the changes made in women's lives in the 1960s, 1970s, and 1980s and that many of them have felt very angry about what they perceive as the usurpation of male privilege. Some gains must also have been made in the world of development with women, for there has also been a backlash in this arena. There are fewer funds available for gender issues and development with women; the preparations for the Fourth World Conference showed up a struggle to achieve consensus on aspects of the Beijing Platform for Action on language which had already been agreed in Nairobi in 1985, and a pulling back on issues such as reproductive rights and the language agreed in Cairo in 1994. The backlash is in part responsible for what UNICEF calls the gender 'fade-away', where policy statements and objectives include gender empowerment statements, but project activities contain little to challenge male dominance and facilitate women's empowerment. Women, despite making personal commitments to trust individual men, are distrustful of males in general, and are particularly concerned that partnership should not mean taking over.

In development practice, the most fertile area for building bridges of understanding between men and women is also the most difficult. Poor women and men share common, but distinct, problems as they attempt to claim their entitlements.[3] Women, for example, have difficulty claiming even direct entitlements such as control over their own body or gaining prestige and respect. Nonetheless, patriarchy severely disenfranchises poor men. It is only the illusion that male hegemony endows all males with power which successfully prevents many men from acknowledging the truth of their powerlessness.

The majority of the world's citizens are trapped in the morass of poverty. But the morass provides fertile ground for change. Robert Chambers (1983) identifies the resistance to change displayed by elites which destroys projects fighting poverty and programmes aiming at empowerment. Replace 'elites' with 'patriarchy' and the analysis fits the reality of both women and poor men. Despite the fact that the poor have so little, they are often unable to take chances on change strategies and/or invest in opportunities which might change their condition. Development interventions should focus more on fostering an understanding of common oppression and, informed by this awareness, shaping mutually beneficial approaches, activities, and interventions. These will continue to break down gendered prejudices and will eventually form the basis of healthier relationships between women and men. These approaches will have to be highly participatory, and concentrate on developing practical examples of the uses of power which focus on using 'power *to*' (where you situate yourself relative to other people, to issues, and to solutions), rather than 'power *over*' (where you situate other people). Building alliances between women and men has added benefits: elites have hitherto been able to isolate poor women from poor men, and to invalidate empowering activities in this way.

The above is not to suggest that men and women and poor women and men have never worked together. They have and they do. Unfortunately, in most cases their joining forces has been predicated upon the requirement that women put aside relational issues of relation, issues of gender inequality, 'until the battle against racism, for independence, for the revolution is won'. When the desired situation is achieved, men remained the power brokers, and women's role in the struggle and gender equality is forgotten. Movements that have been led by women, such as the Chipko movement in India, have been more inclusive.

Building trust means making space for men to work as partners, and making space is as difficult for women as it is for men. When the feminist movement challenged men to share in domestic chores and childcare, many women who did begin to share those areas of responsibility found that they had to school themselves to relinquish their 'space'. They found it uncomfortable; humans find it difficult to unlearn the habits of centuries. Part of the challenge about letting men in is to find the men who want to hear the message — and then giving up space to them to create a place where the togetherness can happen.

Many nodes of change already exist where there are men and women with an extraordinary commitment to break down gender barriers. In the Caribbean, the Centre for Gender and Development Studies at the University of the West Indies has been working in partnership with men to understand their gendered reality. A particular issue has been the high drop-out rate of young males from the education process, and a number of men's groups work with them. In India, *Sumedhas*, The Academy for the Human Context, runs fellowship programmes directed at human resource practitioners in industry and development. These examine the self within the family, in work organisations, and wider society. The group has a strong commitment to breaking down the areas of silence between women and men and building understanding and friendship between them.

The issue of domestic violence is a real point of entry for working with men. Traumatic events can become cathartic and stimulate action. On 6 December 1989, a man shot and killed 14 women engineering students, because they were 'a bunch of feminists'. This horrific crime galvanised men all over Canada to act against violence. Their continuing commitment to changing society has developed into a wide network bound together by the White Ribbon Campaign. The anniversary of the massacre is Canada's National Day of Remembrance and Action on Violence Against Women. Countries in the North and South are developing their own White Ribbon campaigns, and there are also US chapters. White Ribbon seeks to build awareness among men of the issues of violence in the society and of the need for them to make conscious commitments to stamp this out. Some groups have been working in support of feminists by trying to overcome male resistance to feminist messages. Several of the groups have developed anti-violence sensitisation programmes, particularly targeting young men. These groups support the work of women's crisis and counselling centres and shelters. In the words of one of them:

> All this leads into the very rich territory of supporting men to deal with the pain and power in their lives (the personal and the political). Our work is to invite men to explore the middle path of the healthy and assertive expression of feelings and the healthy choices that can go along with that. My philosophy on men and accountability works on the belief that all men, myself included, have three choices: 1) be violent, sexist and abuse power and control; 2) remain silent while it happens around us; or 3) speak out, connect with other men and work as allies with women for positive change and social justice.[4]

All over the globe there are men who, witnessing violence against women they care about, become activists for change (the websites of some of these organisations are listed in endnote 4).

One of the problems development fieldworkers face in confronting violence against women is their need to validate their own presence in the community, and their fear that to intervene would compromise the effectiveness of their work. These same workers, however, try to change a number of other practices and attitudes that are equally sensitive. In Bangladesh, for instance, BRAC decided to challenge the practice of dowry. All fieldworkers knew that this was part of their role, they knew the issues and the arguments. Interestingly, few organisations take such a determined approach to wife-beating.

Although organisations may say that violence against women is an important issue for them, their lack of concrete interventions suggests to the people they serve that in fact they condone it. Development workers need skills to introduce interventions which are necessary, appropriate, and safe; interventions which do not assign blame but open up issues for discussion. Training is needed to upgrade negotiation and processing skills, and development workers need examples of how to intervene without demeaning the abuser and making the situation even more difficult for the woman. North-South and South-South linkages with the men who work on this issue would help to build this capacity in the field.

Male hegemony can only be dismantled and eroded by working with men; it has to implode from within. Women can not do it alone. Perhaps the most important act of subversion, the most important aspect of turning the inside out, is the issue of power. Instead of being concerned with the literature that bemoans women's fear of power and competition, women need to reclaim the types of power with which they *are* comfortable.

'Nature has made women so powerful' ... What power is this? It is a positive, rather than a negative use of power. Power *to* rather than power *over*; power to create, power to nurture, to share, to change a world. The power *to* can undermine power *over* if enough people are committed to making that change. Mahatma Gandhi taught the effectiveness of the use of non-violence. Choosing not to confront, not to abuse, not to fight back is one means of using power *to*. Sharing this power with enough men will begin to disrupt male hegemony.

What is at issue is not an abstract measure of the words 'equality' or 'equity', but the construction of a climate of mutual respect and value between women and men. Essentially, what the feminist movement has been trying to achieve is not a label of equality stamped onto every man and woman, but individual and social acceptance, respect, a deep awareness of the humanity of both sexes, and an equal valuing of men and women, different as they may be. As an ideology, feminism is not exclusive of men, as patriarchy is of women. Its values support the creation of an alternative moral universe, one which is not focused on power and control, or on the accumulation of the material at the expense of human or environmental systems. It allows for sustainability and mutuality and for choices. It offers a vision for the future which should encourage men to want to strike off the shackles of male hegemony all by themselves.

One of the unifying threads which informs women's experience is the consciousness that women's movements have existed throughout history. Like Penelope of old, women have used subterfuge to preserve 'spaces' for themselves within patriarchal systems. In ancient Greek mythology, Penelope achieved this: she distanced herself from her predatory suitors by weaving a burial cloth for her husband Ulysses, whose return she awaited, and then unpicking at night what she had woven during the day. Like her, the women's movement across the centuries has been kept alive by maintaining and subverting processes, by weaving and unpicking, by changing and undoing, by (outward) compliance and by subterfuge. In the twenty-first century, the lessons of all those ripped seams and broken tapestries need to be pulled together and woven into a new cloth.

Notes

1 Interview with Gloria Scott, first Advisor on Women and Development, World Bank.

2 Special sessions of the General Assembly will focus on the follow-up to recent conferences: the Fourth World Conference on Women (2000); the World Summit for Social Development (2000); the second UN Conference on Human Settlements (2001); and the World Summit for Children (2001).

3 After Amaryta Sen's work on 'entitlements'.

4 Personal communication from Peter Davison, Men for Change, Halifax, Nova Scotia. Other websites on men's networks include <www.conscoop.ottawa.on.ca/mensnet/>; <www.chebucto.ns.ca/CommunitySupport/Men4Change/m4c_back.html>; and <www.whiteribbon.ca>

References

Chambers, Robert (1983) *Rural Development: Putting the Last First*, London: IT Publications.

Clark, Alice (1968) *Working Life of Woman in the Seventeenth Century*, New York: A.M.Kelley (originally published in 1919).

Faludi, Susan (1991) *Backlash: The Undeclared War Against American Women*, New York: Crown Publishers Inc.

Eade, Deborah (ed.) (1997) *Development and Patronage*, Oxford: Oxfam.

Griffiths, Naomi (1976) *Penelope's Web*, Toronto: OUP.

French, Marilyn (1985) *Beyond Power: On Women, Men and Morals*, New York: Summit Books.

Hall, Catherine (1996) *Another Poor Cow*, London: Minerva Press.

Jackson, Cecile (1997) 'Sustainable development at the sharp end' in Eade (ed.) (1997).

Kantor, Rosabeth Moss (1983) *The Change Masters, Innovation and Entrepreneurship in the American Corporation*, New York: Touchstone (Simon and Schuster).

Newsweek, 'The market for misery', 3 August 1998.

Rogers, Barbara (1980) *The Domestication of Women: Discrimination in Developing Societies*, London: Tavistock.

■ **Dorienne Rowan-Campbell** *is a citizen of both Jamaica and Canada. For several years, she was responsible for establishing and taking forward the Women and Development Programme at the Commonwealth Secretariat, and later instituted what became the Centre for Gender and Development at the University of the West Indies (UWI). She was a founding member of the Canadian Research Institute for the Advancement of Women, the Ottawa Immigration Service Centre, Inter Pares, and MATCH (a feminist development agency). Now working independently, Dorienne Rowan-Campbell is a research associate at the Institute of Social and Economic Research at UWI, an associate fellow of the Institute of Development Studies (IDS) at Sussex, and a board member of the Global Fund for Women. She is actively involved in promoting organic Blue Mountain coffee, one of Jamaica's premier exports.*

Targeting women or transforming institutions? Policy from NGO anti-poverty efforts

Naila Kabeer

The case for gender-awareness in anti-poverty programmes

The incorporation of a gender-based perspective into research on development issues has established the significance of gender as a central dimension of poverty (Agarwal 1990; Kabeer 1994). There is persuasive evidence to show that women are disproportionately represented among the poorer sections of the world's population, and that households maintained by women tend on balance to be poorer than households whose primary breadwinner is male (see for instance, Buvinic 1983; Bruce and Lloyd 1992). There is also evidence which suggests that women are making up an increasing proportion of the poor, and this is leading to a 'feminisation of poverty'. Thus a major report by the International Fund for Agricultural Development (IFAD) on rural poverty (still accounting for the major share of the world's poor) points out that

> The total number of rural women living below the poverty line in developing countries was estimated in 1988 to be 564 million. This represented an increase of 47% above the numbers in 1965-70, as compared with 30% for rural men below the poverty line. (Jazairy et al., 1992:273).

While the changing distribution of poverty is often an aspect of broader events and processes — natural disaster, wars, depletion of environmental resources, or unjust macro-economic policies — it is always mediated by the institutionalised structures of rules, norms, entitlements, and practices which shape individual access to and control over resources within given societies. The gender-related dimension of poverty arises from a combination of interlocking systems of disadvantage embedded in these various social institutions.

Disadvantage in the private and public domains

Research on intra-household relations has revealed the asymmetrical distribution of resources and responsibilities embedded in domestic norms, and pointed to its implications for men and women's access to broader marketbased opportunities (Standing 1991; Bruce and Dwyer, 1988; Palmer, 1977). Other research has explored the extent to which market-based institutions are themselves sites of gender-based discrimination, so that women tend to be less successful than men in translating their labour and education into command over income and purchasing power (Beneria and Roldan 1987; Humphrey 1987; Appleton et al. 1990; Amsden 1980). Unfair advantages for men within domestic and market institutions interact with inequalities created by class relations, to ensure that women in poverty are generally among the most disenfranchised sections of society. At the same time, these institutions do not lend themselves easily to attempts to alter their internal dynamics in the interests of equalising the positions of women and men. Thus, whole households are frequently targeted as the front-line implementing agencies in a range of schemes that aim to increase productivity and reduce poverty. Most policy-makers are reluctant to be seen to be intervening directly in intra-household norms and relations: the 'private' domain. In as much as market-based institutions belong in the public domain, they may be seen as more acceptable sites for public intervention. But here again there is reluctance in many quarters to interfere with market forces, for fear of distorting price signals and the achievement of efficient allocation of resources.

It is therefore primarily through the efforts of the State, as well as formal and informal organisations within the community, that anti-poverty schemes are formulated and implemented. Within these, attention to women's needs has not always been a priority or even a consideration. Early efforts tended to be formulated for broad generic categories of people: the community, the poor, the landless. The possibility that women — and children — within these categories might not benefit equally with men from these efforts was rarely considered. However, with the advance of a Women in Development (WID) constituency within the development community, these neglected questions began to be explored. A two-fold case was made for the specific targeting of women: that women were among the poorest of the poor; and that resources in the hands of women were more likely to be shared fairly within the household than those in men's hands (Bruce and Dwyer 1988; Buvinic 1983; Palmer 1977).

'Women's projects' and integrated projects

Initially this new awareness was translated into policy in the form of income-generating projects for women. However, a decade of experience has shown that women-specific projects will do little to challenge the marginal place assigned to women within development as long as the norms, practices, and procedures which guide the overall development effort remain fundamentally unchanged. Instead, women-only income-generating activities serve to perpetuate a form of segregation within development polices, with productivity-related efforts targeted at men, and welfare-related efforts targeted at women (Rogers 1980; Buvinic 1986). The labelling of certain projects as 'women's projects' has also given women as a category an exaggerated visibility in the policy rhetoric, one that is not matched by the actual share of development budgets invested in such projects. The absence of the corresponding label of 'men's projects' disguises the fact that by far the largest proportion of development resources continues to be invested in schemes which directly benefit men. While women may — or may not — receive indirect benefits from such schemes, the fact remains that these schemes are generally drawn up without any consideration of the existing gender-based division of tasks, activities, and rewards. The extent to which such schemes achieve their full productive potential, and the extent to which their benefits are fairly distributed among household or community members, are consequently matters of assumption and speculation, rather than properly grounded analysis.

The success of policy efforts to address the problems of women in poverty is emphatically not about separate versus integrated interventions, since different circumstances warrant different approaches. Rather, a gender-aware approach to the design of anti-poverty programmes and projects requires that policy-makers are *clear, consistent, and well-informed* about the relevance of gender in specific contexts to their goals, objectives, and strategies. This will allow them to explore and select from a range of old and new options in their attempts to ensure equal opportunities in anti-poverty programmes, rather than engaging in futile debates over women-only versus integrated projects.

Some important progress in this field has been made by a number of NGOs, sometimes working in partnership with local or national government. The innovative nature of these NGOs does not necessarily imply greater sensitivity to women's needs and potential from their inception. Rather it reflects their greater flexibility, compared with the more rule-bound culture of most bureaucracies, and consequently their greater ability to respond to the lessons of experience. It also reflects their routine face-to-face interactions with their grassroots constituencies, compared with the more remote, formalised modelling exercises undertaken in the upper echelons of bureaucratically-managed planning institutions. This closer contact with the everyday realities of poverty has allowed some NGOs to adopt a process-based approach to policy design, rather than the rigid 'blueprint' approach which characterises conventional planning. In the rest of this article, I want to draw on the experiences of a number of NGOs from the South Asian context, in order to identify some key pointers for ensuring greater gender-awareness in the formulation of anti-poverty interventions. Although these examples relate to one geographical area, I believe that the lessons they offer have a much broader application. In addition, while I am here focusing on the gender-related dimension of policy design, I believe that the discussion here can offer lessons for 'good practice' in policy efforts in addressing all forms of marginalisation.

Participation and needs-identification

Poverty-reduction programmes are generally seen in terms of meeting the basic needs of those who lack the resources to do so for themselves. They may be designed to meet such needs either directly, through the provision of basic goods and services, or indirectly by improving people's entitlements to basic resources. The first step in the design of poverty-alleviation programmes is thus establishing what constitutes 'basic needs' in a given context, and identifying priorities among them.[1]

This is not a neutral process: which needs are recognised, whose priorities are adopted, and consequently whose participation can be relied upon further 'downstream' in the policy process, are all critically dependent on how planners go about the business of needs-identification. Women's needs and priorities have suffered in many conventional poverty-alleviation efforts, because the preconceptions of those responsible for the design of programmes have often led them to impose their own definitions of what women need. Either women's needs are subsumed (and then forgotten) under the collective needs of the household, or, when they are addressed separately, they tend to be those associated with their roles as mothers, wives, and carers within the family. That women, like men, may value interventions which increase their self-esteem, their control over their own labour, or their sense of being active rather than passive, is seldom allowed to surface in poverty-reduction schemes.

What emerges from the experience of the more innovative NGOs is that, where a space is created for women's own voices to be heard, a very different set of needs may emerge. This space can be created by encouraging women to participate in the process of identifying a community's needs. It can also be created by operating with an open rather than closed agenda, so that organisational practice is constantly monitored and revised in the light of experience.

The case of Grameen Bank

An early example of a more participatory approach to needs identification comes from Grameen Bank (Huq and Sultan 1991). This has its origins in an action-research project in the early 1970s which helped to counter many conventional preconceptions about the rural poor which were enshrined in the development literature in Bangladesh: that they were primarily waged labourers; that their poverty resulted from inadequate access to waged employment; and that they were (implicitly) men. What the action research revealed instead was that the rural poor earned their livelihoods from a variety of self-employed activities, rather than relying primarily on waged labour; that they were women as well as men; and that their major constraint was perceived not as the lack of agricultural wage labour, but lack of access to mainstream financial organisations. Grameen was set up as a poverty-reduction programme to deliver credit to this excluded group. From a fairly early stage it focused most of its efforts on landless women, whom it found to be a better credit risk. Women, it also turned out, were more likely to use their credit to improve their family's welfare, rather than their own. The Bank now enjoys higher repayment rates than most official credit schemes for poor people in the region.

A women's sanitation project

In the case of the Grameen Bank, the primary need identified was an economic one, dealing with the inadequacy of financial entitlements. Encouraging women to take part in the process of needs identification may also help to identify hitherto hidden welfare needs. An example of this comes from SEWA (Self Employed Women's Association), a trade union started to organise self-employed women in urban Gujerat in India. Here, participatory action-research carried out before SEWA's entry into rural areas uncovered hitherto hidden health needs. Inadequate sanitation facilities meant that most of the poorer villagers had to use open spaces (Jumani 1993). This posed particular problems for women who, in the interests of modesty, were forced to use the fields under cover of darkness. Cases of rape were common in the spaces kept aside for toilet facilities, while long delays before relieving themselves caused bowel and bladder problems for women. Indeed, the low priority, the shame, and the embarrassment invested in women's bodies in many societies have given rise to the wider problems described by Mary Kiseska (1989) as a 'culture of silence' concerning women's sexual, reproductive, and general health questions.

A women's housing project

From an urban context comes the example of SPARC (Bapat and Patel 1992), which works with those sections of the urban poor who live in hovels on the pavements of Bombay. These are people for whom the 'ordinary' problems of poverty are exacerbated by the constant threat of demolition which they face from the municipal authorities. Through a series of public meetings held with the pavement dwellers in 1986-87, both women and men within the community recognised that shelter was one of women's key concerns and responsibilities: it was women who made a pavement dwelling into a *home*; women who had to deal with demolitions, since these normally occurred while the men were out at work; and women who expressed the need for secure shelter as a first priority, mainly for the sake of their children and grandchildren. SPARC's programmes of popular education based on housing are consequently conducted primarily with women pavement dwellers.

To sum up, participatory approaches to needs-identification should not be seen as a question of the 'right' methods and techniques alone, but also about the possibilities created for democratic participation in the process of needs-identification. No set of methods is *in itself* sensitive to differences and inequalities between men and women; each method is only as good as its practitioner. It can be argued that the qualitative, dynamic, and interactive methodology advocated by Participatory Rural Appraisal makes it more likely to challenge gender-linked stereotyping about needs and opportunities (the men = production/ women = welfare formula), and to uncover categories of needs which might remain submerged in more conventional approaches to policy design. At the same time, SPARC has used quantitative techniques to generate information about the needs of the 'invisibilised' poor, both to the public and to the authorities. At the start of its activities, it conducted a 'people's census' to enumerate pavement dwellers (a group routinely left out of more conventional censuses), both as a strategy to mobilise the pavement dwellers, and as a way of mobilising public opinion against mass demolitions. The active creation of an information base to mobilise people was later adopted as a methodology by the National Slum Dwellers' Federation; collective enumeration also forms a key tool in SPARC's training methodology.

Participation and needs-satisfaction

Identifying needs is clearly only one aspect of the planning process. A major factor behind women's disenfranchisement from most conventional institutions of development is that, except where the resources in question correspond specifically to 'women's roles', these institutions, implicitly or explicitly, target men. The more innovative NGOs, — by adapting their operating rules, practices, and procedures to take account, not just of women's needs, but also of the constraints which often prevent them from claiming their fair share of resources, — have sought to compensate for this. These NGOs' own rules and procedures embody a very different set of assumptions about potential 'beneficiaries', recognising in particular that the unequal division of resources and responsibilities within the domestic domain is likely to constrain women's ability to secure access to resources, services and opportunities distributed through conventional market or State channels. Thus, in addition to prioritising a more gender-aware set of 'primary' needs around which to organise development interventions, these NGOs have sought to respond to a 'secondary' set of needs which arise from the specific constraints that women face in taking advantage of development opportunities. A number of examples will make this clear.

Women's credit schemes

Returning to the question of credit, what has become abundantly clear is that formal financial institutions have failed to reach the poor, and particularly poor women. Even where such institutions have sought to implement special credit schemes for the poor — such as the Uganda Commercial Bank's Rural Farmers' Scheme and the Differential Rate of Interest Scheme in India, both implemented through mainstream banking institutions — women's participation has been poor. Research into these efforts has helped to identify the mis-match between banking norms and procedures and women's needs and constraints. These constraints are:

- Lack of collateral to underwrite loans.
- Inflexible procedures, formidable paperwork, and literacy requirements. The study of the Uganda Bank scheme found that the number of visits required to get loans applications processed and money released was a major reason given by women farmers for not participating in the scheme.
- The small scope of most women's enterprises, which means that they are considered less credit-worthy.
- The costs of transactions, such as the expense incurred in acquiring information about a group that is generally more isolated and less mobile, and the relatively high costs of administering small loans.
- Ambiguous goals for employees in commercially-run banking organisations, who are required to pursue conventional profit-oriented aims in the administration of most of the Bank's loans, but to adopt a different attitude when dealing with the Bank's poverty-alleviation projects. This is clearly a problem, when there are no internal incentives to reward achievements in lending to the poor.
- The social distance between bank employees, who are mainly middle-class men, and poor women.

Gender-sensitive responses to women's credit needs have taken a number of different forms. Some, like Mahila Milan, the Federation of Women's Collectives in Bombay (Patel and D'Cruz 1993), operate their own crisis credit scheme, funded by the savings of low-income households. The Federation works closely with SPARC, which initially put aside an equivalent amount of capital to compensate for any losses. While the actual money raised is modest, it does satisfy urgent needs for cash among members. Others, like the Working Women's Forum in Madras, India, have acted as financial intermediaries between women in the urban informal sector and the mainstream banking system. Still others, like Grameen and SEWA, operate as poverty-focused banks. What these initiatives have in common is that they have sought to overcome some of the gender-specific constraints that women, particularly poorer women, face in getting access to credit, by putting in place a number of innovative institutional practices. These include:

- *Compensating for the absence of material collateral through other mechanisms.* For example, the Uganda Bank adopted character-based lending. In the case of Grameen, reliance was on 'social collateral': the principle of groups of borrowers with joint liability for each other's debts. The member knows that, unless loans are repaid, the chances of other group members receiving loans in the future are jeopardised.

- *Guaranteeing physical access*, as for example by Grameen's strategy of 'barefoot banking', through a dense network of branches and outreach by bank staff.

- *Simplified procedures and minimal form filling.* Grameen's borrowers undergo a training workshop to learn to sign their names. SEWA's members carry identity cards with their photographs. Mahila Milan overcomes the problems posed by the illiteracy of its members by oral and memory processes and the use of symbols. Women keep track of their accounts in plastic bags with different-coloured squares of paper, representing sums of different denominations.

- Interest is generally set at commercial rates; the emphasis is on *subsidising access rather than interest rates.*

A women's health and vocational training scheme

A similar attempt to meet the needs of the poor, with a special emphasis on the needs of poor women, is to be found in Gonoshasthya Kendra (GSK 1991), also in Bangladesh. In Bangladesh, as in much of the Third World, poor people cannot easily take advantage of official health services. This is due to the urban bias of such service-provision, its cost in terms of money and time, and a social distance between (generally male) professional providers and poor rural women. In the Bangladeshi context, it is compounded by cultural norms which dictate female seclusion and restrict women's physical mobility. GSK seeks to service the community through a network of female paramedics, who have been given training in preventative and basic curative care. It relies on young women who have completed a minimum level of schooling, rather than asking for the formal qualifications necessary in conventional nursing. Through a system of monthly household visits, using bicycles to cover distances, GSK overcomes the problems of physical and social constraints on women's access to health care. While it runs a health-insurance scheme to recover some of its costs, contributions are fixed on a sliding scale to reflect household income. However, since the case of an attempted suicide by a young woman in the early years of its life, GSK has also attempted to improve the quality of women's lives, as well their health. It runs vocational training schemes for women, focusing on non-traditional skills (carpentry, metal work, fibre-glass fabrication, shoe-making, and the operation, repair, and management of irrigation-pumps). Such skills are not just likely to bring higher financial returns, but also help to challenge prevailing stereotypes about women's competencies and skills.

Providing resources is not enough

It is beyond the scope of this article to discuss in detail the full range of examples of institutional innovations undertaken by NGOs. However, this brief discussion suggests a key lesson for the design of gender-aware interventions for poverty-reduction. All institutions are made up of rules and norms, practices and procedures which determine which categories of people are likely to be included in — and excluded from — its various operations. Many of these norms and practices where developed at a time when the issue of equity for women and men was not on the agenda, and they now need to be re-thought. More recent analysis reveals that interventions are likely to by-pass women, unless they are designed to address the more complex set of constraints that differentiate women's access to resources and opportunities from men's: mere provision is not enough. Beyond basic needs, generally regarded as the main entry-point for poverty-oriented intervention, there is a further set of 'needs' (often less visible), stemming from gender-specific constraints which differentiate men's and women's terms of access to service provision. Unless institutions are organised to accommodate these secondary needs, they are unlikely to achieve equity for women and men in their outcomes. If the existing mainstream institutions cannot be transformed overnight to take account of the logic of women's lives, gender-aware poverty-reduction requires institutional mechanisms that can help to bridge this gap.

Participation and strategic gender interests

The emphasis so far has been on the participatory identification and design of projects that addressed perceived gender-specific needs, opportunities, and constraints. However, if poverty-reduction is to be combined with fair treatment for women, we must address the underlying structural conditions which generate and sustain inequality and inequity. A study of the different strategies used by the more innovative NGOs provides insights into how the question of women's empowerment is conceptualised at the grassroots level. Most of the NGOs we have been discussing use women's basic needs as an entry point for their work within the community, rather than tackling structural inequalities head-on. The transformative potential of their efforts lies in *how* they attempt to meet these needs: the extent to which they result in building up the self-organisation and self-confidence of poor women sufficiently for them to participate further upstream in the policy-making process. The need for 'upstream' participation is essential, since this is where key decisions about the economy are taken and priorities for resource allocation are determined. Until this occurs, poor women will remain at the receiving end of development, however much they participate in the design, implementation, and evaluation of projects. Thus a more accountable development requires that women are actors in the making of decisions *at the policy level*. The empowerment of women clearly entails a more political agenda, in that it challenges the existing status quo within the community, and here a number of elements in NGO strategies which appear to have this transformative potential can be identified.

First of all, there is a stress on the provision of new economic resources, rather than resources which merely reinforce women's traditional roles within a given society. Such provision sends out an important signal about the productive potential of poor women, against the general tendency to regard the existing division of resources as culturally immutable. It suggests that poverty-reduction programmes could help to continue pushing back the boundaries of what is considered possible or permissible for women to do in a given society.

Secondly, there is an emphasis on building new forms of collective relationships. A considerable body of research has found that where women are members of associations beyond the household, and where these associations are based on solidarity and mutual self-help, they are likely to exercise greater bargaining power within the household, as well as to participate more actively in community life. This provides some of the rationale for the stress which many NGOs place on building new collective relationships among poor women, and between poor women and men. It is worth noting that, with this broader perspective, the issue of whether the process begins with the building of women-only groups or integrated groups becomes irrelevant. The question is to what extent these groups are seen as isolated from the rest of the community, and to what extent they are seen as part of the building up of the broader organisations of the poor.

However, unless such relationships are mobilised to develop organisational power, their transformative potential is unlikely to be fully realised. Consequently, a third common element is the emphasis on collective action around self-defined priorities. The evaluation literature about these NGOs points to a variety of actions, initiated by both women-only groups and by women in alliance with men. Actions range from protests against dowry customs, wife-beating, male alcoholism, and cheating by public works officials, to taking on local government structures — village tribunals, local elections and community action. Such collective action breaks down past isolation, and helps to link women and other hitherto marginalised groups to broader political currents of their societies. And this is critical. Unless women are empowered to move beyond the project-trap and to take part in the making of policy where the key decisions about resource allocations are taken, they will always be a residual category in development.

Notes

1 The focus on the politics of needs interpretation in this paper draws on ideas put forward in Fraser (1989).

References

Agarwal, B. (1990) 'Social security and the family in rural India: coping with seasonality and calamity', *Journal of Peasant Studies* 17/3: 341-412.

Amsden A. (1980) *The Economics of Women and Work,* Middlesex, Penguin, pp.11-38.

Appleton S., P. Collier, and P. Horsnell (1990) *Gender, Education and Employment in Cote d'Ivoire,* Social Dimensions of Adjustment Working Paper No.8. Washington: World Bank.

Bapat M. and S. Patel (1992) 'Beating a Path: Towards Defining Women's Participation in Shelter Strategies of the Urban Poor', paper presented at the International Conference *Shelter, Women and Development — First and Third World Perspectives*, University of Michigan, Ann Arbor, USA, May 1992.

Beneria, L. and M. Roldan (1987) *Crossroads of Class and Gender,* Chicago: University of Chicago Press.

Bruce J. and D. Dwyer (eds) (1988) *A Home Divided: Women and Income in the Third World,* Stanford: Stanford University Press.

Bruce J. and C.B. Lloyd (1992) 'Beyond Female Headship: Family Research and Policy Issues for the 1990s', paper presented at the International Food Policy Research Institute/World Bank Conference on Intrahousehold Resource Allocation: Policy Issues and Research Methods, 1992, Washington.

Buvinic, M. (1983) 'Women's issues in Third World poverty: a policy analysis' in M. Buvinic et al. (eds): *Women and Poverty in the Third World,* Baltimore: John Hopkins Press.

Buvinic, M. (1986) 'Projects for women in the Third World: explaining their misbehaviour', *World Development* 14/5: 653-64.

Fraser, N. (1989) *Unruly Practices. Power, Discourse and Gender in Contemporary Social Theory,* Cambridge: Polity.

Gonoshasthya Kendra (1991) 'Development of Nari Kendra: Vocational Training Centre for Women', Nayarhat, Dhamrai, Bangladesh, mimeo.

Humphrey, J. (1987) *Gender and Work in the Third World;* Sexual Divisions in Brazilian Industry London, Tavistock Press.

Huq M. and M. Sultan (1991) '"Informality" in development: the poor entrepreneurs in Bangladesh', in A.L. Chickering and M. Salahdine (eds): *The Silent Revolution. The Informal Sector in Five Asian and Near Eastern Countries,* San Francisco: International Centre for Economic Growth.

Jazairy, I., M. Alamgir and T. Panuccio (1992) *The State of World Rural Poverty,* New York: New York University Press.

Jumani, U. (1993) *Dealing with Poverty: Self-employment for Poor Rural Women,* New Delhi: Sage.

Kabeer, N. (1994) *Reversed Realities: Gender Hierarchies in Development Thought,* London: Verso.

Palmer, I. (1977) 'Rural women and basic needs' *International Labour Review* 115/1.

Patel S. and C D'Cruz (1993) 'The Mahila Milan crisis credit scheme: from a seed to a tree', *Environment and Urbanisation* 5/1: 9-17.

Rogers, B. (1990) *The Domestication of Women: Discrimination in Developing Societies,* London: Kogan Page.

Standing, H. (1991) *Dependence and Autonomy. Women's Employment and the Family in Calcutta,* London: Routledge.

■ **Naila Kabeer** *has worked in Bangladesh, India, and Vietnam, and has been a Fellow of the Institute of Development Studies at the University of Sussex since 1985. She has been involved in directing and teaching on the MA course in Gender and Development and on the 'Women, Men and Development' course. She is an economist, with a special interest in household economics, poverty, gender, and human-resource issues. Her book* Reversed Realities: Gender Hierarchies in Development *Thought was published in 1994 by Verso Press. This article is an expanded version of a paper prepared for the Conference on Social Development and Poverty, Oaxaca, Mexico, September, 1993, and was first published in* Development in Practice, *Volume 5, number 2, in 1995.*

Women in the informal sector: the contribution of education and training

Fiona Leach

Introduction

Contrary to the images projected worldwide of women fulfilling primarily domestic and child-rearing roles, the reality of most women's lives is that they are obliged by poverty and deprivation to seek an income outside the home, either as the sole breadwinner, or to supplement male earnings. In developing countries, when women are not engaged solely in subsistence agriculture, they tend to be involved in the so-called informal sector (also known as the 'hidden' or 'shadow' economy). In the poorest countries, competition for the better-paid and more secure jobs in the small and under-developed formal or modern sector (which may account for as little as 10 per cent of total employment) is fierce, and women cannot usually compete for these with men.

Within the informal sector, women are generally found in low-income activity which barely guarantees survival. This is likely to be in self-employment or in casual or seasonal paid labour, often of an unskilled and physically demanding nature, with low productivity, long hours, and little opportunity for upward mobility or for acquiring or improving skills. Typical activities for women are petty-trading and street vending (of vegetables, poultry, processed food, or handcrafts), paid domestic work, casual employment in unregulated small enterprises, and on construction sites and agricultural schemes. Such work is rarely protected by labour legislation, and its precarious nature makes women an easy prey for unscrupulous money-lenders and contractors. Often women resort to illicit economic activity such as unauthorised street trading, brewing of alcohol, and prostitution, which makes them even more vulnerable to persecution and harassment. While some women do succeed in setting up profitable businesses, for example in the fashion and service industries, and in certain kinds of trading, these constitute a tiny minority.

It is difficult to assess the exact extent of women's involvement in the informal sector, for much of their activity is 'invisible' or is not counted as 'work'. For example, in those parts of Asia where seclusion of women is encouraged and a man is expected to provide for his wife and family in full, a common form of female economic activity is home-based piece-work for a local contractor (for example in the garment industry), usually at exploitative rates of pay. Likewise, when women are required to work as helpers in a family unit — preparing yarn for weaving, or fetching water and clay for making pots — their contribution is not recognised as 'work'. Women themselves tend to undervalue their economic activities.

As agricultural mechanisation and the commercialisation of farming have denied women access to land traditionally used for growing food, they have turned to the informal sector for a source of income. Economic recession, structural adjustment, and the growing incidence of female-headed households (an estimated one-third of households worldwide) have increased the pressure on women — and children too — to contribute to the family income.

For many women, the informal sector provides their only opportunity for work, especially if they have few skills to offer. The modern sector labour market favours men (except in certain areas, such as the electronics industry, where women's 'nimble fingers' are valued on the assembly line; Mosse 1993). Access to the informal sector is relatively easy, and work can be combined with domestic responsibilities. However, as Moser (1991) points out, this usually means a much longer working day for women, who have to add this to their existing roles and responsibilities.

Formal education and training

A sound general education provides young people with the best foundation for their future participation in the employment market. This applies as much to the informal sector, where the basic skills of literacy and numeracy are essential for most (legitimate) profitable activity, as to the modern sector. Not surprisingly, those whom the educational system has failed to reach, or failed to retain in school, are likely to be found in the least profitable economic activities. Women form the majority in this category, as is obvious from the fact that at least two thirds of the world's adult illiterates, who make up the world's poorest people, are female.

From the 1960s, governments have invested heavily in formal education for girls as well as boys as a means of promoting social and economic development. Many developing countries have also adopted strategies, often with the support of international donors, to get more girls into school. However, despite enormous gains, in some countries there may be as many as five male students in higher education to every female, and schools have failed to equip young women with the necessary skills to compete in the labour market on equal terms with men.

Vocational opportunities for girls, when available, have been restricted to (or girls themselves have chosen) traditional 'feminine' subjects such as home economics, secretarial studies, tailoring, hairdressing and beauty care, which are largely an extension of home-based activities, and are usually poorly remunerated (assuming that jobs are available).

Thus, the function of education has been largely to prepare young women for their assumed adult roles as housewives and mothers, whereas boys have been prepared for jobs and careers. Schools have thus served to reflect and to reinforce the male bias that prevails throughout the labour market, as in all social relations, which usually places power in the hands of men.[1]

Initiatives to introduce education for entrepreneurship into the school curriculum, as in Kenya, Ghana and Malaysia, are unlikely to help women significantly, for the informal sector reflects the same gender bias as the modern sector. Women everywhere experience prejudice and practical difficulties in establishing themselves in economically independent activity, while the school curriculum continues to project conventional images of acceptable activities for women and men.

A wide range of factors, many of them deeply embedded in the gendered nature of culture and society, serve to prevent women from participating in formal education and training, and thereafter in employment and self-employment, on equal terms with men. The most important factors include poverty (where choices have to be made, parents usually choose to educate boys before girls); the greater demand for girls' labour in the home; and the 'hidden curriculum' of everyday school practice which presents a male-dominated hierarchy of authority, and socialises girls into accepting a subordinate adult role — which inevitably means that girls lack self-confidence, and have low expectations of themselves.

In general, formal education and training in developing countries appears not to acknowledge the heavy involvement of women in economic activity, and does little to provide them with relevant skills. The gendered nature of the curriculum serves to reinforce rather than weaken the social and economic constraints operating against the equal participation of women in a labour market which is both highly competitive and discriminatory.

Non-formal education and training

Non-formal education (NFE) has expanded considerably in recent decades, with enormous diversity in terms of aims, content, target audience, and teaching methods, and a wide range of providers. Much of it is intended to give a 'second chance' to adults or adolescents who have failed to complete the primary or secondary cycle, and is directed at basic literacy. NGOs have played a major role in reaching poor and disadvantaged people with NFE programmes which seek either to supplement formal education (as for example through accelerated courses of basic skills for out-of-school children provided in rural Bangladesh by BRAC, and in urban Nicaragua by the evening school programme) or to complement it, as for instance through vocational training schemes for primary-school leavers or drop-outs, such as those provided by the Village Polytechnics in Kenya, and the Botswana Brigades.

Given that much NFE is aimed at those who have missed out on formal education, it might be expected that women, being the majority in this category, should be over-represented in NFE programmes, which would seek to compensate for the failure of the formal system to provide them with marketable skills. Unfortunately, most NFE programmes have continued to reflect the same disparities and biases that prevail in formal education. For example, basic literacy for women has often been conceived in terms of enhancing their role as housewives and mothers, focusing on literacy in the context of family health, nutrition, and community development, rather than on literacy (and especially numeracy) for employment. And in vocational skills programmes, female participation rates have been low in many countries. Vocational training has traditionally been directed at males — carpentry, metalwork, masonry, and motor mechanics — and at modern sector employment, where women are under-represented.

Attempts at positive discrimination and the introduction of quota schemes for women in some countries, to persuade them to enrol on vocational courses that are outside those deemed 'appropriate' for them, have not lived up to expectations, with places often remaining unfilled. Socio-cultural convention and the fear of ridicule and harassment by male students and teachers have deterred girls from joining courses traditionally dominated by boys.

The same constraints affecting formal education for girls apply to NFE for female adolescents and adults. Indeed there are additional constraints facing agencies trying to improve training opportunities for women and girls, including:

- low levels of literacy and numeracy among adult women;
- social constraints on females who have reached puberty or who are married (male members of their family may not allow them to leave the home to take up employment or to attend training courses);
- lack of time, energy, and mobility for women, already overburdened by domestic duties, to attend training programmes;
- lack of child-care facilities in both training and employment locations;
- lack of flexibility in the scheduling of courses to recognise women's daily and seasonal workloads and timetables;
- the inappropriateness of training offered (especially when courses are designed by men);
- lack of part-time and flexible working hours, job-sharing opportunities, and transport for those with child-care responsibilities (even when they have received some training).

In addition, difficulties for women in obtaining credit, restrictive labour laws, unequal pay, and the encroachment of technology on women's traditional skill areas have all contributed to the problem of assisting women into employment.

Income-generating projects for women

Training is often a core activity of income-generating projects (IGPs), and in this respect such projects form part of the non-formal approach to education. Training may be either in basic literacy and numeracy or in specific skills for employment or self-employment. IGPs for women have mushroomed in developing countries, the majority funded and set up by NGOs. Some are free-standing projects, while others are part of a broader programme of community development or welfare. Whatever the framework, IGPs for women have largely concentrated on support for the provision of goods and services which are an extension of traditional female activity in the home, such as handcrafts or food production. In this respect, as Goodale (1989) points out, they reinforce a narrow view of women's work, which views female income as supplementary to the male's (as 'pin money'), and a woman's productive activities as secondary to her reproductive ones. In this sense 'income generation' is for women, but 'jobs' are for men.

There is growing recognition that women's projects which focus on traditional feminine skills for income generation, and are often combined with welfare, have not served women well. They have neither brought those involved much financial reward, nor reduced their subordinate and dependent position in society. Cynics would say that they often serve to keep women in low-paid and low-status economic activity. To some, women have become pawns in a flourishing NGO business, where additional (income-generating) roles are proposed for already over-worked women which require considerable inputs of time, money, and energy, often without the women having any clear notion of what they will gain (Mukhopadyay and March 1992). Traditional female crafts are often very time-consuming, and provide little sustainable income, while the more lucrative crafts are generally monopolised by men.

This is not the place to detail the numerous reasons for such a disappointing record. Rather, I want here to consider issues regarding training in IGPs for women, with a view to establishing the extent to which inappropriate approaches to training have contributed to their generally poor performance.

Caroline Moser, well known for her work on gender planning, suggests that women's projects have largely failed because they have sought only to address the question of increasing women's productivity and income, without attempting to improve their status in society (Moser 1991). In other words, they are only addressing women's practical, immediate needs for survival. Conventional formal and non-formal training opportunities for women can be viewed as subscribing to this approach. However, women's projects need also to address women's strategic needs to overcome their subordinate position in society. This requires challenging patriarchal social structures such as the legal system, property rights, and labour codes, which maintain men in positions of power. Likewise, if the educational system is to become a true source of economic and social mobility for women, it needs to address these issues.

Women's programmes which have sought to do this have tended to adopt an 'empowerment' approach. In India, SEWA (The Self-Employed Women's Association), founded in 1972, is an early example of a grassroots organisation which essentially seeks to empower and mobilise women, in this case in the workplace. More recently, in the UK, Oxfam, through its Gender Team (formerly known as the Gender and Development Unit) and WOMANKIND offer support to more ambitious initiatives where women seek to challenge their subordinate status in society. This bolder approach is also beginning to attract funding from some official donors, who appear ready to give support through NGO channels to programmes which they might not wish to fund through direct bilateral aid. However, most grassroots women's organisations are small and, despite increasing recognition of their effectiveness in improving women's position in society, they remain largely unsupported by national governments and international agencies, because of their commitment to radical social and political change.

Lessons to be learned from training initiatives for women

A number of common characteristics, and weaknesses, in the supply of training for women in the informal sector emerge from a brief review of the literature. The most significant lessons are summarised below.

Education and training alone are not enough

Access to education and training for women is not sufficient to increase their participation in the labour market on equal terms with men. While training may sometimes improve women's (and men's) income-earning opportunities, expectations of the impact of training on work opportunities for women are often unrealistic. As long as gender discrimination continues to exist in the labour market in both the formal (or modern) and informal sectors of the economy, women will be disadvantaged in their search for work, and they will need additional support in order to succeed in obtaining a greater share of worthwhile jobs.

Unfortunately, training is often offered with little or no knowledge of the potential market for a particular product or skill, of the level of start-up capital required, or of the likely problems that women will encounter when seeking to enter a new market. One of the strengths of SEWA, for example, has been its insistence on undertaking surveys of the socio-economic conditions in which women work, and assessments of market opportunities, before offering training in a particular skill area (Jumani 1989, Goodale 1989).

An integrated approach to training is required

Women's projects need a supportive environment within which to operate. For this, an integrated approach which combines a number of strategies (which may include training) is necessary. This has been one of the strengths of SEWA. In other successful projects, the integration of training, production, and employment is cited as contributory factors.

Access to credit may be more important than training

In some cases, training may not be as important as access to credit, whether through a sponsoring agency or through the banking system. Often a small amount is all that is required to get a small business or cooperative off the ground. Some argue that providing credit is the most cost-effective form of support to poor women.

Gaining access to credit is rarely easy for the poor, but women are likely to experience much greater difficulty than men in procuring even small loans, especially from High Street banks, which treat poor illiterate women with disdain. Sometimes, large organisations like SEWA have started their own banks through frustration with the regular banking system. This was the rationale behind the famous Grameen Bank in Bangladesh.

Banks need to be persuaded, for example through awareness campaigns or government incentives, to lend to women setting up small businesses or cooperatives. They should take note of the increasing evidence that women are more reliable in repaying loans than men. This has encouraged some NGOs to set up loan schemes for women. For example, in the K-REP 'Chikola' scheme in Kenya, the repayment rate of loans from the rotating fund to women's groups over the first two years was 100 per cent, and the scheme has been rapidly expanded. In India, WOMANKIND Worldwide is supporting a rotating loan scheme which helps tribal women to obtain government and bank loans. The women's conscientious handling of the loans has made the banks much more ready to lend to them, and has helped to enhance their economic and social status in the community.

Women need additional support services

In addition to obtaining credit and receiving training, poor women need other support services if they are to initiate and sustain viable economic activities. These might include any of the following: a social security scheme, legal advice, business advice, housing and child-care facilities, employment opportunities through cooperatives, and trade union representation. One of the remarkable features of SEWA's integrated approach is that by providing a range of support services, it has offered some security to women in what are to them high-risk areas of economic activity (Jumani 1989). While cost considerations of providing such facilities and benefits cannot be ignored (and are viewed by many employers as a major disincentive to the employment of women), efficiently and realistically run services can reap benefits in terms of increased productivity and incomes, which allow them ultimately to become self-financing.

One-off training programmes are insufficient

Women, just as much as men, need opportunities to re-train and upgrade their skills, and continuing access to vocational and/or career guidance. Women's training needs have, overall, received less attention than men's, largely because women are seen as marginal to, or invisible in. the employment market (Goodale 1989). Because training opportunities have been denied them, they remain in low-status, low-skill work.

Career advice for women, both within and outside the formal educational system, has been either non-existent or heavily gender-biased. Many women have basic skills acquired in the home or in traditional apprenticeship, but skill upgrading would allow them to produce a wider range of products and enter new spheres of enterprise, and make them more employable.

Training in technical skills is not enough

Training for employment has traditionally been conceived as involving narrow technical and vocational skills. This is insufficient for the majority of young people who will seek self-employment in the informal sector. Technical and vocational training must be combined with basic business, marketing, and entrepreneurship skills.

Women also need to learn to view their economic activities as potentially profit-generating, and to make decisions according to business principles, rather than according to household or kinship considerations (Walsh and Nelson 1991). While some British development agencies still offer only basic skills training (for instance in handcrafts), this is increasingly combined with business skills development.

Traditional 'female' skills offer little opportunity for sustainable income

NGOs have concentrated overwhelmingly on training women in traditional skills such as tailoring, embroidery, knitting, and food production, which offer little opportunity for raising income levels significantly or for future expansion. Markets may not be readily available, or may be already saturated by other local women's products, or by cheap imports. The skills acquired through short training courses may not be adequate to produce high-quality goods.

Women will be particularly disadvantaged in this respect when they try to enter new skill areas where men are already well entrenched. However, in the long term, only skills training which goes beyond existing traditional activities for women can help them to move into genuine entrepreneurship.

Women need help to break into new areas of economic activity

To break into new areas of economic activity, women will need assistance, as they are likely to face hostility and resentment from men who see their livelihoods threatened. In addition, women face social disapproval where there are strongly entrenched social and cultural norms which limit their involvement in the labour market. Change is not impossible, as some small success stories show. For example, in India there are admirable examples of women breaking into the traditional male preserves of dairying, weaving, pottery, and masonry, despite strong male disapproval (Iyer 1991).

Women need training in personal and social development

To counter discrimination and hostility when they attempt to enter non-traditional areas of activity, women will need additional training in personal development. This may include training in leadership, assertiveness, the management of stress and discrimination, and self-confidence building. Women often underestimate their ability to earn an income or to manage non-domestic affairs. More radical approaches may include programmes to increase women's awareness of their rights as workers, to analyse women's subordination in society, and to teach mobilisation techniques.

Some funding agencies, particularly NGOs, have started to provide personal and social development training for women. SEWA has been doing this for a long time. Others such as KYTEC in Kenya provide gender-awareness training for men as well as for women. In the UK, the Commonwealth Secretariat has a manual for trainers — Entrepreneurial Skills for Young Women (1992) — which includes sessions on gender awareness and achievement motivation.

Attitude and behaviour change is essential

Without a change in attitude and behaviour towards women working outside the home, women will not achieve equality in the labour market. Offering training opportunities to women, in particular in the more profitable skill areas, will not be successful until social and cultural conventions concerning appropriate roles for men and women in society change. While women are increasingly taking on male roles, for example in supporting the family economically, men rarely reciprocate by taking on female roles, such as sharing child-care or domestic responsibilities. Governments therefore need to embark on media campaigns to influence attitudes concerning women's role in the labour market and the division of labour in the home, which should be addressed to a wide range of people: teachers and educational personnel, male members of the family, community leaders, career advisers, employers, politicians, planners and policy-makers, and women themselves.

Some attempts have been made to provide gender-awareness training for government and NGO staff (male and female) who work with women. For instance, the Namibian government commissioned a group of British consultants to provide gender training for ministry officials. Some British NGOs run gender training workshops for their own staff, either at their administrative headquarters or in their field offices (for example, Oxfam, Save the Children Fund, and ACORD), though these represent only a tiny proportion of all the NGO initiatives involving support to women. Useful resources include Oxfam's Gender Training Manual (Williams et al. 1994), and the 'Guidelines for Good Practice in Gender and Development' produced by the National Alliance of Women Organisations (NAWO) at the request of ODA (Overseas Development Administration, now known as Department of International Development), for use with NGO personnel. Other agencies, such as

World University Service (WUS) in El Salvador, organise courses for NGO staff. WOMANKIND Worldwide in India plans a gender training course for male NGO staff.

Access to information is important

There is often a lack of information directly accessible to women on training-related assistance, and employment opportunities. Greater publicity is needed, of a kind that will reach women (Goodale 1989).

Literacy and numeracy are essential

Literacy is not only a basic human right; it is necessary for all types of employment, and especially for self-employment, where planning, production, marketing, and obtaining credit all require literacy and numeracy. For rural women (who make up most of the world's illiterate adults) training for income generation may need to start with basic literacy and numeracy. However, such training should both recognise women's existing involvement in economic activity, and avoid passing on the message that they are ignorant in all respects. Women have 'invisible' abilities acquired in the home and they continually innovate with the resources available to them; but their skills, knowledge, and inventions often remain unrecognised due to their lack of visibility in the employment market (Appleton 1993).

Literacy can give women greater confidence and an improved self-image (Bown 1990), which in itself may boost their chances of survival in highly competitive markets. Some literacy programmes have served to encourage women to set up their own income-generating organisations or cooperatives. In other cases, women who were already engaged in the informal sector wished to acquire minimal literacy and numeracy, for example to allow them to keep accounts or to take measurements, and then were motivated to look beyond immediate income generation to press for better health care and greater parity with men. In this respect, literacy can act as a mobilising force for women.

Training methods must be appropriate

Many training institutions offer courses which assume a certain level of literacy and are too abstract and theoretical for poor women. These are the people who most need training but have the least time and mobility, and little or no experience of a formal learning environment. Training needs to be practical, related to women's experiences, communicated in an appropriate way, and of direct relevance to the problems and barriers that they perceive. It needs to be of good quality, with adequate provision of equipment where appropriate. Participatory methods, role play, practical demonstrations, and field visits may facilitate learning. Women teachers may be necessary or desirable, and act as role models for participants.

The pattern of training offered must take into account women's daily circumstances. This usually means that training should be short and recurrent, for most women have little time to spare, and are not used to sitting in a classroom. It should be locally based, with child-care and transport provided where necessary. Timing should also be flexible to fit in with women's existing workloads.

The media can be used to reach illiterate women, and extension workers and mobile trainers, used extensively in health and agriculture, can also provide training to women in remote areas.

There is some debate about whether formal (structured) or informal (unstructured) training is more effective, efficient, and appropriate. Formal training in a classroom situation risks being too rigid and too abstract for the type of participants enrolled. Informal training, consisting usually of business advice and information on a one-to-one basis as and when requested by the client, can be more effective and sometimes cheaper.

Successful women can act as trainers and role models

Some of the most successful small-scale training programmes have been ones where women have started income-generating activities and then have trained others in the same skills. For example, in the SKVIS project in India, funded by Christian Aid, a group of women who set up an IGP received requests from others to train them in making saris, crafts, scarves, and bedspreads. A series of Commonwealth Secretariat leaflets (1991-2) describes how successful businesswomen have taught entrepreneurial skills to other women. In addition these women, as entrepreneurs, offer powerful role models to others.

Group training has important benefits

Some agencies believe that training should be offered to groups, such as members of a cooperative, rather than to individuals. This is a common NGO strategy in community-based development programmes. Training for individuals is considered wasteful, because only a small percentage of those trained may become successful entrepreneurs, whereas all group members will derive some benefit from the training.

There are additional benefits for women of a group approach. While some are dismissive of welfare-type projects which adopt a participatory approach (and are unlikely to become financially self-supporting), the benefits of group efforts in terms of increased self-esteem and self-awareness, and the creation of mutual support and mobilisation mechanisms, are also valuable in themselves. However, it is important to be aware that even a group strategy is likely to exclude the poorest and the most marginalised (ACORD 1992).

Some recommendations

While men also face many problems in seeking employment and self-employment, women face a different set of constraints which must be taken into account when offering training or other assistance within the informal sector. As Goodale (1989) argues, women's access to and control of resources in production processes, and their participation in decision-making, are quite different from that of men. Improving women's opportunities in the informal sector has to respond to the fact that they are largely situated at the bottom end of the labour market, and that there are social, cultural, and economic factors which inhibit them from benefiting from training and employment opportunities on an equal basis with men. At the same time, it is unlikely that IGPs will increase women's income significantly, unless they assist them both to enter new areas of economic activity and to challenge their subordinate position in society.

Recommendations that emerge from this brief review of women's education and training for the informal sector are listed below.

1 With regard to **formal education**, governments need to initiate and enforce policies and programmes which encourage girls to enrol and to stay in school. Girls should also be encouraged to study mathematics, science, and technology in greater numbers, and to diversify into a broader range of vocational subjects. The gender bias in textbooks must be removed and more female teachers should be recruited, especially in the male-dominated vocational and technical fields.

2 Governments need to legislate to remove discriminatory employment practices and to ensure equitable employment and self-employment

opportunities for women, which would make a wider choice of subject specialisation in formal education more attractive to girls. This will require overcoming structural arrangements which keep women in low-paid and low-skill jobs and in subsistence self-employment (such as lack of access to land, credit and other resources, and restrictions on female ownership of land and property).

3 Removing the constraints on the equal participation of girls at all levels of education will require changes in socio-cultural attitudes which determine people's perceptions of appropriate female roles, and will require a fuller awareness of the value and benefit of women's participation in the employment market. In particular, it is important to question the sexual division of labour between the home and the workplace, and to overcome employers' reluctance to engage women.

4 Agencies working in **non-formal education** and promoting the training of women for the informal sector need to move beyond offering training in skills which reinforce women's position in low-skill, low-paid jobs.

5 Agencies must recognise that the provision of technical skills must be supplemented by business, management, and marketing skills. Such training is likely to require specialist agency staff and provision for the training of trainers, and advisers to work with local communities.[2]

6 Training must be flexible to respond to women's different needs and levels of education in terms of length of training, location, course content, child-care and transport facilities, and the language of instruction. Above all, the women themselves must be consulted about what they perceive their needs to be.

7 We need a more realistic assessment of what is feasible in terms of training and employment opportunities for women, with regard to the demands on women's time and their need to generate a profit.

8 Training and back-up need to be directed systematically at the informal sector if women are to survive economically. At the same time, feasibility studies are needed to ascertain areas of market

demand, the level of income that can reasonably be generated, and the likely problems that women will face.

9 While training in business skills may be essential for women to set up and sustain their own enterprises, training needs also to address the broader issue of women's self-development, especially among the poor, and should include sessions on gender-awareness, assertiveness, and confidence-building.

10 Agencies need to provide their own staff with gender training and, where necessary, to make structural changes within their own organisations to reflect a more equitable gender balance. At the same time, they need to employ staff with skills in business, marketing, promotion, and in project management.

11 Governments need to initiate policies which will improve women's access to markets, raw materials, credit, business advice, and other forms of support, and to training programmes geared to local markets and technologies.

In conclusion, this review suggests that there is an urgent need for detailed and policy-related research and evaluation of the most effective strategies for training for employment and self-employment among women; into the constraints faced by women in pursuing careers in male-dominated fields; and into the outcomes of training programmes for women. Agencies working with women need tools with which to weigh up the relative value of offering credit-only programmes against those which offer credit-plus-training, or training-only. They need guidance on the appropriate balance of technical skills, business skills, and personal development in training programmes; and they need to know what style of training is most effective in the long term.

Notes

1 There are of course other biases in both the educational system and the labour market, ethnicity and class being the most important. The school curriculum projects an unreal image of women's lives in part because it is based on a narrow middle-class view of reality, in which the domestic 'ideal' may have some meaning.

2 In the UK, the Durham Business School runs a short training course called 'Women Mean Business' for business advisers and trainers from other countries.

References

ACORD (1992) 'Economic Interest Groups and their Relevance for Women's Development', occasional paper no. 5, Research and Policy Programme (RAPP), London: ACORD.

Appleton, H. (1993) 'Women: invisible technologists', *Appropriate Technology* 20 (2), London: Intermediate Technology Publications.

Bown, L. (1990) '*Preparing the Future: Women, Literacy and Development'*, ActionAid Development Report No 4, Chard, Somerset: ActionAid.

Commonwealth Secretariat (1992) Entrepreneurial Skills for Young Women: A Manual for Trainers, London: Commonwealth Secretariat.

Commonwealth Secretariat (1991-2) A series of leaflets on youth enterprise in the Commonwealth, London: Commonwealth Secretariat.

Goodale, G. (1989) 'Training for women in the informal sector', in F. Fluitman (ed): *Training for Work in the Informal Sector,* Geneva: ILO.

Iyer, L. (1991) *Diversification of Women's Occupations through Training: India,* Training Discussion Paper No 61, Geneva: ILO.

Jumani, U. (1989) 'Training of women in the informal sector: The experience of the Self-Employed Women's Association (SEWA), Ahmedabad, India', in F. Fluitman (ed): *Training for Work in the Informal Sector,* Geneva: ILO.

Moser, C. (1991) 'Gender planning in the Third World: meeting practical and strategic gender needs', in T. Wallace and C. March (eds): *Changing Perceptions: Writings on Gender and Development,* Oxford: Oxfam (UK and Ireland).

Mosse, J.C. (1993) *Half the World, Half a Chance,* Oxford: Oxfam (UK and Ireland).

Mukhopadyay, M. and C. March (1992) *Income Generating Projects. A View from the Grassroots,* Report on a workshop in Kampala, Uganda, Oxfam Discussion Paper, Oxford: Oxfam (UK and Ireland).

Walsh, M. K. and C. Nelson (1991) 'A case for business training with women's groups', *Small Enterprise Development* 2 (1): 13-19.

Williams, S. et al. (1994) *The Oxfam Gender Training Manual,* Oxford: Oxfam (UK and Ireland).

■ **Fiona Leach** *is senior lecturer in education at the University of Sussex, specialising in education in resource-poor contexts. She has worked extensively in Africa on DFID-funded projects in education and has recently conducted research into the training of women for the informal sector and the abuse of girls in secondary schools in Zimbabwe. This paper is based on research which formed part of a study commissioned by the British Overseas Development Administration (ODA) in 1993 entitled 'Education and Training for the Informal Sector' (by S. McGrath and K. King with F. Leach and R. Carr Hill). It draws extensively on the published literature and on reports which a number of NGOs kindly made available to me, for which I remain indebted. It was first published in* Development in Practice, *Volume 6, number 1, in 1996.*

The evaporation of gender policies in the patriarchal cooking pot

Sara Hlupekile Longwe

Inadequacy of a consensus discourse

The basic problem is this: the 1985 Nairobi World Conference on Women set out ambitious goals and strategies, but in the years since then, little or no progress has been made. Ten years later in Beijing, we had to admit that the level of women's representation in national politics has not improved, and there is an increased feminisation of poverty. In many Islamic countries, the decade has seen increasing gender discrimination and oppression.

This lack of progress is despite the fact that the policies of development agencies have been considerably changed by the *Nairobi Forward-Looking Strategies*[1]. By the early 1990s, almost every agency had improved its stated goals and strategies, incorporating intentions to contribute to the process of women's empowerment. Most agencies have also adopted policies of 'gender mainstreaming', to address gender issues in all projects and programmes.

How does the Beijing *Platform for Action* respond to the lack of progress since 1985? The response has not been a re-consideration of the goals and strategies defined in Nairobi. Rather, the *Platform* aims to set out a more detailed plan to achieve these same goals. Firstly, it demands more specific commitments from governments; secondly, it sets out in more detail the ways to achieve these commitments; and thirdly, it proposes improved international machinery for monitoring and evaluating progress. In short, the formula is more of the same.

The *Platform* is written as if we are all pulling together in tackling common problems. It is underpinned by an implicit assumption of good will, as if the international push for women's advancement were like the eradication of polio — which nobody opposes, and no government is likely to subvert.

If the assumptions underlying this apparent consensus were to be made explicit, how many of us would consider such assumptions to be appropriate or realistic? What is lacking in such discourse is any admission of the extent to which women's advancement faces patriarchal opposition. The consensus discourse conceals the essence of the problem. We are up against a hidden agenda of patriarchal opposition which needs to be seen, understood, and analysed, as the prerequisite for progress.

Gender policies have a strange tendency to 'evaporate' within international development agencies. Are we going to recognise and discuss this, or pretend the problem isn't there? Are we still to treat it as a 'hidden' problem? Surely, it is obvious enough to any feminist who has ever tried to work with one of these agencies.

This article[1] looks into this problem, which lies hidden within the official vocabulary, but is otherwise clear. We shall consider the case of the development agency as a 'patriarchal cooking pot' in which gender policies evaporate. We shall explore this process of policy evaporation: why it happens, and how it happens. This 'patriarchal pot' is not introduced merely for theoretical amusement. It aims to illuminate current problems which demand better explanation.

Welcome to SNOWDIDA

For a concrete example of a patriarchal cooking pot, it would be most useful to look at the real-life world of a particular development agency and its programmes in a specific country. Therefore, I shall take the reader to Snowdia, a very isolated nation in the North which no foreigner (except myself) has ever visited. Snowdia has its own government development agency, SNOWDIDA, which is an administrative extension of the Ministry of Foreign Affairs in the Republic of Snowdia. We shall look at SNOWDIDA's development activities in the People's Republic of Sundia, one of the least-developed countries in Southern Africa.[2]

Policy evaporation

Imagine a gender consultant who has been called in to look at how gender issues are addressed in a SNOWDIDA programme in Sundia. The consultant is instructed to look at the SNOWDIDA Country Programme.

This provides a summary of the overall policy and goals, and of the objectives and activities of all the projects in the SNOWDIDA-supported programme. Table 1 summarises the consultant's assessment of the level of attention to gender issues in the SNOWDIDA Country Programme in Sundia.

Table 1: Gender assessment of the Snowdida Country Programme for Sundia

Aspect of programme	Assessment
Programme Policy	Policy rationale is mainly concerned with supporting government policy and endeavours. There is a brief mention of SNOWDIDA interest in supporting the process of women's empowerment, which is defined as women's increased participation in the development process and increased control over resources.
Situational Analysis	There is some identification of gender gaps, mainly in access to resources and skills training. There is no mention of gender discrimination, or lack of women's representation in decision-making positions.
Programme Goals	Here there are several goals which are concerned with women's increased access to resources, and increased participation in the development process.
Project Goals	There are no specific gender-oriented objectives. When a target group is mentioned, this is sometimes followed by the phrase 'especially women'.
Project Activities	There are no activities which are gender-specific, nor which are concerned with closing gender gaps, overcoming discrimination, or increasing women's participation in the process of project planning and implementation.
Project Implementation	Despite the Country Director's claim that the projects are implemented in a 'gender-sensitive' way, the consultant's visits to various project sites reveal that there is no attempt to identify and address gender issues during the implementation process.

Looking at the 'gender assessment' of the SNOWDIDA Country Programme shown in Table 1, the reader may get the uneasy feeling of already having visited Sundia, or at least somewhere very similar. The assessment shows a gradual diminution as the programme moves from policy statement to policy implementation. This process of diminution is here called *policy evaporation*.

One common aspect of policy evaporation is that, although the policy goals are concerned with women's increased 'participation and control over resources', project objectives have re-interpreted this as 'increased access to resources'. The (bottom-up) strategy of women's participation and empowerment has been reversed into a (top-down) strategy of service-delivery.

Gender-policy evaporation is a common phenomenon. Sometimes the policy evaporates bit by bit, between the formulation of a policy and its implementation. Sometimes you have only to turn over a page of a development plan, and all the gender issues previously mentioned have suddenly disappeared. Evaporation can be a very rapid process!

But this is only the surface evidence of policy evaporation. Now we come to the more interesting question: who is doing what, and why?

Is SNOWDIDA a bureaucracy?

We cannot entirely understand SNOWDIDA's treatment of gender issues if we regard SNOWDIDA as a normal bureaucracy. This is because bureaucracy is supposed to implement policy. According to the 'proper' theory of bureaucracy, evaporation of policy cannot be understood, since the purpose of the bureaucracy is to implement policy, not evaporate it.

More specifically, from a Weberian theoretical perspective of bureaucracy, policy evaporation is incomprehensible at three levels: policy, planning, and organisation. Let us look at each of these in turn.

Policy

SNOWDIDA does not make policy. Policy is made at the political level of government, and the job of SNOWDIDA is to implement policy. According to the Weberian theory of bureaucracy, implementation of policies is the central purpose of the chain of command (from the government). Bureaucratic rules and procedures are primarily concerned with ensuring that policy guidelines from the top generate appropriate action throughout the organisation. It follows that wilful policy evaporation within SNOWDIDA cannot be explained within Weberian theory.

When a SNOWDIDA official dilutes or ignores the policy on women's advancement, the official is actually re-making policy. Negation of a policy automatically becomes policy intervention, entailing the assumption of powers which are not given in the chain of command and which therefore contradict a basic principle of bureaucracy.

Whereas in other areas an official's repudiation of policy would merit dismissal, in the area of women's advancement the official may instead be praised for being honest and pragmatic. There must a different value system operating here. *Something else is going on.*

Planning

Similarly, policy evaporation during the planning process is incomprehensible, according to Weberian principles. The bureaucratic planning process works according to given rules and procedures. Development plans are formulated to address the problems which have been identified in the process of setting the development policy against the facts of the reality in Sundia.

This identification of problems should lead into the formulation of goals, since goals should be concerned with overcoming the problems. Goals give way to objectives which will address the problems. This is part of a logical planning sequence which is an essential aspect of the due process of a Weberian bureaucracy.

Therefore, the gradual evaporation of policy during the planning process is bureaucratically irrational. It entails slippage from the rationality of the proper process, and this slippage contradicts a basic ideal of Weberian bureaucracy. It can be understood only as a mistake, which must be corrected if procedures are being followed properly. However, if there is a pattern of evaporation throughout the area of policy on women's advancement, then this cannot be a mistake. *There must be other norms operating, quite outside bureaucratic norms.*

Organisation

A third aspect of Weberian-style bureaucracy is that it adapts to new policy and new demands by developing specialised departments, staffed by professionals with specialised training. But when one asks the SNOWDIDA office in Sundia why the Country Programme has overlooked gender issues, the answer is likely to come back like a shot: 'We have nobody with the training to understand these things'.

The policy has been in place for ten years, and still there are no personnel with the training to implement it? This is incomprehensible within a Weberian theory of bureaucracy. It demands some other form of explanation. For, from a Weberian perspective, bureaucrats' official opinions are formed only in terms of given policies, and given rules and procedures. Officially, they do not have their own personal opinions; or, if they do, their opinions must not interfere with their work. For Weber, the whole point of a modern bureaucracy is that it made a break with earlier and medieval systems of administration which were patrimonial, patriarchal, autocratic, arbitrary, inconsistent, irrational, and so on. Thus the whole point of a modern bureaucracy is that it follows policy and due process, *and there is not something else really going on.*

Overt bureaucracy and covert patriarchy

It is not enough to say that policy evaporation occurs in SNOWDIDA's programmes because SNOWDIDA is a bureaucracy, and bureaucracies are automatically patriarchal. On the contrary, the bureaucrats are trained to follow rules and procedures, and to implement policies. And yet, if SNOWDIDA adhered to bureaucratic rules, it would actually be implementing the policy on women's advancement. Therefore, SNOWDIDA can be seen encompassing two very different forms of organisation: the overt and the covert.

- The overt organisation is the development-agency bureaucracy, with its explicit policies and procedures, and legal-rational system of analysis. The Weberian model is its legitimating ideology.

- The covert patriarchy, or the 'patriarchal pot', is within the organisation, which runs counter to the Weberian model and enables the subversion of those policies and directives which threaten covert patriarchal interests.

When presented with feminist policies, the overt and the covert organisations have opposing interests, values, rules, and objectives: bureaucratic principles demand implementation; patriarchal principles demand evaporation.

The culture of the patriarchal pot

If we apply the label 'patriarchal pot' to the organisation which subverts female gender interests, we need to understand more about the way in which the patriarchal pot can exist alongside the bureaucracy, given that they would seem to be antagonistic. We need to know more about the structure and behaviour of the pot, and how it maintains its existence.

Let us look at the interests which are served by the pot, and the procedures by which it is maintained. If it is actually antagonistic to bureaucracy, we need to know how this contradictory and cancerous state of affairs can continue to survive and thrive in partnership with bureaucracy.

Internal interests of the patriarchal pot

The patriarchal interests within SNOWDIDA are not hard to find. First, of course, like other bureaucracies North and South, it is male-dominated. Gender inequality in recruitment, conditions of service, and promotion are essential for maintaining the SNOWDIDA tradition of male domination and male culture. SNOWDIDA is run as a wing of the Snowdian Ministry of Foreign Affairs, which has always been a male preserve.

Implementing a development policy for women's advancement therefore threatens the male domination of SNOWDIDA. It immediately suggests the need to recruit more women and — even more threatening — to recruit feminists. Herein lies the internal threat to SNOWDIDA: that feminist recruits would not confine their interests to the advancement of women within Sundia, but would be equally interested in the advancement of women within SNOWDIDA!

External interests of the patriarchal pot

Here we have to understand the common patriarchal interest between SNOWDIDA and its cooperating Ministry, the Sundian Ministry of Planning (MOP). Both are government bureaucracies, and, therefore, both have common experience and procedures when it comes to delaying, subverting, or ignoring government policies which threaten the privileges of class, tribe, religious group, gender, and so on. In fact, when it comes to subverting Weberian ideals of legal-rational behaviour, the Sundian Ministry outdoes SNOWDIDA.

In the area of gender, the Sundian MOP has exactly the same problem as SNOWDIDA. It also has a government which, at the political level, has handed down policies on women's equality and advancement. In fact, MOP officials have a more serious interest in ensuring policy evaporation: the government policy on gender threatens not only male domination within MOP, but also the continuance of the patriarchal control of society as a whole. The Sundian government policy on gender equality would challenge the customary laws and traditions which have always maintained male domination of Sundian society.

Whereas the North-South relationship has many underlying conflicts and tensions, common patriarchal interests can provide the basis for brotherhood.

The men's club alliance

The easy and cosy relationship between the officials of SNOWDIDA and MOP needs also to be understood in terms of the 'men's club' culture to which they both belong. Officials on both sides are part of the Sundian male culture of meetings, cocktail parties, and the golf club.

The men's club infects both the office and the social world of the high-level bureaucrat in Sundia. At the office, the privileged male activity of high-level decision-making is supported by the menial female work of office-cleaning, secretarial services, and document-production. Similarly, at the domestic level, the husband's full-time professional occupation is enabled by the wife, who looks after the home, children, schooling, and shopping. Leisure hours at cocktail parties and golf clubs are financed by the unpaid or exploited labour of the lower classes, especially their female members.

In the Sundian men's club, women are not discussed as equals or even as human beings. Women are sexual objects or commodities, to be hunted as sexual prey or acquired for additional wealth and prestige. SNOWDIDA officials who attempt to introduce policies of gender equality into the development discourse not only upset the workplace, they upset the whole patriarchal culture. In particular, they upset the men's club, which is not only the centre of their social life but also their essential meeting place for informal contacts and influence in Sundia.

The structure of the patriarchal pot

We have now looked at the common interests and culture of the alliance which sustains the patriarchal pot. But we still need to look at how this pot actually works. How are we to understand the process by which a particular policy can evaporate, when other policies do not? We have to look at the structure of the pot in terms of its relationship to the overt bureaucracy and its legitimating theory and ideology.

Diplomacy in defence of patriarchy

The Country Director's simple formula for implementing a SNOWDIDA development-support programme in Sundia is, as far as possible, to reduce SNOWDIDA policy in Sundia to the selection of the particular MOP programmes for which SNOWDIDA will provide support. Such a selection process is usually conducted as if there is complete Snowdian-Sundian consensus on development policy.

However, this smooth diplomatic gloss conceals the need for policy-level negotiation in areas where in fact there is lack of consensus. All SNOWDIDA development principles have implications for changes in the structure of Sundian society. Therefore, all development co-operation between Snowdia and Sundia needs to be based on initial negotiations to ensure that the policy priorities of both sides are being pursued. For example, in the area of SNOWDIDA policy on structural adjustment, policy is enforced by conditionality. On structural adjustment, the Country Director's diplomatic gloss disappears, and he (it is likely to be a 'he') talks tough.

But in the area of gender equality, SNOWDIDA behaves more like a diplomatic mission than a development agency. When it comes to SNOWDIDA gender policy, the Country Director suddenly becomes very diplomatic, and states that 'we cannot interfere with the internal affairs of Sundia'.

When the Country Director talks of structural adjustment, he is in charge of a bureaucracy. When he talks of gender issues, he is in charge of the patriarchal pot.

Theory in support of pot preservation

The most important aspect of preserving the patriarchal pot is that it should remain invisible. One important way of enabling the pot quietly and invisibly to evaporate the policy is to adopt a vocabulary in which a discussion of women's empowerment becomes impossible. This may be achieved by adopting a technical vocabulary which is not appropriate for the analysis — or even the recognition — of the political and ideological dimensions of the development process.

In order to maintain the technical level of discourse, the Country Director has advised all SNOWDIDA staff that, as technical advisers, they should avoid all politically loaded words — especially in writing. They should avoid the phrase 'gender inequality' and instead talk more diplomatically about 'gender differences'. Also the word 'equality' should be replaced by 'equity', or some other non-threatening term.

Another essential element in de-politicising the vocabulary is to reduce the discourse on women's advancement to the level of *providing for women's basic needs and increasing women's access to resources.* By this means, awkward words such as 'control' or 'discrimination' can be avoided. The word 'oppression' should in no circumstance be entertained. Within this vocabulary, it is possible to discuss women's advancement *within the existing social system,* and not in terms of the need to reform this system.

Addressing gender issues must be treated as a secondary concern which relates only to improved project efficiency. The project has its own primary purpose, concerned with purely technical objectives of increasing the water supply, improving institutional capacity, or whatever. Gender is to be treated as an 'add-on'. Of course, if it can be added, by the same token it can be subtracted.

The implicit ideology of the patriarchal pot

Here we see that the technical vocabulary of development is ideology masquerading as theory. The underlying ideological principle is that systems of male domination in Sundia are not to be the subject of development interventions. Any such intervention is to be labelled as 'interference'. In the area of gender, SNOWDIDA works within the existing patriarchal structure. (Although there is the awkward ideological contradiction that in other areas the policy is structural adjustment!)

This, of course, must remain covert ideology — for the simple reason that the overt principles are the exact opposite of the covert principles. Both SNOWDIDA and Sundia have explicit development policies concerned with promoting gender equality and ending practices of gender discrimination.

This points to the absolute importance of technical rationalisation as a mode and vocabulary of discourse. Within a technical and non-political vocabulary, the ideological contradiction between policy and practice never comes up for discussion. It remains invisible.

Covert procedures of the patriarchal pot

Policy evaporation cannot remain invisible simply on the basis of applying vocabulary control. For instance, there may be vocal members of the women's movement in both Snowdia and Sundia who want to know why there seems to be no action on SNOWDIDA's policies of women's advancement.

So if a gender issue does actually get on to the agenda, how is it to be dealt with? The answer is that it must apparently be dealt with by normal bureaucratic procedure. But this must be done in such a way that the gender issue will slowly evaporate down to nothing.

The procedures of the patriarchal pot are concerned with mocking bureaucratic procedure, making sure that what goes in never comes out. The patriarchal pot implements a strange slow-motion parody of the procedures of Weberian bureaucracy. What looks on the surface like bureaucracy is actually the slow and destructive boiling of the pot.

Let us suppose that a visiting gender consultant has pointed out to the Country Director that family-planning clinics refuse to provide women with contraceptives unless they bring a letter of permission from their husbands. In effect, this makes contraceptives unavailable to most married women and to all single women, and a major part of the SNOWDIDA Health Sector budget is to provide support for family-planning clinics.

The consultant seems to have revealed the lack of attention to the SNOWDIDA gender policy on ending discriminatory practices. The Country Director has to respond to this criticism, and may even have to be seen to take action and make changes in the office. There are various ways in which the Country Director may do this. We may divide his responses into three types of action: verbal defence, diversionary action, and organisational change.[3]

Let us look at each of these in turn. If possible, the Country Director will want to confine his reaction to *verbal defence*, which involves demonstrating that the consultant's criticisms of the programme are mistaken.

Procedures for verbal defence

Denial: The Country Director claims that 'The gender consultant was here for only a day, and has misunderstood the problem. It is Sundian policy that contraceptives are made available only to couples. Therefore, the clinic is only following government policy, to which SNOWDIDA also must also conform.' (But flat denial is a dangerous strategy for the Country Director, because it usually involves obvious lies. Success depends on the triumph of authority over truth.)

Inversion: 'There is a problem here, but it originates in the home and not in the clinic. Husbands who insist that wives cannot be given contraceptives without their permission, and Sundian wives accept this situation. This is therefore a domestic problem, in which the Sundian government cannot interfere, let alone SNOWDIDA.' (This should be recognised as yet another version of the old strategy of blaming the victim.)

Policy dilution: 'SNOWDIDA policy is concerned with increasing access to resources, which we have done by providing more clinics and stocking them with a variety of contraceptives. The rules of who is eligible to receive contraceptives must remain in the hands of the government.' (It is not true that SNOWDIDA policy is limited to providing resources to government. The policy also involves enabling women's empowerment and overcoming the obstacles of discriminatory practices.)

Since verbal defence must entail misrepresentation, the Country Director may choose alternative procedures, admitting the problem and proposing action to address it. This is the basis of *diversionary action.*

Procedures for diversionary action

Lip service: 'The consultant has pointed to a problem which has been worrying us for some time. We are most grateful for her clear analysis of the problem. We intend to establish a Consultative Committee to look at these recommendations, which have implications for improving our attention to gender issues in all SNOWDIDA programmes.' (This is often a procedure for sounding good at the time, but with absolutely no intention of taking any action.)

Research study: 'The consultant has pointed to just one aspect of a larger problem, which is very sensitive and touches on matters of Sundian custom and tradition. We have decided to appoint a team from the Sundian Research Institute to look at gender issues in all sectors, in the context of structural adjustment, and to make recommendations on the implications for SNOWDIDA.' (By the time the report comes out, at the end of next year, the original problem should have been forgotten.)

Shelving: 'The research report "Gender Issues in the Context of Structural Adjustment in Sundia" has recently been completed. It has been sent to headquarters in Snowdia for their consideration.' (The report has been shelved. It will never be seen again.)

Procedures for ineffectual organisational change

Even more diversionary is organisational change. This will require significantly more time, which is viewed as a positive aspect on the road to doing nothing. Moreover, if the organisational change is inappropriate for addressing gender issues, there never will be any appropriate outcomes.

Compartmentalisation: 'We are now establishing the new post of Women in Development (WID) Counsellor to head the new WID Section in the SNOWDIDA office in Sundia. The WID Counsellor will advise on gender issues in all projects, will supervise the planning of support for women's projects, and will be in charge of gender training for SNOWDIDA staff and counterparts.' (Since the SNOWDIDA office is divided into conventional sectors, the creation of a separate WID Section effectively treats gender as a separate sector, when it is actually supposed to be an inter-sectoral concern. This compartmentalisation contradicts the SNOWDIDA policy of mainstreaming gender issues in all sectors of development assistance.)

Subversion: 'I have appointed our Programme Assistant, Mrs Patrison, to take on the additional responsibility of WID Counsellor in our office here in Sundia. I know she is very young and has no previous experience in gender issues. But I am sure she will soon pick it up.' (This appointment is an act of pure cynicism. Patrison is a junior official well known for incompetence and administrative confusion, and famous for immediately losing any document given to her.)

Tokenism: 'I am pleased to announce that the wife of the Vice-President, Mrs Charity Wander-Wander, has agreed to sit on our Sundia-SNOWDIDA Health Programme Committee. Until now the Sundian members of this Committee have all been men, but now we shall hear the woman's voice on some of these difficult issues concerning tradition and custom.' (Mrs Wander-Wander is a well-known traditionalist. In fact, she is known for telling women to obey their husbands. Mrs Wander-Wander has been invited as a token woman. In any meeting she will be allowed to speak for five token minutes to ensure that 'the woman's point of view has been heard' before the men take their decision.)

Conclusion

To examine the process of gender-policy evaporation, this paper has introduced the notion of a development agency as a 'patriarchal pot'. A development agency is here seen as a complex cooking pot, on which the lid normally remains closed. The pot is filled with patriarchal bias, implicit in the agency's values, ideology, development theory, organisational systems, and procedures.

This is the pot into which policies for women's advancement are thrown. It is a strange patriarchal pot, with much input but no output. Officially the policy exists, and the pot does not. But this paper says that the policy has evaporated, and what remains is the pot.

International programmes for women's advancement must be based on an analysis of the various forms of patriarchal opposition to gender-oriented policies. In particular, we must take an interest in the workings of government bureaucracies. If we want to change the world, we cannot treat bureaucracy as politically neutral. This paper analyses how bureaucracy can play a major role in the maintenance and social reproduction of patriarchy. Women's global advancement depends on the transformation of patriarchal bureaucracy into feminocracy, beginning with development agencies.

In other words, as we know more about the patriarchal cooking pot, we must prepare to break it to pieces.

Notes

1 Outcome of the Third UN Conference on Women, Nairobi, 1990.

2 Some readers may be familiar with some aspects of Sundia from my discussion of an earlier visit in 'Towards Better North-South Communication on Women's Development: Avoiding the Roadblocks of Patriarchal Resistance', presented at a Women in Development Europe workshop on gender planning, February 1992, Dublin. I am grateful to my partner, Roy Clarke, for the endless discussions which led to the invention of Snowdia and Sundia. My analysis of patriarchal resistance within development agencies was carried further in 'Breaking the patriarchal alliance: governments, bilaterals and NGOs,' *Focus on Gender* 2:3 (1995).

3 An earlier interpretation of these 'procedures' appears in Sara Longwe (1990): 'From Welfare to Empowerment: The Situation of Women in Development in Africa', *Women in International Development,* Working Paper No 204, University of Michigan at East Lansing, a paper originally written for the 1988 inaugural meeting of the African Women's Development and Communication Network (FEMNET), Nairobi.

■ **Sara Hlupekile Longwe** *is a consultant in women's development and an activist for women's rights. She has published widely in the area of gender analysis, and is on the Editorial Board of* Gender and Development. *This article is a shortened version of a presentation at the seminar 'Women's Rights and Development: Vision and Strategy for the Twenty-first Century', organised by One World Action, Oxfam UK and Ireland, the Gender Institute of the London School of Economics, and Queen Elizabeth House, at the University of Oxford in May 1995. The original paper appears in* Women's Rights and Development, *edited by Mandy Macdonald and published by Oxfam UK and Ireland; this version was first published in* Development in Practice, *Volume 7, number 2, in 1997.*

Participatory development: an approach sensitive to class and gender

Dan Connell

Introduction

The farmers in a small village in the Indonesian province of Irian Jaya in western New Guinea had rarely, if ever, seen a cow before provincial government officials announced the imminent arrival of a boat-load of them. If villagers were shocked, they did not register it, for they had grown accustomed to bizarre surprises from the visiting experts, who periodically dropped by to tell them how to 'develop' their community. But the incident triggered a series of events that typify the evolution of the debate over 'people's participation' in development.[1]

This article will use the Irian Jaya experience as a vehicle for clarifying the centrality of popular participation to the development process. It will then explore the ways in which a focus on class and gender takes participatory development to a new level. Finally, it will consider ways in which development agents can support transformational development.

Integrating the strengths of political economy and gender planning into a participatory methodology yields an approach that puts people first; that does not isolate or privilege particular sectors for special, and often separate, remedial attention; that places subjugation alongside poverty as social evils to be decisively overcome, not simply alleviated. The outcome is an emancipatory concept and practice of development, in which inequalities and inequities are addressed together, not with a view simply to redistribute wealth and income on a transitory basis, but to re-configure society to the benefit of the majority of its members, while empowering them to develop themselves as they see fit. Fostering this demands a delicate and evolving balance between guidance and support, facilitation and response, on the part of the development agent.

The 100-to-1 cow project

In the early 1980s, when the Irian Jaya cattle-raising project was first conceived by development professionals, the target village consisted of some 300 households. Most people eked out a living from small-scale, subsistence farming. They supplemented this by raising a pig and a few chickens, and by hunting. There were no regular links to the few towns in the district, and, apart from government officials and the occasional itinerant trader, the village had infrequent contact with the outside world. Villagers had to walk a half-day to reach the nearest road, where they often waited another half-day for a 'bus' plying the rural routes. No one owned a boat large enough to travel more than a short distance away.

Government development planners were anxious to introduce beef cattle to the region, a former Dutch colony which fell under Indonesian administration in the 1960s, in order to provide a new source of meat for the country's rapidly growing urban centres. As the people of the village had migrated to the coast from upland areas known for breeding pigs, the planners assumed that these people would adapt easily to the challenges of cattle-raising.

The visiting experts convened a one-day training programme to introduce the idea to the villagers. Soon afterward, 100 beef cattle arrived. Almost at once, they began wreaking havoc. Knee-high fences designed to keep pigs from entering the village centre were no barrier to these animals: they trampled gardens, damaged homes, broke tools, and fouled fresh water sources. When the cows were shooed out of the populated area, many wandered into the bush and disappeared.

Within days, the farmers met to organise themselves to deal with this menace, known as 'development'. Deciding to hunt the cattle down before they did any more damage, villagers armed themselves with bows and arrows and set out into the surrounding countryside. One by one they encircled and killed the cows, until there was only one single animal left alive. Satisfied that the danger was past, they spared the lone survivor, a living memorial to the futility of the 'blueprint' method of development, in which experts designed projects far from the community for which they were intended, with little or no input from the members of that community, and then set out to implant them. In Irian Jaya, development planners learned a hard lesson about the value of participation — but the learning process had barely begun.

A few years after the infamous '100-to-1 cow project', as it came to be known, members of a development team from the provincial university visited the village to make an assessment of community needs. They were committed to drawing up a development plan that grew out of village input, so they brought no fixed plan with them.

The team convened a village assembly, and told the people that this time things would be different. They asked villagers to tell them what they needed, and they promised that they would do their best to oblige them. When the farmers asked to delay their decision until they could consider it more deeply, the team agreed and left. When they returned a few days later, they convened another assembly, where village leaders announced that they had come to a decision: they wanted cows!

Now it was the development agents' turn to be shocked, for they knew the story of the ill-fated cow project. They asked: how could the farmers risk another debacle after their earlier experience? Why cows, and not pigs or poultry? Why not agricultural extension assistance with their gardens? Why not new infrastructure for transportation to the market, or food-storage facilities? What about health care, literacy, income generation, or any number of innovative approaches to rural development?

Once they began asking these questions, the answers were deceptively simple: cows were all that the people knew of development. Since outsiders brought cows, the question for villagers, as they saw it, was only: did they or did they not want more cows? In the end, said most villagers, at least the animals could be a source of meat or something to sell to passing traders. Better to take them than not.

Reconceiving people's participation

Fortunately for the villagers, the visiting team grasped the fact that participatory development involves more than simply asking people what they want and then providing it, regardless of the probable consequences or of the prospects for success. They declined the request for cows and set out instead to engage villagers in a thorough process of self-assessment, in order to ascertain what would benefit them over the long term. One researcher came to live in the village, reporting regularly to the supervising team at the university, and assisted by a student-team of two women and two men. Several team members spoke the local dialect. The new field team held a series of meetings with segments of the community. Team members also talked at length to individual villagers, and they mapped out the village economy.

What they discovered was that many households supplemented what they produced for personal consumption with the sale of fruit and vegetables in the nearest district market, several days' journey from the village. Produce was sold in small lots, almost always by individual producers who had no knowledge of weights or prices. Invariably, they were cheated and came back with far less than their goods were worth. What was needed, at least initially, was not production assistance to grow more, but rather marketing assistance to get more out of what they had. This knowledge provided the basis for the village's first participatory development project.

The project began with a training component, as the development agents set out to teach villagers about weights and measures. Once again, however, the outsiders ran head-on into the limits of their own assumptions. Residents lacked numeracy, a precondition for mastering the complex system of weighing and pricing through which they were being cheated in the marketplace.

Once this became clear, the team restructured the training component of the project to prepare villagers on several levels, starting with instruction in simple mathematics. Then the team acquired scales, not only for practising concepts, but for weighing produce prior to taking it to the market. Next, they worked with villagers to establish small marketing cooperatives, largely on the basis of extended family units, in which four or five people pooled their produce before sending it to town for sale. Finally, they helped to estimate payment options for these lots of produce, relating weights to potential unit prices, before villagers confronted the fast-talking middlemen in the town.

However, their entry into the local market also brought new problems and challenges. Once villagers mastered the system, they discovered that prices continued to fluctuate, sometimes wildly. Their conclusion was swift: they were being cheated again!

Yet a closer investigation revealed that the problem lay elsewhere. The local market was responding occasionally — and, from the standpoint of local producers, unpredictably — to the downward pressure of over-supply from outside the region, as, for example, when a boat-load of onions or dried fish arrived from Surabaya and caused a sudden collapse of local prices. This had devastating consequences for those becoming dependent on income from these sources.

With these new challenges came several important lessons: it is not enough to consult beneficiaries and then to act on their behalf, however benign one's intentions. Nor is it usually enough to engage people in a development process if the conceptual orientation and the language of that process do not relate to their experience, and if they lack the tools to assess their needs effectively and to know what options are available to them to bring about constructive change.

Even then, there is more. The most remote Southern communities exist today in a global context, about which their members and those who would act to support their development must know — at least in bare outline — if they are not to waste both their time and their increasingly scarce resources. Project participants need information and perspective on the economic and political context in which their project is operating.

Participation as a strategic goal

People's participation is not only about achieving the more efficient and more equitable distribution of material resources: it is also about the sharing of knowledge and the transformation of the process of learning itself in the service of people's self-development. Key aspects of this knowledge start within rural communities and extend outwards in ever-widening circles, like ripples in a pond, which determine the limits and the potential for development at the local level. For this process to be effective, knowledge located outside needs to be transferred into the community, just as knowledge within the community needs to reach the development agents and sponsoring agencies.

While development agencies need greater access to community knowledge in order to play a more effective role there, rural villagers need increased access to tools and information that these agencies can provide about the wider context in which they live and work, in order to make informed and appropriate decisions about their development. This is where the development agent comes in: as a bridge linking these parties together in a working partnership.

People's participation is both a methodology and a strategic goal of development. As such, it is not something to be added on to or inserted into a development model. It is an alternative model that proposes both to improve people's standards of living and to give them a measure of control over the standards themselves. The process starts with the identification and description of problems, needs, and opportunities. This takes specific tools and a grasp of context — local, regional, and sometimes even global — to be carried out effectively. It continues through grassroots involvement in the conception, planning, and implementation of a solution, which also demands particular skills and information. And it carries on through monitoring and evaluation, which lays the groundwork for the next phase of project identification and planning. People's participation is an on-going process of mobilisation and self-organisation that reshapes the community itself, as it is applied and developed through involvement with specific, discrete projects.

But suppose, in the case of the Irian Jaya village, that knowledge was flowing in both directions and the community was participating in the conception, planning, and implementation of the project. A host of new questions arises. Through whom and to whom does the new information flow? Who, within the village, controls the newly generated surplus, and how is it used? How is the production process affected, particularly in terms of the gender-determined division of labour, as women were in this case both the primary producers of fruit and vegetables and also the ones who took the produce to market? How does the improvement in the return on agricultural products from the distribution end affect the value, allocation, use, and exchange of land (and how is this structured in the first place)? How is the level and quality of village self-identity and organisation affected? What new issues/needs will now come forward from sectors of the community who did not benefit from this development? What issues/needs from those who did not benefit equally? What other issues/needs, if any, might now come forward from disadvantaged or exploited sectors of the community unrelated to this project? Has self-awareness of need changed in the community as a result of this experience? If so, how, and among whom? Perhaps most importantly, will the outcome of future encounters with outside development agents be any different in the light of this experience?

Who participates?

Building popular participation into a community's self-development, in order to transform its social relationships and not merely to ameliorate the misery of a few, is a complex and difficult process. The quality of community participation cannot be effectively measured in statistical tallies or sociological summaries alone: by judging one's success, for example, by noting the percentage of the adult population of a village that attends a public meeting, or by totalling up the opinions voiced by a survey sample. Which sectors of a village participate and how they do so may be far more important than how many do so, in gauging the success or failure of popular participation — and more difficult to assess. Invariably, if an active intervention is not made to avoid it, those at the bottom of the socio-economic and political ladders will remain where they were, despite the establishment of new development projects, no matter how many members of the community are consulted or involved in project development.

Power relationships reproduce themselves, regardless of how 'participatory' or 'democratic' a setting is, unless a conscious, sustained effort is undertaken to alter them. Gather members of a community under a tree in the centre of a village and invite them to select a committee to manage a new project, and the results are fairly predictable. The meeting will be dominated by those who traditionally exercise influence in the community, with the most skilled orators and debaters monopolising the exchange. With few exceptions, these will be older men from the dominant clan or ethnic group — often landowners, merchants, mayors, or village headmen, who occupy the upper end of the socio-economic spectrum as it exists in this particular community.

To know whether and in what way the less powerful members of a community are participating, we must have a clear picture of how power and influence are exercised within a village, and how wealth and access to productive resources are distributed within the community. We need a clear idea of who fits into the primary social, economic, political and cultural categories and how these categories interact (or not) when it comes to making community decisions. For example, are members of a particular social group — village women, an ethnic minority, a sub-clan, a caste, landless tenant farmers, farm labourers — present but not truly engaged? Are the opinions which they publicly voice truly their own? Do they say the same things when their husbands or wives or village elders or employers or other authority figures are not present?

The answers to questions like these can be acquired only through deeper investigation into the economic and social constitution of the communities where projects are to be sited, and by checking the observations at public gatherings against information gained through other means and in different venues. This is particularly true for issues of class and gender.

The intersection of participatory methodology with gender and class

In the early 1970s, an awareness started to grow among those working in the field that standard approaches to rural development were not eliminating poverty. Economic growth was not promoting equity; in many cases, projects even widened the gap between rich and poor. In India during the 'Green Revolution', for example, the introduction of new agricultural technologies increased over-all output, while often making worse the conditions of the rural poor who lacked access to land, credit, input supplies, and extension services. The benefits went mainly to large landholders, who expanded their acreage by evicting tenants and buying or leasing land from smallholders.[2]

In the 1970s, FAO sponsored a series of field workshops in eight Asian countries to assess the successes and failures of rural development projects, before launching the Small Farmers Development Programme. The common findings included the following observations.

- The vast majority of the rural poor were not reached by existing programmes.
- Few small farmers in the project areas were even aware of government programmes. Often, those who were thought they were meant only for the more important people in a village.
- Very few were active members of any community organisation.
- Most were heavily indebted to local money-lenders or rich relatives. Though they badly needed credit, most thought they were ineligible for it through established institutions.
- Most government extension staff relied on progressive farmers to disseminate improved practices to the rural poor, inadvertently following a trickle-down approach to development.
- Every country had pilot rural development projects which were initially successful but then collapsed when originating staff were withdrawn.
- Few programmes were suited to the needs of landless labourers, women, or poor youth.
- Most programmes were planned from the top, with little consultation with either field staff or the small farmers themselves.
- The status of small farmers was steadily declining from ownership to sharecropper and labourer, while that of large farmers with access to new technology, inputs, and services was increasing, resulting in a widening gap between rich and poor.
- Most rural development programmes were strengthening the capacity of government line agencies to deliver their inputs and services to the rural population in general, with little attention to reaching the poor or women, or to helping these sectors to improve their capacity to compete for and utilise these inputs and services.[3]

At this time, researchers and analysts in many countries were arriving at similar conclusions. The common thread was a recognition that the absence of grassroots participation in these projects was a principal cause of their failure. Yet there were major shortcomings in the flurry of attention to people's participation, especially with regard to women. Between 1974 and 1980, for example, only four per cent of the projects funded by the US Agency for International Development, which was increasingly emphasising 'participation' in its stated project criteria, involved the participation of women. In half of these, women were minority participants.[4]

A gender-based critique of development policies and programmes also began to take shape in the 1970s, marked initially by the publication of *Women's Role in Economic Development*, the influential book by Danish development analyst Esther Boserup. This critique gained force during the UN Decade for Women between 1975 and 1985 and was a central theme of the international women's conference in Nairobi at the end of the decade. From there on, most development agencies began to incorporate attention to women's needs into their programmes and projects. By the time of the next global women's conference in Beijing in September 1995 — and much in evidence at the UN-sponsored Cairo and Copenhagen summits on population and social development that preceded Beijing in September 1994 and March 1995 — this critique had come to define mainstream development discourse, though there remained substantial differences in its application.

Throughout this period, gender-sensitive development underwent several permutations, starting with the 'welfarist' approach usually identified with Women in Development (WID) programmes, and running through the 'equity' approach associated with Women and Development (WAD), to the 'anti-poverty' approach of Gender and Development (GAD) programmes. With the deterioration of the global economy in the 1980s and the widespread implementation of economic stabilisation and structural adjustment programmes throughout the South, a variation of GAD, known as the 'efficiency' approach, has gained prominence. This puts the stress more on development than on women, and argues that all projects are more efficient and effective where women actively participate. In an era of increasingly scarce resources for development programmes and with the growing recognition of past development failures, this approach is growing in popularity and is frequently cited by multilateral agencies, such as the World Bank, as undergirding their current approach to development.[5]

However, an 'empowerment' approach, with roots in women's organisations of the South, is also gaining increasing attention, focusing not on women as a strictly economic target but rather as a force for transforming social relations. In this framework, women's subordination is understood to be the result of both gender relations and broader political factors, such as colonial and neo-colonial oppression. What is needed, in this view, is structural change in gender and class relations, as well as economic growth.[6] Such new thinking is reflected in the critical exploration of the relationship between economic growth and human development by the UNDP in its annual Human Development Reports.[7] This perspective is also at the core of the writings of the late Nigerian political-economist Claude Ake, who argued that sweeping political change is necessary to unlock the potential for development in Africa.[8]

Attempts to synthesise the strengths and insights of this approach with those of participatory methodologies are leading to a new radically new approach to development, whose intent is to reconsider and redefine the very notion of what 'development' is and to re-insert women, together with other exploited and oppressed social groups, into the process as 'agents' of transformative change, rather than as 'beneficiaries' of it.

Socio-economic and gender analysis

In this new approach, sometimes termed Social and Gender Analysis (SAGA) or Socio-Economic and Gender Analysis (SEGA), 'development' is conceptualised as a multifaceted process of increasing not only standards of living but also control over and definition of those standards.[9] Development has social, political, and cultural dimensions, as well as economic components. It is a liberating process with qualitative and quantitative aspects that cannot be separated from each other — a process by which formerly excluded and subordinate social groups not only transform their physical environment, but also gain power over their economic and political environment and over the knowledge, skills, and other resources needed to sustain this transformation. A socio-economic and gender-sensitive approach to this process promotes equity and equality within the community that enjoys the fruits of these projects and programmes, and not only changes the position of social groups within the community but transforms the community itself.

In linking development objectives to relationships that are characterised by complex forms of domination, subordination, and exploitation, we profoundly redefine the meaning of development, shifting our focus from one limited to quantitative economic 'growth', to one that includes social emancipation as well. Social and gender transformation become central not only to the methodology of development but to its end result, for the full and equal participation of formerly excluded members of a community in the initiation, design, implementation and outcomes of projects is in itself an important advance in social development. However, if this is to be self-sustaining, participation must rapidly translate into dynamic self-organisation.

A commitment to sustainable organisations needs to be integrated into all project efforts, not only to facilitate the direct, immediate participation of the poor and women, but also to ensure that these efforts support long-term engagement, education, and action. Most rural communities have rich traditions of mutual aid that reflect non-institutional forms of common action. Though there may not be written rules, custom is likely to dictate strict adherence to procedures and clearly understood structures of decision-making and action. Discovering these traditions, whether or not they are consistently practised today, can offer important starting points for extending or reviving common, interest-based action. Efforts should be made to identify, support, and extend them where they exist and to support the efforts of the poor and women to organise in new ways. One role which outside agents can play is to familiarise community members — women and men — with similar efforts elsewhere, and to link these community-based organisations with each other in order to facilitate the growth of regional, national, and even international networks.

Constraints on transformative participation

The rural poor do not participate in development on an equal basis with the rich, nor do women participate on an equal basis with men, owing mainly to their pre-existing, subordinate positions in the society. This is, of course, also true for dominated ethnic groups and others whose exclusion or subjection within a society is reproduced in development interventions. Any approach to development within a specific community inevitably reflects these inequalities. Efforts to challenge them are likely to come up against a number of powerful constraints:

The political conditions and power structures of the country and the community. These may vary from those of a decentralised, laissez-faire system to those of a highly centralised, planned economy. Government responses at the national and local levels may range from indifference, to outright hostility, to full support.

Legislative obstacles, put in place by those in power or with access to power. They may prohibit the poor from organising themselves, or limit the right of women and other social groups to participate in public political activities.

Administrative opposition. This occurs when highly centralised bureaucracies control decision-making, resource allocation, and information and either formally discourage popular participation or impede it through the imposition of complex procedures.

Socio-cultural impediments. They may include deeply ingrained mentalities of dependence and frustration, as well as distrust of outsiders based upon past disappointments or destructive experiences. Conflicting perceptions of interest among various social groups — based, for example, among different class, caste, gender, ethnic or religious constituencies — can also disrupt participation if not approached with care and sensitivity. In some countries, women do not hold title to the land they farm and are therefore ineligible for credit.

The limitations imposed by daily life. These may include the isolation and scattered habitat of the rural poor, their low levels of living and their heavy workloads, especially among women, as well as poor states of health, low levels of education, and a general lack of experience with organised activities such as these.

The chief constraint on transforming people's participation in most countries is political will; but political constraints on popular organising can change suddenly. This occurred in Grenada, after a US-led intervention in 1983 installed a new government which moved swiftly to dismantle the network of subsidised cooperatives set up by the previous regime; and in Nicaragua, after the 1990 elections brought to power a government that immediately limited credit and cancelled subsidies for agricultural cooperatives established by the former regime, causing many to close within months. In similar fashion but with opposite results, the collapse of the Marcos regime in the Philippines in 1987, the fall of the Mengistu regime in Ethiopia in 1991, and the transition from military rule in Brazil in the 1980s, led in each case to an explosion of new community groups, trade unions, and sectoral organisations representing landless peasants, urban poor, women, indigenous minorities and others, as laws governing such organisations changed.

External events and socio-cultural factors may also combine to create new constraints on popular participation in village-level development projects. The outbreak of ethnicity-related conflict in Rwanda in 1994 generated human migrations on a massive scale that disrupted all development programmes there, while injecting divisive (and heretofore incidental) ethnic factors into participation in individual projects. In mid-1994, an eruption of controversy in Bangladesh over the writings of a local feminist, temporarily constrained women's groups from carrying forward gender-based development initiatives throughout that country. The signing of a peace accord between Israel and the Palestine Liberation Organisation in September 1993, triggered a sudden shift in foreign funding for projects in the West Bank and Gaza Strip away from local NGOs to the newly constituted Palestinian National Authority, causing many projects to collapse. The Jerusalem-based Union of Palestinian Medical Relief Committees, for example, was forced to close three of its 19 rural clinics, while the Palestinian Agricultural Relief Committee lost nearly one-fourth of its annual $3 million budget.

What can be done

While it is not possible at the local level to avoid the effects of such externally generated constraints, development agents can assist villagers to anticipate their impact and support efforts to cope with them. In the Palestinian territories, for example, indigenous NGOs organised a broad network in 1994 that quickly came to include over 400 popular organisations, service groups, and charitable societies to make their case for continued funding for village-level development projects from donor agencies and governments, including the new self-rule Palestine Authority. Key donor agencies with in-country field staff assisted in this mobilisation, responding to Palestinian initiatives.

Donor agencies can also facilitate and fund South-South exchanges that give members of affected communities the opportunity to share experiences and to learn from each other. The Centro de Estudios Internacionales in Nicaragua, and the South African Foundation for Contemporary Research, for example, have sponsored a series of exchange visits by development agents from their respective countries, while Latin American women have organised annual 'encounters' to come together to broaden their perspective — and their impact — on development issues and projects within their respective countries.

Another kind of constraint occurs where political movements, parties, or governments set up formal structures to represent the rural poor and women without involving them in a direct, sustained, and meaningful way, except as objects of centrally directed campaigns and projects. In Nicaragua during the 1980s under the government of the Sandinistas, for example, the Party-sponsored national women's organisation, Asociación de Mujeres Nicaragüenses Luisa Amanda Espinosa (AMNLAE), operated social services, literacy campaigns, and income-generating projects for women but, especially in the late 1980s, under the pressures of the US-backed Contra war, it resisted efforts by members to organise activities to deal with gender-specific issues, such as male violence, reproductive rights, pregnancy, or marriage and divorce, and it sought to maintain tight control over all rural projects. In the early 1990s, many frustrated AMNLAE members left the organisation to form autonomous women's organisations.[10] In Brazil, a highly organised rural and urban women's movement pressured the transitional regime in 1985 to set up a government-funded Conselho Nacional dos Dieitos da Mulher (National Council on Women's Rights), that included women legislators and grassroots organisers and was intended as the precursor of a full-scale Ministry of the Status of Women. Yet four years later the original councillors and most of the CNDM staff resigned, amid charges of politicisation and manipulation by the government, and with little to show for the time and effort invested in the committee.[11]

The initial challenge for the development agent is to assess local structures which purport to represent women, the rural poor, and other dominated groups. Once engaged in this process, the outside agent is likely to run head-on into perceived conflicts of interest among dominated and exploited groups, such as peasant associations, trade unions, and women's organisations, or worse, into rivalries among competing groups based in the same population. In Brazil in the 1980s, community-based women's organisations became divided over their positions on reproductive rights and began competing with each other for project funding, often for projects in the same communities. In the West Bank and Gaza each of the four major political factions of the Palestine Liberation Organisation set up competing organisations of farmers, women, workers, and youth to organise village-level development projects and services.

The over-arching challenge is to foster conditions in which rivalries can be subsumed, to some degree, within an alliance for community change that benefits the oppressed and exploited members of the community in tangible ways. The five leading Palestinian women's committees found, for example, that they generated greater resources than before for each of their day-care projects after they formed a Higher

Women's Council in the late 1980s to do joint fundraising. However, continuing political differences among the sponsoring parties undermined this cooperation, until three of the committees insisted on organisational autonomy and formed the Women's Affairs Technical Committee to carry out joint advocacy work for women in the national political arena, as well as to coordinate project work.

Contention is inevitable

People's participation enhances economic equity and social equality, and it encourages democratisation in other realms. For this reason, it is inherently challenging to pre-existing power structures, both within a community and between the community and its broader surroundings, particularly when it is centred directly on socio-economic and gender issues. If effective, it is bound to trigger opposition. For example, when peasants in one Indian village, acting on the advice of a development agent, formed a credit union to break the cycle of perennial debt that had caused a number of them to lose their land, money-lenders charged the organisers with being communists and threatened them with dire consequences. After development agents in another community encouraged farmers to start a pig-selling group to increase their bargaining power, local middlemen, fearing this would cut into their profits, beat up the leader and warned him that, if he continued his activities, he would be further punished.[12]

This aspect of participatory development becomes all the more sensitive in instances where large sums of money are at stake, as is often the case with large-scale projects sponsored by multilateral agencies. Knowing this, the development agent must pay extremely close attention to the social and political environment and use caution in challenging traditional seats of authority before such challenges can be defended and sustained. This is important not only for the prospect of success for the project, but also for the sake of those who respond positively to the invitation to participate in new ways of reshaping their communities and, in doing so, become vulnerable to recriminations after the outside agent leaves the scene. For example, residents of a remote village in the southern Philippine island of Palawan were attacked by powerful timber smugglers after a visiting development agent went to local authorities to report finding a large cache of illegal hardwood logs taken from a nearby rainforest. Development agents themselves can also become targets, as occurred when field workers for Nijera Kori, a Bangladesh NGO, were badly beaten and one was killed after farmers' groups with whom they were working protested against corrupt local officials.

Opposition to gender-sensitive planning can take many forms, from ridicule to resistance. Often it gets personal, with women or men who advocate gender equality being singled out for criticism or attack. There is a great need to provide support for those who take the risk of standing up for equality and change, to carry out education among those who are perhaps confused and uneasy but not adamantly opposed to it, to win allies within the community who have status and command respect and to find ways to demonstrate widespread acceptance elsewhere.

Another major challenge — and a potential danger — is that posed by ethnicity-based organisation and advocacy work, a rapidly growing phenomenon throughout the world since the end of the Cold War. It is important to be clear from the outset that what is being proposed is an inclusive model that rejects ethnic, racial, or other forms of exclusivity rooted in or aimed at structural domination of one group over another.

Meanwhile, development agencies bring their own constraints to full popular participation. The most serious of these are time pressure and a lack of flexibility in the field. There is often a demand from the sponsoring institution and the supporting government to produce quick results, undermining the participatory process. Many sponsoring agencies are structured for centralised planning, decision-making, and implementation, particularly budgets in allocating for prospective projects. Finally, most agencies lack field staff with extensive experience in people's participation — though with time this is likely to improve, as many are now facing the need to develop staff in this area.

Conclusion

The central challenge to the development agent, whether acting alone or as part of a team, is to engage key sectors of the local population in the process and then to nurture this engagement until it blossoms into direct, active participation at as many levels as are possible under the particular circumstances and constraints where he/she is working. As such, the development agent is more a catalyst or a facilitator than an independent initiator — presenting ideas but not issuing orders, encouraging local initiatives but not organising people around his or her preconceived ideas of what is best for them.

There are no simple formulas for this process, as it may vary widely from one situation to another, based upon the specific economic, social, political, and cultural circumstances at play in a community — or upon such unpredictable factors as the chance exposure of one community member to a successful project in another village, or the impact of recent climate patterns on village agriculture.

Class- and gender-sensitive people's participation is interactive. For it to develop successfully, the development agent must participate in the community, getting to know it from the inside out to the greatest degree possible, as members of the community participate in the process of identification and formulation of the project. For its part, the community needs to get to know the outside agent and what he or she brings to the process from prior education and experience, as well as from the mandate of the sponsoring organisation. This takes time, for which there is no substitute, no matter how sophisticated the 'tools' of the development agent. It also demands patience, attention, and flexibility, with development agents spending far more of their time listening than lecturing, especially in the early stages, and adapting their ideas of what is best for a community to those developed by disadvantaged groups within the community itself.

Guiding people's initial efforts at self-analysis and priority-setting may be the most important contribution made by the development agent. In this process, it is not only communication that is needed between the outsider and the disempowered or oppressed sectors of a community, but also *trust* — which must be earned, not learned. Under these circumstances, success will come when the development agent is no longer needed to nurture the process.

Notes

1 This account comes from a development agent with extensive experience in this village, who asked to remain anonymous.

2 See 'Structural characteristics determine who benefits', *Rural Development* No. 15, FAO: Rome, January 1994, p.15.

3 See Antonio J. Ledesma, *A Tree Grows in Village Asia, Cagayan de Oro City,* Philippines: South East Asia Rural Social Leadership Institute, Xavier University College of Agriculture, 1991, pp.1-3. Most rural development projects also ignored the possibility of exacerbating environmental risks, and few took into account the question of long-term resource sustainability (impact on the water table, decreasing fertility, and so on).

4 See UNDP (1982) *Integration of Women in Development*, UNDP: New York.

5 For a review of the literature and policy debates, see Valentine M. Moghadam, WID, WAD, GAD: *Integration of Women, Women's Concerns and Gender Issues in the Development Process,* Gender and Society Working Paper #3, Women's Studies Programme, Birzeit University: Birzeit, Palestine, September 1995, pp.1-30.

6 For more on the empowerment approach to development, see Maruja Barrig, 'Gender in institutions: an inward look' in Barrig and Wehkamp (1994) and Sara Hlupekile Longwe, 'Gender awareness: the missing element in the Third World development project', Gender Aware Project Planning and Evaluation, pp. 149-57. See Moser (1993) pp. 55-79, for an explication of the relation between strategic and practical interests in gender planning.

7 See the UNDP's Human Development Report 1996, UNDP: New York, for detailed statistical information on the failure of economic growth to improve the lives of people in countries with almost half the world's population. It concludes that more growth is needed, but calls for more attention to the structure and quality of that growth to see that it reduces poverty, protects the environment, and ensures sustainability.

8 In Ake (1996), he charged that post-colonial African elites had little if any concept of or commitment to development. Instead, African leaders focused on how to service their constituencies with patronage, while sub-contracting 'development' — in the form of externally designed projects randomly inserted into their economies — to outside agencies, effectively disempowering their own populations. The only solution he saw was political change from below.

9 In the early 1990s, FAO commissioned papers and convened a series of conferences on SEGA under the direction of Patricia Howard-Borjas and John Hourihan. The results were incorporated into *A Manual for Socio-Economic and Gender Analysis: Responding to the Development Challenge,* produced by the ECOGEN Project of the International Development Programme at Clark University, Worcester, MA, USA in October 1995.

10 See Randall (1994) for narratives by women who were active in the FSLN in the 1980s and who came to play leading roles in the autonomous women's movement.

11 See Alvarez (1990) for an account of the debates within the Brazilian women's movement on whether and how to participate in government, as well as an analysis of the movement during the transition from dictatorship to democracy in the 1980s.

12 An account of this incident is cited in K. Bhasin (1979).

References

Ake, Claude (1996) *Democracy and Development in Africa,* Washington, DC: Brookings Institute.

Alvarez, Sonia E. (1990) *Engendering Democracy in Brazil: Women's Movements in Transition Politics,* Princeton, NJ: Princeton University Press.

Barrig, Maruja and Andy Wehkamp (1994) *Engendering Development: Experiences in Gender and Development Planning,* The Hague: NOVIB.

Bhasin, K. (1979) *Breaking Barriers: A South Asian experience of training for participatory development,* Bangkok: FAO.

Boserup, Esther (1970) *Women's Role in Economic Development,* New York: St. Martin's Press.

Moser, Caroline O.N. (1993) *Gender Planning and Development: Theory, Practice and Training,* New York: Routledge.

Randall, Margaret (1994) *Sandino's Daughters Revisited: Feminism in Nicaragua,* New Brunswick, NJ: Rutgers University Press.

■ **Dan Connell** *is the founder and former director of the Boston-based development agency Grassroots International and the author of* Against All Odds: A Chronicle of the Eritrean Revolution *(Red Sea Press). He is writing a book on political and social movements in Eritrea, South Africa, Palestine, and Nicaragua with support from the MacArthur Foundation. This article was first published in* Development in Practice, *Volume 7, number 3, in 1997.*

Sanctioned violence: development and the persecution of women as witches in South Bihar

Puja Roy

Throughout society, violence pervades the lives of women in ways that are blatant and cause tremendous physical and psychological trauma. Overt expressions of violence encompass rape and molestation, domestic violence and battering, dowry-related torture, female genital mutilation (FGM), and female infanticide and foeticide. There appears to be 'a visible increase in all forms of violence on women, including rape, dowry murders, *sati* and witch-hunting.'[1] *Sati* (a widow's immolation on her husband's funeral pyre) and witch-hunting, in particular, fall within the boundaries of social sanction. Thus these practices are not always condemned as violent, but seen as culturally acceptable and necessary for upholding traditional values and beliefs. Local communities usually condone these practices and often collude with the perpetrators.

In his address at the 1995 Fourth World Conference on Women, Dr Boutros Boutros-Ghali recognized the importance of viewing 'human rights of women as an inalienable, integral and indivisible part of universal human rights; of violence against women as an intolerable violation of these rights.'[2]

The very essence of a woman's right to self-respect and dignity is ravaged by the practice of identifying and torturing women as *dains* (witches) — something that in 1994 claimed the lives of 15 women in the district of West Singhbhum in South Bihar, and of 24 women and children there the following year.[3] This reflects the number of reported witchcraft-related crimes in the area and indicates the alarmingly common practice of subjecting a woman to torture by accusing her of witchcraft. Given that social sanction prevents most cases from being reported, the potential proportion of the problem and its impact on the lives of women are of urgent concern.

The persecution of women accused of witchcraft is usually seen as being linked with local superstitions, so that any intervention requires a sensitive approach 'without hurting the pride and sentiments of the local population' and creating a 'tribal — non-tribal divide.'[4] However, a significant number of cases have been among non-tribals, so the problem is not exclusive to tribals. The belief that superstition and illiteracy are the main causes of witchcraft-related persecution is also debatable. The case-studies presented below suggest that there is usually a complex background of female economic subjugation, sexual exploitation, and the persecution of widows and independent, vocal women. As in the case of *sati*, victimizing women as witches can be seen as the height of patriarchal suppression, which devalues and undermines a woman in society, and 'keeps her in a propertyless and resourceless state.'[5]

The issues

Aspects of this form of violence are examined in four case illustrations, and drawing on consultation with people involved in this issue. The core concern is that women are subjected to brutal and socially sanctioned forms of violence, making it very difficult for them to obtain any support or immediate assistance.

Communities profoundly believe in the evil spirits which exist in *dains*, and in the need for them to be annihilated. However, these beliefs and fears are usually exploited by a few community members who have ulterior motives in suggesting that a woman is a witch; in order to expropriate her, to exploit her sexually, or to exact vengeance for past grievances or family feuds. Once a woman has been named as a witch and the accusation has been verified by a witch doctor, action against her is swift and remorseless.

The role of an *ojha* or *sokha* (a village witch doctor) is critical. Faith in their powers and skills is deeply entrenched in people's minds. 'All evils: worry, sorrow, disease, even death are caused by bewitchment involving some individual, some spirit...'; the role of the witch doctor 'is the removal of the numerous ills that afflict the community.'[6] It is common and simple to use this person to collaborate with any accusation made against a local woman, especially if the witch doctor is amply compensated for doing so. It is very lucrative for him to identify a woman as a witch since he charges the hapless woman and her family exorbitantly for exorcising evil spirits.

The implications of subjecting a woman to this socially sanctioned torture profoundly affect development agencies and non-governmental organizations (NGOs), especially those concentrating on gender-focused development. The belief that a woman is evil and should be subjected to violence for this evil to be removed, coupled with strategies to prevent all women from becoming economically and socially independent, poses many challenges to agencies that seek women's empowerment and gender equity throughout the development process.

Background

South Bihar covers 17 districts and is a drought-prone area mainly inhabited by tribals whose survival depends on a depleting forest. Over three-quarters of the population are rural. The total female literacy rate in Bihar is 23 per cent, under half that of men (52 per cent).

Extraction of iron ore, coal, dolomite and granite is carried out by large Government and private companies. Mining, together with three big dam projects, have resulted in the displacement and land alienation of tribals. Just under half of the non-forested land is used for agriculture, but most of this is mono-cropped and rain-fed, due to the lack of proper irrigation facilities. The rocky, undulating terrain and poor soil conditions add to the problems. Health facilities are inadequate, with less than one primary health care centre for every 100,000 people in all but two districts of South Bihar.[7] That this may contribute to people turning to witch doctors and believing in their powers[8] is commonly argued, and will be assessed here in relation to witch-hunting.

Since South Bihar is a predominantly tribal belt, it is important to understand the system of tribal administration and the role it plays in the practice of identifying and victimizing women as witches. The two most common systems are the 'Manki-Munda', belonging to the Ho and Munda tribes, and the 'Majhi-Harram' which is followed by Santhal tribes. In the former, the village headman is the *Munda*, and twelve villagers form a committee headed by a *Manki*.[9] The 'Majhi-Harram' system consists of a village headman and a council of five. In both systems, leadership is non-democratic and hereditary, and there is no provision for women's participation. The leaders decide village disputes and problems and handle routine administration, which includes fixing wage rates that are usually unequal for men and women. The reliance on village headmen to settle contentions makes them very powerful figures. So if a village headman agrees that a woman is a witch, he places a seal of approval on the violence that will be meted out to her by the other villagers.

Women charged with witchcraft: four illustrations

The following illustrations have been gathered from personal testimony from the victims of this violence, and their account of the torture and despair they experienced. Pseudonyms have been used to protect their identity.

The case of Kunti

Kunti is a 35-year old woman from a backward caste (non-tribal) in the West Singhbhum district of Bihar. She is married and has three sons and a daughter. There was a lot of opposition to her marriage by her in-laws who wanted their son to marry someone of their choice. Since Kunti and her husband married against their wishes, the in-laws were unhappy and resentful. Kunti's husband owned land on which the family planted paddy and vegetables, both for subsistence and for income. The children attended the village school, and Kunti's work involved the usual tasks of housework, child-care, and fetching fuelwood and water. The family led a peaceful and comfortable life. On 3 September 1995, a young girl from Kunti's in-laws' family, who would venture close to Kunti's house in order to cut grass to sell, fell ill. The witch doctor immediately declared that the girl had been possessed by a witch. He studied the young girl's hands and said that Kunti was responsible for her illness, by practising witchcraft on her. The girl's father (Kunti's husband's cousin) threatened to kill Kunti. Kunti was summoned to the girl's house and asked to cure her. Kunti insisted on taking the girl to hospital, but was not allowed to do so, and the witch doctor and the girl's family continued to insist that Kunti was a witch. Kunti and her family approached the local Member of the Legislative Assembly for help, but he showed little interest.

On 4 September, the village chief called a meeting of the council, along with the witch doctor and the young girl's father. It was an all-male assembly that dragged Kunti from her house to this meeting where her fate would be decided. In spite of Kunti's protests that she was not a *dain*, the assembly decided to punish her for her 'crimes'. She was pinned down and forcibly fed human excreta which, according to the villagers, would reduce her evil powers. Members of the council then threatened to kill her if she did not leave the village. So Kunti and her family had to leave their land and property, and move to Kunti's mother's village.

Kunti's husband now works as a daily wage-labourer, and the family has to struggle to make ends meet. The children have had to leave school. The family's land and property have been taken by Kunti's accusers. They cannot consider returning to their village, since Kunti's life is still at risk. Kunti firmly believes that her accusers had other motives for labelling her a *dain*. They have wreaked havoc on her life. She was the victim of a degrading and perverse form of violence, the horrors of which she relives every day.

Kunti is a very strong and vocal woman who refuses to accept this situation. She has filed a criminal case against her accusers and although there has been pressure on her to drop this, she feels that unless they are convicted, the persecution of women as witches will continue. Although Kunti is determined to obtain some form of justice, she also feels that by labelling her a *dain*, her accusers have attached a permanent stigma on her and have violated her self-respect and dignity.

The case of Parul

Parul is a physically disabled tribal woman aged about 20, from a village in West Singhbhum. She used to live with her parents, five brothers, and two sisters. Her family owns about seven acres of land, which was once used for agriculture. Over the years, there had been a boundary dispute; some villagers felt that their land was being encroached by Parul's family. There were constant disagreements and arguments about it, and Parul feels that the main reason for this was the villagers' deep-seated resentment against her family for owning a lot of land. In April 1995, two of Parul's neighbour's children died from an illness. The neighbour and other villagers accused Parul's mother of being a witch, claiming that she was responsible for the deaths of these children, and for the illnesses of other children in the village. On the night of 3 April 1995, villagers armed with sticks and knives entered Parul's home and dragged her father away. They then attacked her mother, who protested that she was not a *dain*. The villagers killed Parul's mother, four of her brothers and one sister, the youngest of whom was a one-year old baby.

Parul was raped by three men. When she became unconscious, the attackers left her for dead. As soon as Parul regained consciousness, she fled to her uncle's house in another village. She did not tell him immediately about the night's tragedy for she was unsure about how he would react to her mother's having been accused of being a witch. The next morning, Parul and her uncle went to the headman in Parul's village to report the murders. The headman seemed very helpful and accompanied them to the local police station to file a formal report.

However, as soon as they reached the station, he slipped away, on the pretext of getting a cup of tea.

The police raided the village and found the bodies of the murdered family, also including Parul's father. Parul managed to identify six of the men responsible, but to date they have not been arrested; they escaped from the village, and no-one appears to know where they are. Parul was helped by the local administration; she was given employment in a local girls' hostel, and a room to stay. She says that the other girls regarded her with suspicion, fearful that she might have learnt witchcraft from her mother. Parul and one brother and sister who were away from their village on that fateful night, are trying to rebuild their lives. Parul's life is still under threat; she lives in a government building, and is locked inside all day by the guard so that the men she identified cannot harm her. Parul finds it ironic that she is a prisoner while the men responsible for these gruesome crimes which have ruined her life, are still free.

Parul believes that the villagers wanted her family's property, and labelled her mother a witch for that purpose. She does not believe in witches and is very sad that most of the villagers believed that her mother was one. She also feels that some men in the village wished to exploit her sexually, and used the opportunity to rape her. She cannot return home, nor would she like to, since the place holds many unpleasant memories for her. The family property has been entrusted to the village headman by Parul's uncle, until further decisions are made.

Parul does not know if she will ever forget or erase the memory of that night's tragedy from her mind. She lives in constant fear and is very unsure of her future. Her main aim now is to be a mother to her younger brother and sister, and see that they get a proper education and a good chance in life.

The case of Champa

Champa, a tribal woman of about 40, lives in a small hamlet in the Deoghar district. Her husband works in a colliery, and the family owns a little land on which they grow crops to meet their subsistence needs. Champa has six children, though only the youngest live with her. In 1996, a family from her village employed a young girl to tend their livestock. Champa's daughter also looks after animals, and the girls became friends. One day, for no apparent reason, the girl ran away. Champa's daughter was blamed and the villagers began saying that Champa was responsible for using witchcraft to send the girl away. The accusations took no further shape until there was an illness involving the same family. The witch doctor was called and he rubbed two leaves with oil and declared that he could see in them the face of the person responsible. He blamed Champa and accused her of being a witch.

The family was enraged, especially after the child subsequently died. They pondered grimly on the injustice of the situation; Champa had six children who never seemed to fall ill, but other children in the village fell ill regularly. Champa must indeed be a witch, since she kept her own children healthy and cast spells on others' to make them ill. On 9 May 1996, the villagers marched to Champa's house and dragged her out. They stripped her, tied her hands and legs, and beat her mercilessly. They then forced her to eat cow-dung, in order to reduce her 'evil powers'. Champa's husband, brother-in-law, and son attempted to intervene, but they were attacked by the villagers. It was the intervention of the leader of a women's organization which probably saved her life. The villagers released Champa as soon as Sarojini demanded that they solve the matter in a non-violent manner. The villagers called a meeting and it was finally decided that Champa should consult a prominent witch doctor whose verdict must be accepted by all concerned. The villagers would decide which *ojha* she should consult. When Champa was interviewed, she had not visited him since the villagers were still deciding the issue.

However, Champa feels confident that the witch doctor will not pronounce her a witch since she is definitely not one. She wants to see the witch doctor since she wishes the matter to be settled finally. She cannot tolerate or live with suspicious, frightened villagers. The NGO that formed the women's group in the village is evolving a strategy to protect Champa from them.

The case of Phulmani

Phulmani lives in a town in West Singhbhum district of Bihar. She is a 26-year old tribal with two sons aged five and 18 months. At the time of her interview, Phulmani and her younger son were staying in a Government hostel. Phulmani is employed by the district authorities. The problems began when Phulmani's husband and his brothers had a major dispute over property. The fact that Phulmani and her husband had converted to Christianity intensified the general discontent in the rest of the family, which was opposed to this. One day, Phulmani's brother-in-law had a boil on his leg and immediately accused Phulmani of being responsible. It was not difficult for him to place the blame on her since he is an *ojha* of some repute. That same day, he had spread the news that Phulmani was a witch to the other villagers.

That evening, when Phulmani's husband was returning home from the fields, the villagers attacked him with bows and arrows. He managed to escape and lock himself and his family in his house. The villagers surrounded the house and hurled bricks and stones, damaging the house in the process. Phulmani's husband attempted to reason with them, suggesting that they settle the matter the next day, but the villagers did not listen. It was only when Phulmoni threatened to counter attack with their own weapons that the villagers finally dispersed.

However, they kept harassing and attacking the family; they insisted that Phulmoni should leave the village since she was a witch. Phulmoni and her husband reported this at the local police station but did not receive a helpful response, and the threats against her and her family continued. The family finally decided that it would be wisest to leave the village and stay at Phulmoni's mother's home temporarily; Phulmoni was expecting her second child and needed a safe place to stay. They stayed three weeks with Phulmoni's mother, where Phulmoni's son was born. On their return, they found their house had been looted by the villagers; they had lost all their possessions.

Phulmoni approached the missionaries nearby for help, who encouraged her to stay with them. Phulmoni and her baby lived with them until people in the area began to question and oppose her presence once they learnt that she had been accused of witchcraft. Finally the missionaries were forced to escort Phulmoni to town and place her in the care of the district welfare officer. The district administration employed Phulmoni and gave her and her baby a place to stay. However, Phulmoni's husband and her older son live in the village to protect their property. The boy goes to school and her husband farms their land, but the villagers have socially boycotted them. There is pressure from Phulmoni's husband's family for him to remarry, but he refuses to leave Phulmoni. Phulmoni meets her husband and son once a week when they visit her.

Phulmoni realizes that this arrangement cannot continue indefinitely but is not optimistic about her chances of returning home. The family is very doubtful and uncertain about its future, and hopes that the villagers will eventually stop harassing them. Phulmoni, at the end of her interview, insisted that she did not believe in witches; that witchcraft was a belief invented in the minds of people and that it was used to harass innocent victims.

The implications for development work

The power of social sanction

During the process of interviewing women who had suffered witchcraft-related violence, one woman requested a certificate from NGO representatives stating that she was not a witch; this certificate, she insisted, would be a passport to a trouble-free existence in her village. This request reveals the strength of the social sanction which forms a tight web of consent and silence which traps the victim of violence and protects its perpetrators. In each of these cases, social sanction and agreement prevented the women from gaining any form of support and assistance from the villagers; indeed, most of the women had to flee their homes. In Champa's case, the intervention by the women's organization's leader probably saved her life, but the villagers are still adamant that Champa should consult a prominent witch doctor of their choice. Parul did not immediately confide in her uncle about her family's murders, since she was unsure how he would react to the accusations of witchcraft levelled at her mother.

The illustrations further reveal that social sanction is not only limited to the villagers. When the MLA whom Kunti approached did nothing to help her, he was, in effect, sanctioning the villagers. The police were ineffectual where Phulmoni and Parul were concerned; the murderers of Parul's family are still free, and the police did not intervene in Phulmoni's case when they were approached. How deep rooted are superstitions, and how important are they in contributing to the power of social sanction in witchcraft-related crimes?

During the interviews with the victims, members of the village community, and various witch doctors in South Bihar, it was evident that the belief in evil spirits (including witchcraft) is part of a villager's life. An NGO in East Singhbhum interviewed a man who had murdered a woman suspected of practising witchcraft. He justified his actions, claiming that he had cleansed society by killing a witch, and served his community.[10] The belief is that women learn the rites and rituals of witchcraft on an *Amavasya* (dark night), at a cremation ground. Once a woman is initiated, she is fully equipped to practise witchcraft on the other villagers.[11]

Villagers attribute a range of unpleasant happenings to witchcraft: accidents, unexplained deaths, chronic and incurable diseases, epidemics, crop failure, failure of a woman to have sons, and death of livestock, among other things.[12] It is, therefore, not difficult to instigate villagers against a particular woman by claiming that she is responsible for some misfortune. However, villagers would not translate their beliefs into action unless certain prominent people approved of them doing so, and gave permission for violence. This is because, where the belief is real, there is a genuine fear that the 'witch' would harm anyone who ventured close to her.

This is well illustrated in an interview with women from a village in East Singhbhum. Discussing witchcraft, the women (many of whom belong to a women's group associated with literacy programmes) expressed fear about a spinster who lived alone and whom everyone suspected was a witch. This woman had been attacked by the villagers at the instigation of a few local men, but the police intervened, and the attacks stopped. On further investigation, it was discovered that the instigators had managed to extort some property from the woman and so were probably allowing the matter to rest. The villagers, however, genuinely believe that the woman is a witch and have boycotted her since they fear her evil powers. They want her to leave, but without the headman's sanction they cannot take any action against her.

The key issue, then, concerns certain powerful people in the community who exploit the villagers' superstitious belief in persecuting women as witches. That initial push ultimately leads to a drastic crime. The conspiracy of silence, and the sanctioned violence in the case of witchcraft-related crimes, have major implications for development work in the area. The most difficult aspect of development involves encountering a society's belief system, especially when this is part of a community's ethos and culture. A tribal political party member reacted sharply to proposed legislation against witchcraft since he felt that this would 'aggravate tribal sentiment against non-tribals'.[13] Hence development agencies may find it a highly sensitive question; few readily comprehend the complexity of the issue and the range of factors it encompasses. A community might see development agency interventions as a direct attack on their own beliefs and culture. Strategies for intervention must find ways to pierce these social sanctions — which are an expression both of the interests of certain powerful persons and a genuine belief in witchcraft — in ways that will not offend or alienate the community.

Witch doctors

Witch doctors and village headmen are important in understanding the issues behind witchcraft crimes. In all the cases illustrated, the witch doctor played a significant role. It was his ultimate pronouncement that made people sure that a woman was a witch. This stamp of approval is usually given by the village headman too and seals a woman's fate. Discussions with witch doctors revealed that their belief in witchcraft was secondary; their primary concern is to earn money and exercise their power in society by exorcising evil spirits. A widow in Bokaro district had to give the witch doctor her livestock, utensils, some land, and a substantial amount of cash for conducting a session of *jhadpok* (a ritual of exorcism) on her.

Witch doctors are not always seen as medicine men but as men with extraordinary powers, who can combat evil. One witch doctor explained that there were two categories of illness; one that was caused by disease and the other by possession, or an 'evil eye.' The former could be dealt with by administering herbal medicine, but the latter would need extra preparation; systematic worship and rituals. The witch doctor revels in the power accorded him by society. One witch doctor proudly boasted that villagers from other states often consulted him on a range of problems, including that of witchcraft in their villages. He went on to describe the case of a woman whom he had caught practising witchcraft, and whom he beat into submission. He explained, with satisfaction, that the woman never dared to practise witchcraft again.

Evidently, witch doctors are not the main reason behind the systematic persecution of women as witches. But they are one of the main players and are useful tools for people who have a real motive for branding women in this way. Hence, the crux of the issue lies in the way a witch doctor is revered by society, so that his word is seen as the ultimate truth. His hold over a village is something that development workers must consider seriously in terms of its detrimental effect on their programmes. If a witch doctor's power was questioned by development agencies and subsequently by the villagers themselves, especially in relation to witch-hunting, his stature might eventually decline.

The gender dimension

As with rape, domestic violence, and other forms of violence against women, witch-hunting is essentially about gender-based control; it is about men asserting and reasserting their power and control over women's sexuality and individuality.

Witches, a personification of evil, are almost always women; and witch doctors, the symbols of power and good, are always men. 'Only men can receive the training to be *ojhas*', which equips them with the power to heal and protect.[14] The relationship between witches and the witch doctor is clearly a reflection of deeply embedded patriarchal values within society. These reinforce the idea that it is the men who are authorized to control and prevent women from going astray; their power is strong, necessary, and positive, and any power that a woman acquires is regarded with suspicion, and seen as negative and destructive. In other words, men use their power constructively and legitimately, whereas women's power is unauthorized, harmful, and needs to be controlled by men. Men and women are conditioned to believe and perpetuate this belief, with serious consequences for gender equity.

Witchcraft-related crimes keep women in a constant state of subjugation by denying respect for women as human beings, and denying them the right to live with dignity and freedom. In regions where witchcraft-related crimes are common, a woman dare not protest or oppose the social system, for fear of being labelled a witch. This too can have severe ramifications for development, since development workers are working against a tide of patriarchal values that do not allow women to come to the fore. Hence, the promotion of women's leadership in these areas is likely to be opposed by societal structures.

Once a woman is pronounced a witch, she is subjected to horrific forms of violence, including rape, physical and mental torture, and humiliation. She is socially boycotted and often forced to flee her village for fear of being killed. Widows, unmarried women, and woman who speak out, are usually singled out for attack. In a village in Hazaribagh, a widow and her daughter-in-law were forced to parade around the village naked, with hair tonsured, and wearing a garland of slippers. They were branded as witches because they refused to oblige four prominent village men with sexual favours. When they reported this to the police, the villagers retaliated by razing their house to the ground.

Asked why widows were often identified as witches one young man replied that widows and single women are not controlled by any man, hence they have the freedom to harm others. The assumption that women are essentially evil, and that only men can control them, embodies all those values that suppress women in a patriarchal society.

Violence against women is a clear indication of their degraded social status and vulnerability, and witchcraft-related crimes exemplify this. Kelkar and Nathan argue that 'we cannot infer the low status of women' from witch-hunting, for witch-hunting is prevalent where women have a relatively high status, and that it reflects 'an attack on the existing status of women'.[15] This argument is legitimate to the extent that women who have attempted to assert themselves in a male-dominated society, women who have resisted sexual advances from powerful men, and women who are widows with land rights, are among the victims of witch-hunting. In other words, it is usually women who have in some way threatened men's superior position in society who come under attack. Thus witch-hunting discourages any attempt by women to assert themselves and ensures that they maintain their inferior position in society. Where witch-hunting is common, we found that women are denied participation in village council meetings, and have no decision-making power regarding village matters, such as deciding wages for labour; all these decisions are made by men and result in discrimination against women. In addition, women face violence frequently, usually in the form of assault by their husbands.

Given women's low health and education status, witch-hunting, like other forms of violence against women, can be viewed as a means of reinforcing their vulnerable and devalued social status, and as an expression of male power and dominance over their sexuality and individual freedom. Kishwar and Vanita observe that 'unless the consensus within our society changes in favour of a more dignified and self sustaining life for women, any number of repressive laws and policemen are not likely to save women's lives'.[16]

Development workers need to address this basic issue, of which witchcraft-related violence is a stark reflection. For any development programme to succeed, it is necessary to work towards equality between men and women. But where such violence exists, there is evidently an enormous gulf between the two.

Village headmen and the traditional administration system

Village administration, especially in tribal areas, allows the headman unilateral power in deciding village affairs and settling disputes. The system follows a hereditary pattern of leadership and excludes women. In January 1995, a report from a government-instituted committee, popularly known as the Bhuria Committee report, accepted the community 'as the basic unit of the system of self governance in tribal areas'.[17] The report further suggested that all resolutions of disputes, day to day administration, investigation, and adjudication of all matters should be managed by the village community.[18] Thus, on the one hand, the report hopes to promote control over natural resources and usufruct rights over forest produce, while on the other, it accepts a non-democratic, gender-biased, and partisan system of administration which will legitimize a village headman's power and subject women to further subjugation. It is vital for women to be included in village-level administration, and for village councils to be gender-sensitive and provide support to women who face violence.

The larger motives

The case illustrations clearly reveal that persecuting women as witches is pre-planned and systematically perpetrated. The main motive is to ensure that women remain inferior in status to men, and that they have no control over resources or decision-making. Other motives, which are usually part and parcel of this, are for material gain (such as wresting property from the woman by conveniently labelling her a witch), existing family feuds, and sexual exploitation.

Illness is seldom the main reason behind condemning a woman, but an excuse that ignites the villagers into action. Hence development workers must bear in mind the underlying motives, and analyze the role of health and education in this context. Illiteracy and lack of education are not inevitably linked with superstition and ignorance, just as superstition alone is not the main reason for branding women as witches. Improved health services and more health-awareness programmes may mean, however, that people stop using illness as an excuse to brand women as witches, and that the power of the witch doctor in health-related matters diminishes.

Suggested intervention strategies

Interventions must address the root cause of the problem, which means examining the issue in the context of unequal gender relations. NGOs may have a role to play here. Unlike government agencies, NGOs usually have long-term and sustained interaction with communities, especially where they have other development programmes in the area. NGO workers are often from the community and so have a good understanding of the various issues involving witch-hunting, and of the risks of appearing to make an attack on local culture.

NGOs are well placed to intervene when they are closely involved with the community, can form a good rapport, and understand the various aspects of the problem. Such NGOs are also in a position to sensitize government representatives. An intervention strategy must establish from the outset that witch-hunting is a gender and violence issue, and not merely a result of superstitious beliefs or community culture. Once this is clear, it will be easier for community members to accept change and not feel threatened.

The following longer-term strategies may help to reduce the threat to women.

- *Intervening from the angle of atrocities against women* — If development agencies attempt to approach the problem by removing superstitious beliefs, they are not likely to make significant headway, since the main issue is that of a woman's low social status. An intervention that concentrates on removing atrocities against women, and so also focuses on other forms of violence, might be more acceptable.

- *Forming a support group for women:* Women who are branded as witches are usually in danger of being killed and face severe forms of torture. But where there are strong women's groups, a victim's life is usually saved. Hence it is important to strengthen women's groups to provide this crucial support.

- *Sensitizing police and government officials:* This might enable the administration to be more understanding and open about crimes against women, and in to recognize witch-hunting as an issue of violence against them.

- *Incorporating gender into development planning:* Programmes that insist on and promote women's participation and leadership will ultimately increase their credibility in the community; this process will enable women to rise above their subjugated state.

- *Advocating a more gender-sensitive form of administration:* Successful advocacy will increase women's participation in village administration, thereby increasing her status in the community. Sensitizing village council members to gender issues is also important.

- *Increasing access to health and education:* This may help to reduce reliance on the witch doctor, and ultimately prevent illnesses being used as an excuse to pronounce a woman a witch. Training witch doctors in basic health care may also be essential.

Conclusions

In a world where unequal gender relations are the norm, as exemplified by male violence against women, the practice of persecuting women as witches epitomizes the tragedy of gender disparity. Culturally and socially acceptable interventions to overcome this crime against humanity are critical, and will require long-term commitment by development agencies.

Notes

1 Bina Agarwal (ed.) (1988) *Structures Of Patriarchy, State, Community and Household In Modernizing Asia*, New Delhi: Kali For Women.

2 Quoted in *Platform For Action And The Beijing Declaration: Fourth World Conference On Women*, Beijing, China, 4-15 September 1995.

3 From Amit Khare (1996) 'Anti-Superstition Campaign in West Singhbhum District, Bihar,' unpublished report.

4 *Ibid.*

5 Quoted in Gail Omvedt (1990) *Violence Against Women: New Movements And New Theories In India*, New Delhi: Kali For Women.

6 Quoted in W B Crow (1968) *A History Of Magic, Witchcraft, And Occultism*, Abacus.

7 Information and data from an unpublished report by Upsana prepared for Oxfam India Trust, Calcutta, entitled *Bihar, A Demographic Profile*. Most of this data is based on 1991 figures.

8 Taken from Amit Khare (1996) 'Anti-Superstition Campaign in W. Singhbhum District, Bihar', unpublished report.

9 *Ibid.*

10 From *Samadhan* (Jan 1996) An Unpublished Newsletter by Free Legal Aid Committee, Jamshedpur.

11 *Ibid.*

12 From an unpublished report on a seminar, 'Atrocities Against Women', held on 25-26 May 1996 in Jamshedpur, organized by Free Legal Aid Committee.

13 Article in *The Hindusthan Times*, Jamshedpur (4 June 1996) entitled 'FLAC Up In Arms Against Witchcraft'.

14 Taken from Govind Kelkar and Dev Nathan (1991) *Gender And Tribe*, New Delhi: Kali For Women.

15 *Ibid.*

16 Quoted in Madhu Kishwar and Ruth Vanita (Sept to Dec 1987) *The Burning Of Roop Kanwar, Manushi*, No. 42-43, p. 25.

17 Quoted in B D Sharma (1995) *Whither Tribal Areas? Constitutional Amendments And After*, Sahyog Pustak Kutir.

18 *Ibid.*

■ **Puja Roy** *is Regional Coordinator for the India Programme of Terre des Hommes, Germany, and Terre des Hommes, Switzerland, covering Orissa, Bihar, and West Bengal. She has a special interest in helping organisations to incorporate a gender focus. This article was researched while the author was a Project Officer for Oxfam India Trust, Calcutta. It was first published in* Development in Practice, *Volume 3, number 2, May 1999.*

Men's violence against women in rural Bangladesh: undermined or exacerbated by microcredit programmes?

Sidney Ruth Schuler, Syed M. Hashemi, and Shamsul Huda Badal

Violence by men against women in Bangladesh is best understood as part of a patriarchal system that subordinates women through social norms which define their place and guide their conduct. This system isolates women within their families and gives men control over most economic resources. Whereas ideal norms stress male responsibility and women living useful and happy lives within the protected space of the home, in reality women and girls face discrimination in everyday life, rationalised by the fact that they are seen as an economic burden. Women often have no independent sources of income, little or no education and few marketable skills, no independent property or money, and no socially sanctioned identity outside the family. When there is not enough for everyone, women and girls are most likely to be underfed and malnourished, and to go without healthcare and education. As they grow up, women come to see dependence and deprivation relative to male family members as natural, a logic that encourages them to accept men's violent behaviour. The first sexual encounter is unwanted and forced for many women and girls. Wife-beating is common. Women who venture outside the home unaccompanied are all too often seen as 'fair game' for sexual exploitation.

Juxtaposed against this bleak backdrop is a growing presence of women in the public sphere, mainly because of new economic opportunities. In cities this is due especially to the rapid growth of the garment industry, which now employs about one million women (Reuter). Small rural industries such as rice mills also employ women, but in rural areas targeted credit programmes of governmental and non-governmental organizations (NGOs) are probably the most important catalyst for change in traditional gender roles.

Multivariate analyses suggested that women in two credit programmes were significantly more empowered than women in communities without such programmes based on seven of eight empowerment indicators that we developed (Hashemi et al., 1996), and less likely than other women to be beaten by their husbands (Schuler et al., 1996). A subsequent analysis led us to qualify the earlier findings. Although being in a credit programme was associated with a lower risk of domestic violence, the risk of being beaten did not diminish with time in the programme, raising the possibility of selection bias rather than a true programme effect (Schuler et al. 1997). Women's empowerment did increase with time in the programme.

In this paper we present data from open-ended interviews about husbands' violence against their wives to examine the socio-cultural context of wife-beating. We look at whether women who earn independent incomes and contribute to family support are less vulnerable to men's violence. And we also look at the possible role of credit programmes in reducing or exacerbating domestic violence.

Data sources

The data were collected through ethnographic research in six villages from two regions of Bangladesh between 1990 and 1996 (Hashemi et al., 1996). Participant observation and in-depth interviews were used to document women's changing roles and status, and changing reproductive norms, in these villages. The researchers also observed and documented the operations of two microcredit programmes at the village level and interviewed programme participants. Grameen Bank was working in two villages and the BRAC Rural Development Programme in two, while the other two villages did not have credit programmes.[1] One male and one female researcher lived in each village for a period of about two years (1991-1993), and made periodic visits over the following several years. Their observations and interviews were focused on families belonging to the landless or virtually landless population that includes roughly half of all families in rural Bangladesh, whom the credit programmes are intended to serve. A census of all households in the study villages was conducted in early 1994, containing socio-demographic variables, and information related to women's roles and status within the family and community (including their subjection to beating by their husbands), participation in credit programmes, and contraceptive use and fertility.

This paper is based on interviews in connection with incidents of men's violence against women that the ethnographers became aware of during their stay. Most of the incidents involved men beating their wives. In addition to describing situations in which men do this, the ethnographers interviewed both men and women to investigate how violence against women is perceived in the communities, when it is believed to be justified, and women's reaction to it. Members of BRAC and Grameen Bank, and field staff of the two microcredit programmes, were interviewed regarding the problem of domestic violence against members, and how the credit groups and programme staff respond to it.

Prevalence of wife-beating

Near the end of the final section of the census, concerning women's roles and interactions with their families, were two questions about domestic violence. First the woman was asked: 'We hear in some villages that men mistreat their wives, and sometimes men beat their wives. Has your husband ever beaten you?' Women who said yes were then asked: 'Did he beat you at any time during the past year?' Overall, two-thirds said they had been beaten at one time or another, and in one village the incidence was as high as 87 per cent. Thirty-eight percent of the women said they had been beaten in the previous year, with percentages ranging from 14 to 60 in different villages (Figure 1).

Situations in which men beat their wives

An analysis of the incidents of wife-beating that were described to (and, in a few cases, witnessed by) the researchers showed that men beat their wives over trivial matters, often out of frustration over problems for which the women were not responsible. Their wives were a convenient target, unable to retaliate in any damaging way because of their social and economic dependence. Men also beat their wives to control their behaviour, to reassert their own authority when challenged, and to exploit their wives for financial gain.

Some of the most severe incidents of wife-beating were in connection with dowry. As much of the Indian subcontinent, dowry in Bangladesh has evolved into a system of institutionalized extortion. Dowry is seen as obligatory compensation to the bridegroom's family for taking the bride off her parents' hands. Since the amount of the dowry generally increases with the bride's age, there are many cases in which desperate parents promise more dowry then they can deliver, or promise it but can't give it at the time of marriage. Violence and threats of further violence, in extreme cases even to the point of murder, are used to extort money or property from the young woman's relatives, sometimes even in excess of what was negotiated. A mother told one of the researchers:

> My daughter's husband always beats her because when we arranged her marriage we said that we would get him a job, and we still haven't been able to do that.

In addition to extortion of resources via the institution of dowry, men in the study villages often seemed to feel that whatever their wives brought with them at marriage, inherited, earned, acquired, or even borrowed, was rightfully theirs. One woman complained:

> My husband likes to go to the movies, smoke, and drink tea. When he runs out of money he takes my pumpkins and chickens [and sells them]. If I try to stop him he beats me.

Violence by husbands against their wives is an expression of a patriarchal social system. Women in rural Bangladesh spend most of their time within the confines of the family, and most violence against them is domestic. As women begin to encroach into traditionally male space to take advantage of new opportunities, violence is sometimes meted out to them at home in response to a general social reaction against their violations of patriarchal norms. In one of the study villages a local religious leader was threatening to initiate a *shalish* (traditional adjudication by male elders) against local women who went out in public. After finding out that the wife of his brother's son had visited a neighboring hamlet, he confronted his brother and demanded that she be punished. The brother spoke to his son, who gave his wife a beating. Another woman took a job at a rice mill just outside the village after her husband fell ill and was unable to support them. Her better-off cousins accused her husband of dishonouring their family and beat her up.

Generally, both the perpetrators and the victims of domestic violence perceived it as legitimate. The only real lack of consensus in the study villages had to do with the degree of violence that was justified or appropriate under various circumstances. Most of the men saw wife-beating as men's right. Some said that it was condoned in the religious texts (*Hadith*), and others described it as a normal way to keep women's unruly natures in check and make the household run smoothly. One respondent told the ethnographer:

> Sister, if you don't beat them they'll stop being good. And if they're good, and you beat them, they'll stay that way.

In general, the women in the study acknowledged that their husbands, as their guardians, had the right to beat them if they behaved unacceptably, and some believed this right to be grounded in religious doctrine. The women were also acutely aware of the socio-economic realities that made it difficult for them to resist violence. One said:

> If I ever argue with him he hits me. I don't argue much because he might abandon me, and I would have no place to go. Usually he doesn't beat me unless my shortcoming is serious.

Violence against women plays a large part in maintaining patriarchal norms. It prevents women from exercising their legal rights to property inheritance, constrains their ability to take advantage of economic opportunities, and keeps them in the home. Their isolation within the private sphere makes them particularly vulnerable to domestic violence.

Women's economic empowerment and violence against them

In rural Bangladesh, expanding women's access to economic opportunities and resources does not always make them less vulnerable to domestic violence, at least not right away. There were many cases in the study villages where husbands became increasingly violent as their wives began to earn independent incomes and became more mobile and autonomous. Conflicts often developed over control of assets and earnings, and the women became more inclined to defend themselves against what they see as unfair domination and exploitation. In contrast, we found many women who had nothing of their own, were completely dependent on their husbands, and were rarely if ever beaten. There was nothing to take away from them or fight over, and they tended to be so insecure that they went to extremes to avoid provoking their husbands.

The highest level of violence against women was in the village where it was most apparent that a transformation in gender roles was underway. Sixty per cent of all women of reproductive age in this village said they had been beaten by their husbands during the preceding year. This village also had the highest percentage of women who were contributing to family support (41 per cent). In contrast, the village with the smallest percentage of women who said that they had been beaten in the past year (14 per cent) had very few women who were contributing to family support (10 per cent). BRAC's credit programme was operating in both of these villages. There was frequent conflict over rights to income and assets in the most violent village, and one-third of the women said that their husbands or other relatives had seized their money or assets without their permission during the year preceding the interview. By contrast, only two per cent of the women from the least violent village said this. Asked to explain the high incidence of wife-beating in his village, an elderly man from the more violent village said:

> Our wives would not be beaten so much if they were obedient and followed our orders, but women do not listen to us, and so they get beaten often.

The most empowered women typically emerge from a period of conflict with a new definition of their roles and status in the household. Muneera (a pseudonym) is one example of this, a BRAC member who works outside of the home in a rice-processing enterprise. She now controls and invests her own income, and pays for her own healthcare despite once having been beaten for doing so. She told one of the researchers:

> My husband used to beat me up and take my money. Now he can beat me a thousand times and I won't give him my money. I tell him, 'you had better not beat me too much — I can live without you!'

Women who were most successful economically, or whose incomes provided most of the family's support (cases in which the husband's earnings were inadequate or intermittent, for example because of poor health) appeared to be relatively immune from domestic violence. This suggests that there may in fact be a positive association between women's contributions to family support and reduced violence, but only when such contributions reach high levels.

Credit programmes and violence

A combination of direct questions, case studies, and observation in the six villages yielded ambivalent findings regarding the influence of credit programmes on domestic violence. Giving women access to credit can protect them from violence; bringing home a resource that benefits their husbands and families reduces poverty-related stress in some households, and raises the woman's perceived value. In some cases, however, credit creates a new arena for hostility and conflict.

In one village our researcher went to the place where a Grameen Bank centre meeting was about to begin and said to the group of about 16-17 women who had come, "Many of the women in this village are Grameen Bank members. They get loans from the bank and hand the money over to their husbands. Those who are not members cannot assist their husbands in this way. Does this make any difference in how often a woman is beaten by her husband? Who gets beaten more, members or nonmembers?" This was a village in which many of the women did make part or all of their loan money available to their husbands, and 87 per cent said they had been beaten by their husbands at one time or another. The consensus among those who responded was that access to credit had no influence on domestic violence. As one of them put it:

> A woman is not beaten by her husband because she has done something wrong. She is beaten just because he feels like it.

Later the researcher visited several of the women in their homes. Again, the question was put indirectly (the women were not asked about their own experience but about Grameen members as a group) but rather bluntly: "After so many years with Grameen Bank, have you found that your husbands beat you less, or do they beat you just as much as before?" One woman continued to maintain that men's inclination to engage in wife-beating was a matter of individual character, unlikely to be influenced by access to credit or anything else. Others expressed a variety of sometimes contradictory views. For example, one woman said that the Grameen women were beaten less than others, except when they put pressure on their husbands to hand over money for the loan installments. Several women said Grameen members were beaten less because they provided cash for their husbands to invest, and this improved the family's standard of living, and described cases in which this appeared to be true. Others cases were cited in which men beat their wives in struggles over control of the loan money.

A man who had helped Grameen Bank become established in the village nine years earlier said that some of the men were gamblers who appropriated their wives' loan money. When their wives lost their tempers over this, or when the men felt humiliated because bank staff reprimanded them in front of others, they responded by beating their wives. To ensure that she would have enough funds to repay her loan, one woman re-lent her BRAC funds to another man in the village at a higher interest rate than she was paying. When her husband learned of this he saw it as a challenge to his own rights over his wife. Between blows he shouted at her:

> So then I'm not your husband! The man you gave your money to is your husband — if not, why did you give him the money?

A group of men interviewed in the second of the two Grameen villages was unanimous in saying that Grameen Bank loans engendered conflict and violence within families. Money was scarce, men pressured their wives to take loans, often appropriated the money and then failed to use it productively, and there were weekly fights over payment of the loan instalments. In separate interviews several women disagreed, citing diminished violence or failing to see any relationship between the credit programme and men beating women. But one woman said:

> After joining Grameen Bank we learned to speak out. I argue with my husband... Then he gets angry and wants to beat me up.

In the BRAC villages we encountered similar mixed views of the relationship between credit, domestic conflict, and wife-beating:

> Even before I joined BRAC my husband used to beat me, but now he beats me more often. He wasted the money I got from BRAC, and my cow died...If I ask him to bring anything from the market he beats me.

> My husband no longer beats me like he used to. Nowadays the money stays in my hands. I can visit the doctor, can take the children there if I need to. If I need groceries I can go to the market and buy them myself...We are no longer in such dire need and, so, he no longer beats me.

> You don't hear about women being beaten as often as before [BRAC came here], except when women take loans and the money is squandered [by their husbands]...you do hear about women being beaten in those cases.

Providing women with access to resources — loans — can in some cases reduce and in others exacerbate men's tendency to use violence against their wives, as the above show. Another aspect of credit programmes is public exposure at women's mandatory weekly meetings. This exposure may provide women with some protection against domestic violence. Most of the survey respondents had been in a credit programme for two years or longer by the time they were interviewed; in two years a member attends about 100 group meetings, in which she has contact with other members and with programme staff from outside the village. The group meetings also foster support networks outside of the family, which may provide sources of intervention or sanctuary. Two women in our study made direct statements suggesting that their husbands had refrained from beating them for fear that others would learn of it (they might see the bruises or wounds, or she might say something in public). One of them told the researcher:

> In the past my father-in-law would never stop my husband from beating me. But after I joined Grameen Bank he said to my husband, 'You had better stop beating and scolding your wife. Now she has contact with many people in society. She brings you loans from Grameen Bank. If you want to you can start a business with the money she brings!'

For the most part, the credit programmes do not directly address the problem of violence against women. The ethnographer in one of the villages reported:

> During my two-year stay in the village I never once heard any protest against domestic violence in the Centre meetings. Grameen Bank never wants to know whether the women get beaten by their husbands when they ask for money to pay the instalments [in cases where the husband appropriates part or all of the loan money for his own use]. When the Centre Chief was laid up after a beating by her husband the Bank staff didn't ask her anything about it, although [surely] he could guess the reason. J., the Centre Chief, says, 'When our husbands beat us we do not tell Sir [the local Grameen staff]. How can we tell Sir about this shameful thing? If he asks [what the problem is] we tell him something else. And when he hears that a member is sick he doesn't ask any more questions.'

A BRAC member related:

> Two months ago my husband beat me senseless because of these things. [They had fallen on hard times, he had squandered her

> loan funds, and he became enraged when she asked him for money.] That was the day the loan instalment was due. After he beat me up he went to the BRAC meeting, cursing, and told them he would no longer keep me, he would divorce me. [J., BRAC staff] said "You have three or four children. Why divorce her now?" I heard that he [her husband] said all kinds of insulting things about me. Everyone at BRAC knew that he had beaten me senseless, but no one said anything to him about that. [Even now] I have not heard that anyone said anything to him.

A BRAC member who believed that her husband no longer beat her because of their improved economic situation said, when asked whether domestic violence was ever discussed at group meetings:

> Wife beating is never discussed at the BRAC centre. I have never heard it discussed.

Similarly, a woman who had been chief of her Grameen centre explained:

> All of the women in this village are beaten by their husbands to some extent. Some admit it, some don't. Grameen Bank has never done anything about this. Even my husband beat me a few months ago, because I talked back to him. He had lost a lot of money trading. When I asked him about the money he beat me pretty badly. Many people know about it, but not the Grameen workers. At the centre we don't discuss women being beaten. Except the women may discuss it amongst themselves.

Interviews with credit programme field staff suggest that they have an intuitive understanding of the deeply-rooted connection between men's violence against women and patriarchy. They sense that speaking out against domestic violence would be perceived as a challenge to men's rights over their wives and, thus, could jeopardise the programme's acceptance by the community. Because of this they tend to avoid the issue. One of the Grameen Bank staff said:

> We never directly tell the men in the village not to beat their wives, because they might get angry with us if we did that.

His colleague elaborated:

> Some people in the villages feel that Grameen Bank and other such organizations are trying to bring women out of their homes,

> and that we are giving women more importance than men. They also say that women argue with their husbands more than they used to, and that this is because of Grameen Bank. So we do not protest against these things [wife beating] directly.

But occasionally, one of the staff added, if they learn that a woman is being beaten excessively they may ask one of her relatives, preferably an older woman, to speak to her husband.

Sometimes it is difficult to avoid the issue of domestic violence. Once a member's husband beat his wife while a Grameen Bank meeting was in progress, in front of all of those assembled. He wanted the money she had saved to pay the loan instalment for gambling. The Bank worker admonished him, saying, 'Have you no sense of decency, beating your wife in front of us?! You must repay the money immediately!' The same Bank worker described another case, in which a husband dragged his wife into another room and beat her while the credit group meeting was going on. In this case the Bank worker said to the man's father, who was sitting nearby, 'What kind of son do you have, beating his wife in front of us? If he needs to beat her so badly let him wait until we have gone!'

When we discussed the Grameen Bank worker's responses our research team was divided. Two members initially argued that the male credit programme staff, were identifying with their own gender, and at some deep level accepted the idea that men had the right to control their wives. They felt that the Bank staff should have gone further in defending the women. Others argued that under the circumstances this would have been foolish. At least the man said something to embarrass the husband. The message was 'don't beat your wife', and the words 'in front of us' were necessary to soften the challenge to the man's authority over his wife. Intervening further might even have raised suspicion of a sexual liaison between the Bank worker and the woman.

Men's violence against women undoubtedly is a sensitive issue. It is not addressed in the of Grameen Bank or BRAC credit programme field staff, except indirectly, insofar as they are told to encourage members to support one another. Lacking direct guidance, and perceiving that attempts to intervene in domestic violence could backfire, it is not surprising that field staff tend to avoid the issue.

Conclusions

The findings of this study draw attention to the pervasiveness of men's violence against women in rural Bangladesh, and suggest that along with expanding employment and other income-generating opportunities for women, interventions may be needed to support women who are subjected to such violence. Credit programmes may reduce domestic violence by channelling resources to families through women, and by organizing women into solidarity groups that meet regularly and make their lives more visible, strategies that could be employed in other types of programmes. In some cases, however, providing resources to women and encouraging them to maintain control over these resources may provoke violent behaviour in men, because they see their authority over their wives being undermined.

Given the widespread acceptance of men's violence against their wives, a meaningful attempt to intervene through credit programmes would require extensive awareness-raising efforts directed at programme staff as well as members and their families. Although the possibility of a patriarchal backlash is a real one, the credit programmes might begin with open discussions of the problem of domestic violence in group meetings. In principle, both Grameen Bank and BRAC encourage their members to stand up against injustice and to support one another; collective resistance to men's violence could be explicitly encouraged as ways to put these principles into practice. Separate sessions could be organized for men, or for couples, to stress the idea that violence against women is not morally justified or socially acceptable. BRAC's involvement in education and health programmes could provide an opportunity to disseminate anti-violence messages in communities through various avenues, and to influence the next generation through its non-formal schools.

Some NGOs in Bangladesh are attempting to address the issue of violence against women through consciousness-raising, legal advocacy at the national level, and legal aid; Ain O Shalish Kendra, Nijera Kori, Nari Pokkho, Saptagram, and Mahila Parishad are a few examples. Such efforts to strengthen rights and protection for women in the legal code, and to improve women's access to the legal system, may gradually reduce women's susceptibility to men's violence if pursued on a large scale. BRAC has begun to offer para-legal training in some villages, including one of those in our ethnographic study. According to BRAC staff that we interviewed, rather than intervene directly in cases of family violence and other injustices against women, it is better from a practical as well as a political point of view to raise women's awareness and provide them with the tools to solve their own problems through the legal system. Legal aid services might give women a stronger position in dealing with the legal system.

The success of Bangladesh's national family planning programme in radically transforming reproductive norms may provide a model for addressing the problem of women's social subordination, of which violence is one aspect. In addition to providing contraceptive supplies and services on a large scale, the family planning programme has made extensive use of mass media and interpersonal communication to promote the small family norm. The result has been a dramatic and rapid transformation in attitudes and behaviour related to fertility. The Bangladesh Government, with assistance from UNICEF, is beginning to use television and radio to promote the idea that girls should be treated equally to boys in allocation of food and education. And NGOs are using mass media to condemn the institution of dowry and the violence against young brides that too often results from conflicts over dowry. Expansion and sustainment of such efforts in order to produce an impact comparable to that of the family planning programme will require a strong political commitment at the highest levels of government, as well as among development donors. Further research can provide the data needed both for political consciousness-raising and for development of further interventions to combat men's violence against women as gender roles are gradually transformed.

Acknowledgements

We are grateful to Ann Riley for her contribution to the statistical analysis presented here, and to Shireen Akhter, Sharif Shamshir, Tofazzal Hossain Monju, and Zakir Hossain for their important contributions to the field research. We are deeply indebted to Professor Muhammad Yunus and Muzammel Huq of Grameen Bank; and to Salehuddin Ahmed, Dr Mushtaque Chowdhury, and M. Ghulam Sattar of BRAC for the valuable insights that emerged through discussions; and to the field staff of Grameen Bank and BRAC in Rangpur, Faridpur, and Magura for their generous assistance. Support for this study was provided by Population Action International, The William and Flora Hewlett Foundation, The Andrew W. Mellon Foundation, The Rockefeller Foundation, The Summit Foundation, and International Development Research Centre, Canada.

Notes

1 Grameen Bank and BRAC's Rural Development Programme, the two largest non-governmental credit programmes in Bangladesh, together provide small loans (averaging about $100) to over 3.5 million women (and about 250 000 men). Repayment rates are nearly 98 per cent. The credit recipients consist almost entirely of landless rural poor who are excluded by commercial banks because of their inability to provide collateral and because of the banks' aversion to handling small loans and dealing with poor, semi-literate and illiterate clients. The programmes provide collateral-free banking, using a system in which borrowers must organize themselves into small groups which share responsibility for ensuring that each member pays her weekly instalments. (For further details about the two credit programmes see Bangladesh Rural Advancement Committee, 1996; Grameen Bank, 1997; Hashemi and Schuler, 1997; Holcombe, 1995; Korten, 1989.)

References

Bangladesh Rural Advancement Committee (1996) *Annual Report 1996,* Dhaka: Bangladesh Rural Advancement Committee Rural Development Programme.

Grameen Bank (1997) *Annual Report 1996,* Dhaka: Grameen Bank.

Hashemi, Syed M. and Sidney Ruth Schuler (1997) "Sustainable Banking With the Poor: A Case Study of Grameen Bank", JSI Working Paper No. 10, Arlington Virginia: JSI Research and Training Institute.

Hashemi, Syed M., Sidney Ruth Schuler, and Ann P. Riley (1996) 'Rural Credit Programmes and Women's Empowerment in Bangladesh', *World Development* 24/4, pp. 635-653.

Holcombe, S. H. (1995) *Managing to Empower: The Grameen Bank's Experience of Poverty Alleviation,* Dhaka: University Press Ltd.

Korten, David C. (1989) *Bangladesh Rural Advancement Committee: Strategy for the 1990s,* Boston: Institute for Development Research.

Reuter Asia-Pacific Business Report, 3 October 1996.

Schuler, Sidney Ruth, Syed M. Hashemi, and Ann P. Riley (1997) "Men's Violence against Women in Rural Bangladesh: Undermined or Exacerbated by Microcredit Programs?", Paper presented at the Population Association of America Annual Meetings, Washington DC, March 1997.

Schuler, Sidney Ruth, Syed M. Hashemi, Ann P. Riley, and Shireen Akhter (1996) "Credit Programs, Patriarchy and Men's Violence Against Women in Rural Bangladesh", *Social Science and Medicine,* 43/12, pp. 1729-1742.

■ **Sidney Ruth Schuler** *is a social anthropologist affiliated with the JSI Research and Training Institute, where she started a research programme to investigate relationships between changing reproductive norms and changing gender relations in developing countries.*

■ **Syed M. Hashemi** *is Professor of Economics at Jahangirnagar University, Dhaka. He started and currently directs the Programme for Research on Poverty Alleviation at the Grameen Trust in Dhaka.*

■ **Shamsul Huda Badal** *is a researcher affiliated with the Development Research Centre in Dhaka. He is interested in poverty alleviation, NGOs, and community participation.*
This article was first published in Development in Practice, Volume 8, number 2, May 1999.

Domestic violence, deportation, and women's resistance: notes on managing inter-sectionality

Purna Sen

Southall Black Sisters (SBS) s a small women's organisation in London which combines campaigning, lobbying, activism, and casework. We have worked for over 15 years on issues of relevance to the (predominantly) Asian women who come to seek advice, support, and counselling, most commonly on domestic violence and the associated practical difficulties of ensuring housing, money, and safety. Of course, there are also issues relating to emotional distress, fear, and trauma with which abused women and their children have to deal. However, for many Asian women this constellation of problems is not the full story — the British state and the women's families (both in the UK and in the sub-continent) too often act in ways which restrict the choices available to abused women, continue to threaten their safety, or force the women out of the UK back to their country of origin against their will.

SBS is intolerant of domestic violence and the conditions in which it thrives. We challenge and seek to change the context and experience of abuse, including at the hands of the state which can and does deport women facing domestic violence. Our work cuts directly across a number of social cleavages — those of race, gender, and poverty — and we seek to increase the influence women can assert over their own lives, partly through changing the conditions which give rise to those deprivations. We now handle an average of about 1,000 enquiries per year — the majority of which concern domestic violence, sexual abuse, family problems (such as young girls being forced into marriage), and immigration difficulties. Our staff speak a number of south Asian languages and are thereby accessible to women who do not speak English and who have been disenfranchised from other services. Our advice always prioritises safety for the women and children with whom we work and this brings us into conflict with organisations with other priorities (discussed below).

We engage in deliberate actions for change in individual cases and in the contemporary UK policy context. Over the 19 years of SBS' existence, our casework has provided the anchor for our lobbying and campaigning work: the problems faced by the women who seek our help illustrate failings in mainstream services, policies, and legal provisions. Our work for social change includes challenges to:

- the cultural climate in which women are systematically denied control of their own lives, especially through the endemic practices of violence against women;

- the construction and delivery of services to abused women which are poorly geared to the needs of Asian women, particularly those with little or no English;

- the legal and policy context (at local and national levels) which undermines the ability of Asian women to resist violence and take control of their lives.

Many of our clients who leave their husbands find themselves plunged into poverty. Those who do leave home become economically responsible for themselves and their children, although they may have been dependent on their husbands, families, or in-laws. Employment opportunities are few, especially for women who speak little English and have childcare constraints. Many of our clients find paid work in a twilight zone, untouched by employment legislation and protection, similar to women in informal sector activity elsewhere in the world.

UK immigration rules contain a restriction (the 'one year rule') on incoming spouses whereby residency status is dependent upon the marriage lasting at least one year. It means that the incoming spouse is liable to deportation if the marriage does not last for the specified year and effectively ties women to husbands, no matter how good or bad the relationship. Further, during the 12 month period the incoming spouse is denied access to state welfare provisions — such as housing benefit, the means by which women fund their stay in safe houses (refuges) if fleeing domestic violence.

SBS works in many ways, including casework, lobbying, campaigning, policy work, publications, and public speaking. Our casework includes giving advice, counselling, making clients aware of the possible consequences of certain decisions, arranging alternative safe accommodation, finding appropriate legal counsel, and supporting them through legal proceedings. Legal cases commonly relate to obtaining injunctions (for example, to prevent violent men from harassing their wives), child custody arrangements, and divorce. However, our casework can also take us into pioneering areas. For example, in March 1998 one of our clients won a case against her husband for marital rape (the first by an Asian woman). She also took her in-laws to court for false imprisonment and actual bodily harm and won her case. While this client's success is significant she now has to fight the British state which seeks to deport her as she is caught by the one-year rule. We continue to support her in fighting this injustice by state agencies. This is an illustration of the way in which our casework is the basis for and link to our campaigning work.

The 'community' and the state

It is rarely easy for women to speak out about domestic violence, no matter who they are. Quite apart from their own (perhaps conflicting) emotions they may face disbelief or even disapproval from those whom they tell about the violence. For black and ethnic minority communities in the West there are a number of particular pressures which may be brought to bear upon women — most commonly the potential for internal criticism to be used to strengthen racist stereotypes or actions against their communities (see for example Mama 1989; Bryan et al. 1988). These dangers have been constructed as constraints to action and discussion, both against individual women and against organisations — such as Southall Black Sisters. The construction of knowledge on racial oppression has been allowed to contest the construction of knowledge of gender oppression and means that only those voices and issues which are not critical of the community are sanctioned for public discourse. This allows male 'community leaders' successfully to impose an agenda of race over one of gender (see Sahgal and Yuval-Davis 1992; Trivedi 1984); and some black women themselves have declined to expose 'their men' to further harassment from racist institutions such as the police (Mama 1989; Bryan et al. 1988). Isolated and abused women are denied the first step towards seeking help — speaking about abuse. The feminist imperative to 'break the silence' is at odds with the minority community imperative to maintain a silence.

SBS has refused to be silenced on issues of gender, male power, and violence within the Asian community and on discriminatory actions of the state. This has brought considerable antagonism from within the 'community'. We have been accused of wrecking the fabric of Asian culture and our funding has been threatened because of the nature of our work (Southall Black Sisters 1994; Sahgal and Yuval-Davis 1992). SBS is known in certain circles as 'home-wreckers', a nervous reading of our efforts to support abused women, including their decisions to leave home. Men escape censure for their actions: how sad and significant it is that the men (and their families) who abuse women are not named as home-wreckers — a title of which they are undoubtedly worthy. Nor are violent husbands commonly subjected to calls to protect the community image in the context of racism — if men were to stop using domestic violence, this would both strengthen their own relationships and be a step towards reducing racist-inspired criticisms of the community.

Our campaigning and lobbying work arises from our casework and both in terms of supporting individual clients in terms of seeking policy change. We have run a campaign against the one-year rule which has included commissioned research — it found 512 women caught in this situation in 1995-6 (SBS), and we have given evidence to parliamentary investigations and lobbied politicians. We have had to educate politicians about domestic violence and its particular impact on Asian women both in terms of cultural context and in the immigration legislation. The current government recently faced questioning in parliament on the need to review and change this law. In his reply the Immigration Minister acknowledged SBS' campaigning efforts:

> I pay tribute to the work of SBS who brought this matter to the attention of Ministers and the House... The evidence given by SBS was described by the then Minister — and I endorse the description — as moving and poignant... I have worked closely with SBS to see how we can change the law... (O'Brien 1998).

We expect an announcement soon on changes to the legislation but anticipate that these will not include the abolition for which we have pressed. We intend to encourage a range of organisations to monitor the impact of any changes, will make shortcomings known to the government, and shall continue to press the government for abolition.

Zoora Shah

Campaigns may also be built around the need to gain support for an individual client. A current case involves Zoora Shah who is currently serving a life sentence for the murder of a man who exploited her sexually and economically for over twelve years, while he was married to and living with another woman. Having been brought to England to marry, Zoora suffered domestic violence from her husband and was later abandoned by him, along with three young children; another two children had died. She was illiterate, spoke no English, and found herself homeless and extremely poor. At this time of heightened vulnerability she was befriended by Azam, a man from the criminal underworld, who provided her shelter in return for sexual services. Destitute, Zoora felt she had no alternative and began to live in a house bought by Azam, for which she made the mortgage payments. Azam's sexual demands were relentless — sometimes he would demand sex four or five times in a day, sometimes he would take her to the cemetery where Zoora's children were buried and demand sex there. Zoora was not free of Azam's influence even when he was imprisoned for drugs offences — he sent former prisoners to her in the expectation of getting sex. As Zoora's children grew older Azam began to express his sexual interest in her daughters.

Zoora did try to get help during her years of abuse including turning to Sher Azam — Azam's brother and then head of the Bradford Council of Mosques — but her appeal was unproductive and her ordeal continued. On one visit to Pakistan, Zoora obtained neela thotha (arsenic), which she was told would render Azam impotent, and brought it back to the UK. She used the poison in Azam's food and found relief from his sexual demands for a short period. Azam's interest in her daughters continued to distress Zoora and eventually she gave him a second dose of poison, which killed him. At her trial she said nothing of her history of abuse or of Azam's sexual interest in her daughters. She was sentenced to life imprisonment for murder, with a tariff (minimum period to be served) of 20 years. Zoora made contact with SBS from prison; we appointed a new legal team and over five years we pieced together her history of abuse and exploitation. In July 1997 Zoora won leave to appeal against her conviction for murder. Her appeal — that she was wrongly convicted for murder and her offence should be reduced to the lesser charge of manslaughter (which does not carry a mandatory life sentence) was heard, and dismissed, in April 1998: the judges did not believe Zoora's history of abuse.

Zoora's case exemplifies some of the difficulties discussed above. The nature of community dynamics and power relations severely limit the degree to which Pakistani women in Bradford are able to raise their voices, particularly in relation to the thorny issue of domestic violence. Discourses of shame and honour denied Zoora support within the community and severely limited her access to support elsewhere. The sexual nature of much of the abuse was deeply embarrassing for Zoora to discuss, but sexual matters are anyway beyond the limits of respectable discussion in her social milieu. This shows how effective is male power and control over what enjoys legitimacy as public discourse and what is denied that recognition. Failure to give public space to abuse serves to silence women's voices and to deny abused women recognition of their experiences and support to enable them to change their situation. The Appeal Court decision turned Zoora's reality upside-down by claiming that her relationships with men showed that she was not behaving as Asian women should, and that she thus had no shame left to salvage by remaining silent about domestic violence.

Intersections: challenging many fronts at once

SBS recognises that state and patriarchal systems interlock; and this makes our work difficult as we have to unravel these without becoming simplistic or reinforcing gender/cultural stereotypes. We sometimes strike alliances in our work — with women's groups on gender issues and with anti-racist groups, for example, against deportations. However, alliances are not always straightforward, as a recent example in Zoora's case illustrates.

Leaflets about this case were sent to various groups for distribution and in all but one instance this was unproblematic. However, one group (a well known anti-racist organisation) refused to distribute any leaflets as they thought the literature fuelled racist stereotypes of Asian/Muslim/Pakistani communities. They wanted SBS to re-write some of the leaflet and remove the references to patriarchal forces within Zoora's community. This (predominantly white) organisation told Southall Black Sisters (a black group) that our leaflet strengthened racist understandings by saying that Zoora's culture is patriarchal. Their argument displays a lack of understanding both of the nature of minority women's oppression (especially in the intersection of race and gender inequality) and of the need strategically *to take on* multiplicity, rather than dealing with only one issue at a time. Their response subscribes to the silencing of women which patriarchal dynamics in all cultures seek to impose, and highlights the discomfort of strands of anti-racist thinking in dealing with oppression within minority communities as opposed to oppression from external sources.

The changes they asked for would have decontextualised Zoora's experiences and left us referring only to the inter-personal dynamics of a single relationship. SBS understands the nature of male violence, that it is institutionalised in community and social practices, and we seek legal recognition of the context in which Asian women experience and respond to domestic violence. Like women across the world, we strive to keep gender on the agenda alongside other forms of oppression (e.g. Jayawardena 1986) and do not subscribe to a linear approach. Parallels can be found with the 'poverty-first-gender-later' argument and the cultural relativism which de-legitimises challenges to gender oppression. In the UK context the struggle is to maintain challenges to gender oppression alongside anti-racist struggles. Our history of, and commitment to, challenging both forms of oppression strengthens our work and brings tensions into partnerships with other organisations. SBS is not afraid to take on difficult cases (although we do so with care) and we work with both Muslim and Hindu women (as well as others); we take a clear stand against communalism and against abuses of male power in all communities. There is enough evidence on the widespread prevalence of domestic violence to put any community (not only Muslim or south Asian) to shame for institutionalised abuse of women.

Concluding thoughts

Unlike many other groups in the UK, SBS works against gender and racial oppression (including religious fundamentalism and communalism) and we operate at the level of the family, the community, and the state. There is the possibility and need for work with other groups on various aspects of this work, or on specific campaigns. However, our commitment to challenging the simultaneity of oppressions has brought tension (even conflict) into those alliances and partnerships and ours is a constant struggle to raise and keep a focus on gender in the face of pressure to privilege cultural /religious identity.

I have sought to highlight three key strategies in our work. Firstly, maintaining a strong and dynamic link between our casework and the macro view of policy and social practices which impinge upon women's options in dealing with violence. This grounding facilitates informed and relevant work at the level of the individual, the family, the 'community', and the state and shows a clear relationship from the individual to the macro level. Secondly, we maintain a view on the simultaneity of various forms of oppression, including gender or race/ethnicity relations, communalism, and state practices. Thirdly, working across these areas means that we can and do link up with a range of other organisations as appropriate to the specific work we are doing. However, both cooperation and tension can mark these relationships.

We continue to campaign and lobby for individual women and for policy changes which would benefit women. Sometimes we find our voices isolated but remain determined in our pursuit of justice for women in the UK. Perhaps our greatest strength is our knowledge that our work is both productive and necessary. The constant flow of cases with which we deal reminds us of the need to continue seeking the best possible conditions for south Asian women to be free from both racial and gendered oppression: it is our grounding in the daily lives of women from which our vision, strategies, and determination derive.

References

Bryan, B., S. Dadzie and S. Scafe (1988) *Heart of the Race: Black Women's Lives in Britain,* London: Virago.

Jayawardena, K. (1986) *Feminism and Nationalism in the Third World,* London: Zed Books.

Mama, A. (1989) *The Hidden Struggle: Statutory and Voluntary Sector Responses to Violence against Black Women in the Home,* London: London Race and Housing Research Unit.

O'Brien, M. (1998) Reply to Margaret Moran MP from Mike O'Brien, Parliamentary Under-Secretary of State for the Home Department, House of Commons Hansard Debates for 24 June 1998 (pt17).

Sahgal, G. and N. Yuval-Davis (1992) *Refusing Holy Orders: Women and Fundamentalism in Britain,* London: Virago.

Southall Black Sisters (1994a) *Domestic Violence And Asian Women: A Collection Of Reports And Briefings,* London: Southall Black Sisters.

Southall Black Sisters (1994b) *Against The Grain: A Celebration of Survival and Struggle 1979-1989,* London: Southall Black Sisters.

Southall Black Sisters (1997) *A Stark Choice: Domestic Violence or Deportation? Abolish the One Year Rule!,* London: Southall Black Sisters.

Trivedi, P. (1984) 'To deny our fullness: Asian women in the making of history', *Feminist Review* 17:39-52.

■ **Purna Sen** *has worked for several years on violence against women, both as a researcher and as an activist. She is a member of the management committee of Southall Black Sisters and the UK advisory group for the NGO Change, has taught development studies and gender studies, and worked on race and gender equality in the UK. This article was first published in* Development in Practice, *Volume 9, number 1.*

Women entrepreneurs in the Bangladeshi restaurant business

Mahmuda Rahman Khan

The Bangladesh Rural Advancement Committee (BRAC) is an NGO, involved in multi-sectoral development programmes for the rural poor, in which special emphasis is given to women. The Rural Enterprise Project (REP) was established in 1985 to promote the generation of increased income for rural poor women in a systematic manner. The objective is to find new or improved income-generating activities that can be owned, operated, and managed by BRAC's landless members. The Shuruchi restaurant programme represents one such effort to involve rural women in more challenging entrepreneurial activity in the non-agricultural sector.

The Restaurant Programme was started in 1991. A restaurant may be opened under individual ownership with a maximum loan of taka 6500 (£108), after which a current account for the individual is opened with BRAC. This money is withdrawn in instalments according to the entrepreneur's needs, and repayment is collected as either a daily or a weekly instalment, with an interest rate of 20 per cent. Like most rural restaurants, these enterprises sell tea, snacks, and meals. By January 1993, there were 273 'Shuruchi Restaurants', or 'restaurants for good food' all over the country.

The research

An exploratory study was undertaken by BRAC's Research and Evaluation Division. Five restaurants were selected from Manikganj, Jamalpur, and Sherpur districts. The main focus was to examine how far women's entrepreneurial capacity has developed, and to assess whether women have control over the business. Rapid Rural Appraisal

(RRA)/Participatory Rural Appraisal (PRA) techniques were used for data collection.

Through the introduction of the Restaurant Programme, the field of income-generating activities has expanded and a new dimension has been created for women, aiming to involve them in an untraditional activity. As it has been in operation only for a short period, it was thought to be an opportune moment to address initial shortcomings, in order to improve the project. REP had designed a questionnaire and an arithmetical test for selecting the potential entrepreneurs, to establish their accounting capacity, business experience, understanding of hygiene, and their family responsibilities.

Table 1: Restaurant profile

Indicator	Entrepreneurs				
	Kalpana	Haowa	Aklima	Khodeja	Maina
Length of membership (yrs)	2	3	3	3.6	5
Marital status	married	separated	married	married	married
Educational level	nil	nil	Class V	nil	nil
Amount of BRAC credit (taka)	6500 (£108)	6500 (£108)	6500 (£108)	6500 (£108)	4000 (£67)
Types of worker	family labour	family labour	family labour	family labour	fam. lab. + 1 hired
Monthly profit (taka)	1548 (£25)	1272 (£21)	1670 (£28)	1823 (£30)	9767 (£163)

Table 2: Division of labour in restaurant

Indicator	Entrepreneurs				
	Kalpana	Haowa	Aklima	Khodeja	Maina
Cooking, washing	herself	herself	herself	herself	herself
Time spent on cooking, washing	30%	32%	43%	58%	—
Serving customers	husband or son	herself or sister	husband	husband	son
Marketing	mainly husband	herself or sister	husband	husband	son
Keeping accounts (unpaid)	outside man	outside man	herself	husband	son
Handling cash	husband	herself	husband	husband	son

Observations

Some differences were observed between REP's formal selection process as officially formulated, and the ways in which entrepreneurs are actually chosen. In practice, when the target is set in terms of the number of restaurants, the criteria are not followed strictly. However, REP tends to give preference to women whose husbands or brothers already have a niche in the market-place, which creates dependence on a male member of the family from the beginning.

In terms of how the restaurants are actually run, women are involved largely in traditional work such as cooking, washing, and cleaning (Table 1). However, exceptions arise, as for example in the case of the separated woman who has no male family member to help her in shopping and serving, so that she and her sister have to share all the work. Another restaurant owner often does the shopping, and local opinion is that 'She is Hindu' (and thus exempt from *purdah* regulations). Generally, all the 'public' work such as serving customers, handling cash, and keeping accounts is done by men, and the women's place is still in the kitchen.

In conventional accounting terms, the restaurants are making a modest monthly profit. However, when strict cost considerations (overheads, household consumption from restaurant, and the market wage of the workers employed) are accounted for, the profit margin disappears. All the owners eat their daily meals at the restaurant. They estimated that this cost Tk.50 (£0.83) monthly, but none of them documented it in their accounts. None of the entrepreneurs had any idea of the monthly profit of their restaurants, and they re-invest their daily income as working capital.

Two of the restaurant owners were found to be more entrepreneurial: one has complete understanding of profit and loss, and also does extra business to make money. Another has full control over the restaurant, though her son does the shopping, keeps the accounts, and serves customers. Entrepreneurial activity was not much in evidence in the case of other restaurant owners. For instance, one woman could hardly be called an entrepreneur at all, since her husband is running the business. But because the loan is in her name, she has to live on the restaurant premises. The husbands of all the married women are to a degree involved in the business. Even the women who are separated and widowed are to some extent dependent on sisters and sons. Most of the women surveyed are illiterate, except one who has a good primary school education, and deals with accounts with the help of her husband; the rest have to rely on others for keeping accounts.

The restaurant owners are not facing any problems as borrowers, and all are repaying the loan on a regular weekly basis. It is also evident from the community-level response that these female-run restaurants are socially acceptable. However, local people tend to excuse the unconventional nature of the work by saying that these women are poor, so they do not have other alternatives for earning their livelihood.

Analysis: changing social conditions for women

As shown by the restaurant survey, there has been no real change in the women's condition. In the first place, although women may have gained some mobility in the market-place because they can now leave their homes to work in the restaurants, there is no change in terms of the division of labour. In fact, the restaurant business has increased the women's workload: they now cook for longer hours, or sometimes even several times a day. On the other hand, men do not deal with cooking, except for making tea and sometimes chapattis. Women who have male family members to help are never seen serving in the restaurant, so they are not doing anything to challenge traditional household-based roles.

Secondly, far from becoming more independent of men, the women are increasingly dependent on them to run the restaurants. The women themselves cannot visualise their future in terms of the restaurant enterprise, especially those whose husbands are involved: they do not feel that it is their business. Since they are not independent of their husbands or sons, they lack self-confidence. However, women who are widowed or separated are trying their best to establish the business for themselves, and may have the potential to develop into entrepreneurs.

Thirdly, women's involvement in the restaurant business generally makes no impact on the community in terms of increasing respect for women, or helping others. The one exception is the case of a woman who is not solely dependent on the restaurant business, who could make some money through complementary activities — for example, by doing extra business during Durga Puja (a Hindu religious festival), or renting out a room. So, although BRAC has been successful in bringing women physically from homestead to market-place, it has not necessarily changed their position within the family or the community. For without addressing men's attitudes towards women at the household and social levels, we cannot expect any social change for women. BRAC's efforts to challenge gender-based discrimination focus exclusively on women and do not address men's attitudes and responsibilities. Though it will take time to alter men's behaviour, BRAC will have to make an effort to do so, to bring about permanent change in discriminatory attitudes.

Fourthly, these female-run restaurants tend to reinforce the traditional concepts of the division of space. The restaurants are seen as continuation of *purdah*: the general community response to them is, 'It is good that these women are working in a room, instead of wandering around and working in an open space. They are not violating *purdah*.' The ideal of *purdah* is for women to be fully occupied with their household work, and to do it all within their own homestead. The market, on the other hand, is one of the most strictly male-dominated areas in Bangladesh. It is not that women in Bangladesh do not go out, but that notions of 'inside' and 'outside' are open to complex manipulation, since going out of their households is not necessarily an index of women's power within them (White 1992). When it is a question of earning a livelihood because they are too poor to survive, *purdah* becomes more flexible. So, if this venture challenges neither the sexual division of labour nor traditional notions of gender-specific roles, BRAC's vision of the capacity of the restaurant programme to make an impact on discrimination is called into question.

Finally, while the owners of Shuruchi may have gained a degree of social acceptability, the male members of the family have not seen this as proof of women's entrepreneurial ability, but as means of access to credit.

Women's development as entrepreneurs

An entrepreneur needs some independence, access to markets, and an understanding of business. Among these women restaurant owners, there is little scope for becoming an individual entrepreneur. Though the area managers of the Rural Development Programme (RDP) agree that at the initial stage women do need some support from men, they believe that ultimately they should be self-reliant. Sometimes the programme personnel underestimate the capacity of the group members and shield them from their responsibilities by involving men from the very beginning. It seems difficult for women to be self-reliant when they are helping their husbands, instead of running the business by themselves.

If BRAC wants to develop women's entrepreneurial capacity, it should start doing business with the women alone, and should not rely on the husbands' involvement. It has been suggested that husbands should not be allowed to handle the cash, or that they (or other male relatives) should be entitled to work only as employees. But in our male-dominated society, especially in the rural areas where conservative concepts of the proper division of labour and of space are very entrenched, it is absurd to think of keeping a husband as an employee.

Recommendations

This project is a new venture, aiming to expand rapidly. Given the findings of the study, the following recommendations have been made:

1 The criteria set for selecting Shuruchi entrepreneurs should be strictly followed.
2 BRAC should provide training for the female entrepreneurs before starting the restaurant.
3 The restaurant should start operating in completely new premises, not in a building owned by the husband of the entrepreneur or other relatives.
4 Systems for keeping accounts should be uniform in all areas.
5 A personal file on each woman entrepreneur and restaurant should be maintained at the BRAC area office.
6 BRAC should consider whether a predetermined inflexible level of loan is conducive to developing entrepreneurial capability.

Otherwise, if the husband is much more involved in the business and in fact runs it, while the woman does her traditional work, why not give the loan to the man? Indeed, why even call it a female-run restaurant?

Note

The author would like to thank Dr Anne Marie Goetz, Fellow at the Institute of Development Studies at the University of Sussex, who kindly gave up valuable time to go through the draft and make comments.

Reference

White, Sarah (1992) *Arguing with the Crocodile: Gender and Class in Bangladesh*, Dhaka: University Press Ltd. (UPL).

■ **Mahmuda Rahman Khan** *is currently working as National Professional Project Personnel — Gender Issues, UNFPA (Dhaka) where she is involved in advocacy on reproductive health and gender issues in different ministries. She provides technical support and monitoring through a technical cell for successful implementation of the Fifth Health and Population Project. Her areas of interest are women's empowerment, violence against women, reproductive health and child rights. She is also Secretary and Head of the research and training cell of 'Shishu Aangina-Child and Women Development Center', which is involved in promoting child rights through children's participation in cultural activities. This article was first published in* Development in Practice, *Volume 5, number 3, in 1995.*

Empowerment examined

Jo Rowlands

The often uncritical use of the term 'empowerment' in development thinking and practice disguises a problematic concept. Many development practitioners and policy-makers will have come across the term in Caroline Moser's work (1989) on gender analysis. However, development is not the only context in which it is used. We now hear about empowerment from mainstream politicians such as Bill Clinton and John Major. Its use in some disciplines — adult education, community work, and social work in particular — is relatively advanced, though here too there is room for greater clarity about the concept and its application.

Some of the confusion arises because the root-concept — power — is itself disputed, and so is understood and experienced in differing ways by different people. Indeed, the person invoking 'empowerment' may not even be aware of the potential for misunderstanding. Power has been the subject of much debate across the social sciences.[1] Some definitions focus, with varying degrees of subtlety, on the ability of one person or group to get another person or group to do something against their will. Such 'power' is located in decision-making processes, conflict, and force, and could be described as 'zero-sum': the more power one person has, the less the other has. Other definitions differentiate between various kinds of power, which can then be understood as serving distinct purposes and having different effects in or on society. These include 'a threat power', 'economic power', and 'integrative power'; or 'the power to create such relationships as love, respect, friendship, legitimacy and so on'.[2]

Most frameworks for understanding power appear to be 'neutral': that is, they make no mention of how power is *actually* distributed within a society. There is no consideration of the power dynamics of gender, or of race, class, or any other force of oppression. This absence is tackled by a number of feminist theorists.[3] Conventionally, power is defined in relation to obedience, or 'power over', since some people are seen to have control or influence over others. A gender analysis shows that 'power over' is wielded predominantly by men over other men, by men over women, and by dominant social, political, economic, or cultural groups over those who are marginalised. It is thus an instrument of domination, whose use can be seen in people's personal lives, their close relationships, their communities, and beyond.

Power of this kind can be subtly exercised. Various feminist writers have described the way in which people who are systematically denied power and influence in the dominant society internalise the messages they receive about what they are supposed to be like, and how they may come to believe the messages to be true.[4] This 'internalised oppression' is adopted as a survival mechanism, but becomes so well ingrained that the effects are mistaken for reality. Thus, for example, a woman who is subjected to violent abuse when she expresses her own opinions may start to withhold them, and eventually come to believe that she has no opinions of her own. When control becomes internalised in this way, the overt use of 'power over' is no longer necessary.

The definition of power in terms of domination and obedience contrasts with one which views it in generative terms: for instance 'the power some people have of stimulating activity in others and raising their morale'.[5] One aspect of this is the kind of leadership that comes from the wish to see a group achieve what it is capable of, where there is no conflict of interests and the group sets its own collective agenda. This model of power is not a zero-sum: an increase in one person's power does not necessarily diminish that of another. And, as Liz Kelly (1992) observes, 'I suspect it is "power to" that the term "empowerment" refers to, and it is achieved by increasing one's ability to resist and challenge power over'.

What is empowerment?

The meaning of 'empowerment' can now be seen to relate to the user's interpretation of power. In the context of the conventional definition, empowerment must be about bringing people who are outside the decision-making process into it. This puts a strong emphasis on access to political structures and formal decision-making and, in the economic sphere, on access to markets and incomes that enable people to participate in economic decision-making. It is about individuals being able to maximise the opportunities available to them without, or despite, constraints of structure and State. Within the generative interpretation of power, empowerment also includes access to intangible decision-making processes. It is concerned with the processes by which people become aware of their own interests and how those relate to those of others, in order both to participate from a position of greater strength in decision-making and actually to influence such decisions.

Feminist interpretations of power lead to a still broader understanding of empowerment, since they go beyond formal and institutional definitions of power, and incorporate the idea of 'the personal as political'.[6] From a feminist perspective, interpreting 'power over' entails understanding the dynamics of oppression and internalised oppression. Since these affect the ability of less powerful groups to participate in formal and informal decision-making, and to exert influence, they also affect the way that individuals or groups perceive themselves and their ability to act and influence the world around them. Empowerment is thus more than simply opening up access to decision-making; it must also include the processes that lead people to perceive themselves as able and entitled to occupy that decision-making space, and so overlaps with the other categories of 'power to' and 'power within'.

These interpretations of empowerment involve giving full scope to the full range of human abilities and potential. As feminist and other social theorists have shown, the abilities ascribed to a particular set of people are to a large degree socially constructed. Empowerment must involve undoing negative social constructions, so that the people affected come to see themselves as having the capacity and the right to act and have influence.

This wider picture of empowerment can be seen to have three dimensions.

- **Personal:** where empowerment is about developing a sense of self and individual confidence and capacity, and undoing the effects of internalised oppression;

- **Close relationships:** where empowerment is about developing the ability to negotiate and influence the nature of the relationship and decisions made within it;

- **Collective:** where individuals work together to achieve a more extensive impact than each could have had alone. This includes involvement in political structures, but might also cover collective action based on cooperation rather than competition. Collective action may be locally focused — for example, at village or neighbourhood level — or institutional, such as national networks or the United Nations.

The profound — but often unrecognised — differences in the ways in which power is understood perhaps explain how it is that people and organisations as far apart politically as feminists, Western politicians, and the World Bank have embraced the concept with such enthusiasm.

Empowerment in practice

The idea of empowerment is increasingly used as a tool for understanding what is needed to change the situation of poor and marginalised people. In this context, there is broad agreement that empowerment is a process; that it involves some degree of personal development, but that this is not sufficient; and that it involves moving from insight to action.

In a counselling context, McWhirter (1991) defines empowerment as:

'The *process* by which people, organisations or groups who are powerless (a) become aware of the power dynamics at work in their life context, (b) develop the skills and capacity for gaining some reasonable control over their lives, (c) exercise this control without infringing upon the rights of others and (d) support the empowerment of others in the community'. (my emphasis).

She makes a useful distinction between 'the situation of empowerment', where all four of these conditions are met; and 'an empowering situation', where one or more of the conditions is in place or being developed, but where the full requirements are not present.

Through all these definitions runs the theme of understanding: if you understand your situation, you are more likely to act to do something about it. There is also the theme of acting collectively. McWhirter's definition makes clear that taking action is not about gaining the power to dominate others. Writers on social group work also insist that empowerment must be used in the context of oppression, since empowerment is about working to remove the existence and effects of unjust inequalities (Ward and Mullender 1991). Empowerment can take place on a small scale, linking people with others in similar situations through self-help, education, support, or social action groups and network building; or on a larger scale, through community organisation, campaigning, legislative lobbying, social planning, and policy development (Parsons 1991).

The definitions of empowerment used in education, counselling, and social work, although developed through work in industrialised countries, are broadly similar to Freire's concept of *conscientisation*, which centres on individuals becoming 'subjects' in their own lives and developing a 'critical consciousness' — that is, an understanding of their circumstances and the social environment that leads to action.

In practice, much empowerment work involves forms of group work. The role of the outside professional in this context becomes one of helper and facilitator; anything more directive is seen as interfering with the empowerment of the people concerned. Since facilitation skills require subtlety in order to be effective, this has usually meant that professionals must to some extent re-learn how to do their jobs, and develop high-level skills of self-awareness. In some cases, the professional facilitator has to become a member of the group, and be willing to do the same kind of personal sharing as is encouraged from other participants.

The outside professional cannot expect to control the outcomes of authentic empowerment. Writing about education, Taliaferro (1991) points out that true power cannot be bestowed: it comes from within. Any notion of empowerment being given by one group or another hides an attempt to keep control, and she describes the idea of gradual empowerment as 'especially dubious'. Real empowerment may take unanticipated directions. Outside professionals should therefore be clear that any 'power over' which they have in relation to the people they work with is likely to be challenged by them. This raises an ethical and political issue: if the reality is that you do have power-over — as is the case with statutory authorities or financially powerful organisations, such as development agencies — it is misleading to deny that this is so.

Empowerment in a development context

How can the concept of empowerment be most usefully applied in a development context? Most of the literature about empowerment, with the exception of Freire and Batliwala, originates from work in industrialised societies. Do poor or otherwise marginalised women and men experience similar problems in developing countries? In both cases, their lack of access to resources and to formal power is significant, even if the contexts within which that lack is experienced are very different. McWhirter's definition of empowerment seems equally relevant to either context. Any difference is more likely to show up in the way in which it is put into practice, and in the particular activities that are called for. This is confirmed in one of the few definitions of empowerment which has a specific focus on development (Keller and Mbwewe 1991), in which it is described as:

> A process whereby women become able to organise themselves to increase their own self-reliance, to assert their independent right to make choices and to control resources which will assist in challenging and eliminating their own subordination.

Srilatha Batliwala, writing about women's empowerment, has made a detailed analysis of women's empowerment programmes, looking at Integrated Rural Development (IRD: economic interventions, awareness-building, and organising of women) and at Research, Training, and Resource Support.[7] She notes that in some (especially IRD) programmes, the terms *empowerment* and *development* are used synonymously. It is often assumed that power comes automatically through economic strength. It may do, but often it does not, depending on specific relations determined by gender, culture, class, or caste. Economic relations do not always improve women's economic situation, and often add a layer of extra burden. Often, development work is still done 'for' women, and an exclusive focus on economic activities does not automatically create a space for women to look at their own role as women, or at other problematic aspects of their lives.

Economic activities and the empowerment process

Economic activities may widen the range of options for marginalised people, but do not necessarily enable them to reach a point where they can take charge of creating for themselves the options from which they get to choose. To do that, a combination of confidence and self-esteem, information, analytical skills, ability to identify and tap into available resources, political and social influence, and so on, is needed. Programmes that build on the demands and wishes of the people who participate in them are a step towards empowerment, but they do not in and of themselves tackle the assumptions that those people (and the people around them) make about what they can and cannot do: the point where the internalised oppression works in combination with the particular economic and social context to restrict the options that people *perceive* as available, and legitimate. An empowerment approach centred on economic activity must pay attention to more than the activity itself. The processes and structures through which an economic activity operates need to be deliberately designed to create opportunities for an empowerment process to happen.

The role of outsiders

The role of the professional or the outsider in the development setting is just as important as in the social-work contexts described earlier. Price describes the crucial role played by women staff of an Indian NGO, giving an example of an occasion when a key worker talking about her own personal experience enabled other women to do likewise. This is in stark contrast to the tendency in many development projects, as in Ngau's account (1987) of the Kenyan Harambee movement, for professional-client relationships to be fostered by para-professionals, fuelling resentment and withdrawal among local people. This has implications for the way in which personnel in development programmes and projects — as well as in aid agencies — perform their work. A process of empowerment that seeks to engage poor and marginalised people cannot be effective if the methodology is 'top-down' and directive, or encourages dependency. Empowerment is a process that cannot be imposed by outsiders — although appropriate external support and intervention can speed up and encourage it. It calls for a facilitative approach and an attitude of complete respect for and confidence in the people being worked with, or accompanied.[8] It therefore makes great demands on the change-agents, and may require (and feed into) their own empowerment. Furthermore, since most professionals are trained to work in ways that disempower — and which tell other people what they should do and think — it requires conscious and sustained efforts to modify that pattern of behaviour and to clarify mutual expectations.

Individual empowerment

In discussing empowerment through awareness-building and organising of women, Batliwala highlights an aspect of an empowerment approach that poses a difficulty for many agencies working in development: it can be desperately slow. Most funding agencies are understandably preoccupied with showing results. Yet the work needed for raising levels of confidence and self-esteem among poor and marginalised people in such a way that will enhance their ability to take charge of their own needs is necessarily time-consuming. It is a process that each individual has to go through at her or his own pace. Because of this, there is a temptation to work with people who already have a degree of self-confidence. This is one of the reasons that even empowerment-focused programmes often fail to engage with the poorest and most marginalised. Even to participate in a group, you require a certain minimal sense of your own abilities and worth, as well as being able to overcome the obstacles to making the time to participate.

Collective empowerment

In the context of development, while individual empowerment is one ingredient in achieving empowerment at the collective and institutional levels, concentration on individuals alone is not sufficient. Changes are needed in the collective abilities of individuals to take charge of identifying and meeting their own needs — as households, communities, organisations, institutions, and societies. At the same time, it is important to recognise that the effectiveness of such group and organisational activity does also rest on the individual empowerment of at least some people.

Professionals involved in such empowerment work should repeatedly ask how the development intervention is affecting the different aspects of the lives of the people directly involved. A monitoring and evaluation process that reflects the empowerment process is essential. People need to be involved in the identification of appropriate indicators of change, and in the setting of criteria for evaluating impact. As the empowerment process proceeds, these will inevitably need to be modified and revised. Clarity about the dynamics that push poor and marginalised people to stay within what is safe and familiar is vital, in order to ensure that the empowerment process is kept well in focus. Qualitative indicators are, self-evidently, central to the evaluation of empowerment.

Conclusion

'Empowerment' has much in common with other concepts used by development practitioners and planners, such as 'participation', 'capacity-building', 'sustainability', or 'institutional development'.

There is, however, a worrying temptation to use them in a way that takes the troublesome notions of power, and the distribution of power, out of the picture. For in spite of their appeal, these terms can easily become one more way to ignore or hide the realities of power, inequality, and oppression. Yet it is precisely those realities which shape the lives of poor and marginalised people, and the communities in which they live.

The concept of 'empowerment', if it is used precisely and deliberately, can help to focus thought, planning, and action in development. However, when its use is careless, deliberately vague, or sloganising, it risks becoming degraded and valueless.

Notes

1 See, for example, Bachrach and Baratz (1970), Lukes (1974), Foucault (1980), Giddens (1984), Hartsock (1985 and 1990), and Boulding (1988).

2 These distinctions are from Boulding (1988) p.10.

3 See, for example, Hartsock (1985, 1990), and Starhawk (1987).

4 See, for example, Pheterson (1990), and Jackins (1983).

5 Nancy Hartsock (1985) draws on the writings of Hannah Arendt, Mary Parker Follett, Dorothy Emmett, Hannah Pitkin and Berenice Carroll in her analysis.

6 I do not wish to imply here that there is one 'feminist' model of power. Space constraints have led me to generalise and leave out important variations in analysis.

7 Batliwala (1993). I had access to the second draft and not to the final version.

8 *Acompañamiento,* or accompaniment, is a word widely used in Latin America to describe an outside agent's sense of solidarity and willingness to share risks with poor and marginalised people, and a willingness to engage with the processes of social change in which they are directly involved. It contrasts with the position of outside agents — whether these are church workers, development NGOs, or funding agencies — which maintain a greater sense of distance.

References

Bachrach, P. and M.S. Baratz (1970) *Power and Poverty: Theory and Practice,* New York: Oxford University Press.

Batliwala, S. (1983) *Empowerment of Women in South Asia: Concepts and Practices,* New Delhi: Asian-South Pacific Bureau of Adult Education and Freedom from Hunger Campaign.

Boulding, K. (1988) *Three Faces of Power,* London: Sage.

Foucault, M. (1980) *Power/Knowledge: Selected Interviews and Other Writings,* ed. Colin Gordon. Brighton: Harvester.

Giddens, A. (1984) *The Constitution of Society,* Cambridge: Polity.

Hartsock, N. (1985) *Money, Sex and Power: Towards a Feminist Historical Materialism,* Boston: Northeastern University Press.

Hartsock, N. (1990) 'Foucault on power: a theory for women?' in L.J. Nicholson,(ed): *Feminism/Postmodernism,* New York and London: Routledge.

Jackins, H. (1983) *The Reclaiming of Power,* Seattle: Rational Island.

Keller, B. and D.C. Mbwewe (1991) 'Policy and planning for the empowerment of Zambia's women farmers', *Canadian Journal of Development Studies* 12/1: 75-88.

Kelly, L. (1992) 'The Contradictions of Power for Women', paper presented at the NFHA Women and Housing

Conference. Mimeo.

Lukes, S. (1974) *Power: a Radical View,* London: Macmillan.

McWhirter, E.H. (1991) 'Empowerment in counselling', *Journal of Counselling and Development* 69: 222-7.

Moser, C. (1989) 'Gender planning in the Third World: meeting practical and strategic gender needs', *World Development,* 17:11.

Ngau, P.M. (1987) 'Tensions in empowerment: the experience of Harambee (self-help) movement, Kenya', *Economic Development and Cultural Change* 35/3:523-8.

Parsons, R. J. (1991) 'Empowerment: purpose and practice principle in social work', *Social Work with Groups* 14/2:7-21

Pheterson, G. (1990) 'Alliances between women: overcoming internalised oppression and internalised domination' in A. Albrecht and R.M. Brewer (eds): *Bridges of Power: Women's* Multicultural Alliances, Philadelphia: New Society.

Price, J. (n.d.) 'Women's Development: Welfare Projects or Political Empowerment?', presented at Amsterdam conference. Mimeo.

Starhawk [pseud. M. Simos] (1987) *Truth or Dare: Encounters with Power, Authority and Mystery,* San Francisco: Harper & Row.

Taliaferro, M.B. (1991) 'The myth of empowerment', *Journal of Negro Education* 60/1: 1-2.

Ward, D. and A. Mullender (1991) 'Empowerment and oppression: an indissoluble pairing', *Critical Social Policy* 11/2:21-30.

■ **Jo Rowlands** *worked for over ten years as a trainer and consultant for cooperatives and NGOs in Britain and Latin America. When this article was written she was based at the University of Durham, where she worked on developing a model of empowerment that draws on her fieldwork in Honduras. She currently works as Programme Evaluation Advisor for Voluntary Service Overseas in London. This article was first published in* Development in Practice, *Volume 5, number 2, in 1995.*

The Zimbabwe Women's Resource Centre and Network

Hope Chigudu

In a world where men shape the distribution of material resources, knowledge, and ideology which govern social relations in both public and private life, the Zimbabwe Women's Resource Centre and Network (ZWRCN) is an oasis that generates alternative and critical feminist thinking. As women question patriarchal power and challenge the dominant ethos, they need to draw on different sources of energy. The gender and development debates and networks are valuable resources which provide women with strategies to continue their search for alternative discourses as a basis for action.

It requires great energy for women to cope with the contradictions in our societies, especially if they are critical of it. It is therefore not enough to have a feminist documentation centre or library. It is also necessary to distribute the information in a way that challenges people to examine their own identity. In this respect, ZWRCN differs from ordinary libraries, in that it provides new ways of generating and distributing information which is itself alternative to the mainstream.

The rural libraries and linkage programmes are central in enabling rural women to continue to work towards transforming the structures and institutions which reinforce and perpetuate gender discrimination and social inequality. Group discussions at the rural libraries create a forum for broad-based popular participation. For women, such a forum is important, since self-reconstruction requires a critical mass. The discussion groups enable women to share their common experiences and struggles and confirm that, contrary to what many believe, women do and can organise for their rights.

This article discusses some of the innovative ways in which ZWRCN has generated space for alternative critical feminist knowledge and analysis, which it sees as an essential basis for equitable development.

Objectives and strategies of ZWRCN

ZWRCN was set up in 1990 with the following objectives:

- to promote and strengthen inter-organisational networking activities for the exchange of knowledge, experience, and information on gender and development issues;
- to promote greater gender-awareness through collecting and distributing information on gender and development issues;
- to promote the adoption of gender-sensitive information systems, so that development agencies' programmes are amenable to gender analysis;
- to re-package information in forms appropriate to relevant users;
- to fill information gaps in both formal and non-formal ways, such as research and discussion.

ZWRCN gives women access to a new body of ideas and information which not only changes their consciousness and self-image, but also stimulates action.

The strategies used by the ZWRCN include the following:

Documentation Centre

This is responsible for collecting and distributing information, the bulk of which is 'grey', i.e. unpublished material which is generally inaccessible. The material selected, much of which incorporates a feminist perspective, is often not taken seriously by mainstream libraries and yet is information which can enable women to control their intellectual and ideological resources.

Further, there are few bookstores in Zimbabwe which sell books on either feminism or gender and development issues. ZWRCN networks with a cross-section of international publishers, and so obtains books which are not otherwise easily available.

Information is distributed through communication channels such as the electronic and print media, as well as by exploiting alternative methods (see below).

While the library is viewed as the heart of the organisation, ZWRCN's information work is continued through publications, networking, lobbying, gender debates, and gender-training programmes. These have taken the agenda beyond ZWRCN into the wider community, and it is mostly here that changes take place.

Thematic debates

Two themes are selected every year, on which thorough research reveals gaps in existing information. Ways of producing new knowledge on the subject are discussed, and a bibliography and discussion paper are produced on the theme. Then a workshop is held to brainstorm on the issues raised, most of which arise from the literature review, and follow-up activities are identified.

After each workshop, the recommendations are compiled and distributed to appropriate organisations. For example, after a workshop on the topic 'Is There a Women's Movement in Zimbabwe?', it was suggested that a Women's Federation should be established, to provide Zimbabwean women with a strong political base and a point of unity. The Federation would enable women to articulate a collective voice and demonstrate collective strength. This initiative is now moving ahead.

Thematic debates enable ZWRCN and members of the network to study a chosen subject in greater detail, and to *generate* information. The process deepens our collective analysis of the context, and the position of women locally and internationally. The debates also equip activists with tools with which to bring about changes in their personal and organisational lives.

Talks on Gender and Development (GAD)

GAD talks are held every other month. These create a social and friendly climate in which to discuss women's issues. Initially, the discussions were meant to ground the ZWRCN staff in feminist theory. Eventually, many others expressed an interest in attending. ZWRCN decided to take the opportunity to use the GAD talks as a forum to challenge power relations and patriarchal ideology. These talks have also created a space to examine those areas which are kept un-examined because of sexism and patriarchy.

People considered to be experts on selected topics are asked to facilitate the discussion. For example, one of the most controversial topics selected in 1996 asked 'Why do men hate women?'. The meeting was well attended by both sexes. The heated discussions concluded that men love their daughters and mothers, but fear being disempowered by their wives and the women 'out there'. The conclusion was that when conducting gender-training, the meaning of power should be explored in greater detail.

Gender training

As ZWRCN continues to create space for creating and distributing feminist information, the demand to understand the concept and dynamics of gender has grown not only among government agencies and non-government organisations (NGOs), but also among private organisations.

In order to meet this demand, and to fulfil its objective of enabling women in Zimbabwe to reach their potential, ZWRCN decided to embark on a gender-awareness programme for various government agencies and NGOs. Thus in 1993, ZWRCN started its gender-training activities. Encouraged by the results of the first year, ZWRCN decided to undertake a three-year cooperative venture to enable it to systematise its training activities into a training of trainers (TOT) programme. Having a pool of trainers would enrich the programme by providing different areas of expertise to draw on. Besides, the trainers would continue developing and incorporating gender analysis in their own organisations.

The programme aims to develop the gender-training capability of ZWRCN specifically, and more broadly in Zimbabwe, by focusing on the needs of three groups: development planners and policy makers; programme and project implementers; and community managers, animators, and extension workers. In its TOT programme, ZWRCN is being assisted by two consultants: a woman from the Philippines and a man from Zambia. Coming from developing countries, they are committed to the South-South exchange of experiences and expertise in the areas of gender analysis, needs assessment, and planning, as well as developing local training modules and materials. The TOT is informed by the agenda, perspectives, vision, and actions of Women, Gender and Development and not just those of the more popular Gender and Development (GAD). The latter risks reducing gender training to a mere technology. For ZWRCN, gender training is not something that can be removed from the feminist agenda of women's empowerment. The ZWRCN gender-training programme aims to do the following:

- raise gender issues within the national policy arena;
- introduce a feminist political culture conducive to gender-friendly political action;

- incorporate gender-sensitive policies, programmes, and projects in State institutions;
- re-design societies so that they are based on democratic relationships;
- develop a broader analysis of human rights and social justice;
- create a new understanding of gender and gender relations, as well as destroying old beliefs which construct powerful gender ideologies;
- intensify the campaign for women's empowerment, and ensure that civil servants and others in the private sector adhere to gender-sensitive policies in the work-place;.
- develop analytical tools to evaluate the effects of certain development strategies for the promotion of women's strategic interests;
- transform the structures and institutions that reinforce and perpetuate gender discrimination and social inequality.

In addition to the TOT programme, ZWRCN is housing a United Nations Population Fund project on Women, Population, and Development. This focuses on gender training in the population sector, and is currently concerned with producing manuals. In the second phase, 75 people will receive gender-awareness training as this relates to population issues.

Linkage programme

The major aim here is to create a 'democratic space' for women, through the provision of relevant information. It originates in ZWRCN's networking and information-distribution activities, and is linked to our recent survey of women's perceptions of their situation, the results of which were compiled in a book entitled *Women's Voices*.

The book clearly demonstrates a need for a mechanism through which women can channel their concerns to national-level decision-makers — parliamentarians — so that their needs and priorities are incorporated into national policies and programmes. *Women's Voices* is a testimony to the frustration which arises from lack of information and knowledge about the structure and processes of government. Even well-intentioned pieces of legislation, policies, and programmes are not sufficiently advertised or publicised. Thus, ordinary women do not take full advantage of them.

Parliamentarians are also often not familiar with the issues concerning their constituencies, and so are unable to influence legislation to best advantage.

ZWRCN recently commissioned a study called 'Women's Role and Participation in Central and Local Government Politics'. Indications from the draft report confirmed that lack of information and knowledge on pertinent issues seriously hinders women's proactive political action. Several factors contribute to this situation. Firstly, 'World Affairs' were traditionally men's preserve, so that today most women do not possess meaningful levels of knowledge about political matters. Men construct and control the intellectual and ideological resources.

Secondly, low levels of literacy have hampered women's access to relevant information, little of which has been produced or distributed with this reality in mind.

Thirdly, few providers of information have ever considered women as a specific audience with specific needs for information and knowledge.

The adage that knowledge is power remains true. Empowerment starts with ideas and information which can help people to improve their situation. Recognising this, in October 1993, ZWRCN and another grassroots-based NGO, the Rural Libraries and Resources Development Programme (RLRDP), agreed on a joint strategy to circulate reading material which could contribute to the empowerment of women in selected rural areas. The advantage of the partnership is that, while ZWRCN has over the years identified and collected a significant number of titles of perceived relevance to rural women, the RLRDP has a strong infrastructure for channelling information to rural people.

Although much information exists on many topics, it needs to be repackaged to suit the reading and comprehension skills of women at the grassroots, who have low levels of education. Various strategies are used. In many cases, information is transmitted from readers to non-readers in the form of discussion groups. The responsibility for this process lies with appointed gender and development sub-committees within the communities. The programme also includes workshops and networking for the representatives of different libraries to exchange information and develop cooperative activities.

The perceived benefits of the rural libraries programme are many:

- It helps women to develop skills to challenge oppressive behaviour.

- It enables women to interrogate their own identity and unearth the root causes of their own subordination.
- It ensures that information is used, by encouraging discussion groups among women. This is important, because an empowerment process must involve not only individual awareness but also collective awareness and action.
- It contributes towards building women's confidence.
- It motivates women to join literacy classes, which in turn enable them to gain new knowledge and broaden their horizons.

ZWRCN has also embarked on a pioneering project seeking to promote sustained interaction between parliamentarians and grassroots women. The key objective is to enable grassroots women to contribute to parliamentary debates via their representatives. Ideally, this will become a two-way process which will foster the transparency of parliamentary processes and enhance the accountability of parliamentarians to their constituencies.

Specifically, the programme aims to empower grassroots women by ensuring that they have information on current affairs as a basis for proactive political behaviour, and enhancing women's participation in national politics. It also aims to empower women parliamentarians by giving them more intimate knowledge of ordinary women's concerns. This will enhance their effectiveness in parliamentary debates on issues concerning women, and their role in initiating gender-sensitive reforms, policies, and programmes which will improve the situation of women.

Grassroots women also need an independent and objective source of information and information, that makes sense to them. It is hoped that this project will enable women to stop seeing the world through the eyes of politicians at political rallies.

Lobbying and advocacy

A major objective of ZWRCN in its efforts to bring about women's empowerment in Zimbabwe, is to ensure that those who wield power and make decisions affecting women's lives are held accountable for those decisions. For this, they need to be aware of the constraints which inhibit women from participating actively in the social, economic, and political development of their country.

For ZWRCN, the process of lobbying decision-makers is never-ending. To this end, ZWRCN produces information for raising the consciousness and capacity of the women themselves, so that they demand more economic and political space for themselves; and it lobbies those who make decisions about policies, programmes, and allocation of funds. For example, ZWRCN has just completed a study of development aid and its impact on women in the sectors of education and health. This information will be used to lobby donors to provide more resources for the two sectors.

ZWRCN continues to conduct research on land issues, and to use the information generated to lobby the government to give land to women in their own right. Recently, we carried out a study of mainstreaming gender in the agriculture sector. Such information is used not only to inform but also to lobby relevant bodies.

GAD Base

In 1994 ZWRCN began to develop a database. This registers individuals and organisations active in the field of gender and development in Zimbabwe. Eventually, this database should include a wealth of useful data which can be shared with relevant networks and women activists.

Book fairs

International book fairs are held every year in Zimbabwe, and ZWRCN uses them to distribute information and to purchase exciting new books which may not be easily available.

Conclusion

While women are still treated as just another item on the development agenda, ZWRCN must continue to sharpen its framework of research, analysis, and advocacy on feminist issues — including information about women's gains and successes, so that women can gain more strength from their achievements to date. Ultimately, our goal is to analyse where power really lies in the world, and the implications of that for building a women's movement.

■ **Hope Chigudu** *is co-founder and chair of the Zimbabwe Women's Resource Centre and Network (ZWRCN).* *This article was first published in Development in Practice, Volume 7 number 2 in 1997.*

Dealing with hidden issues: trafficked women in Nepal

Meena Poudel and Anita Shrestha

Nepal is today a source of illegal exports of women to the flesh markets of other countries in Asia and the Middle East. This trafficking consists of the transport, sales, and purchase of women for prostitution and bonded labour. It is estimated that more than 200,000 Nepalese women are in Indian brothels, and that tens of thousands are taken each year to other countries and forced into prostitution or to work in oppressive and inhumane conditions.

Nepal is beset with many problems. More than 70 per cent of the population lives below the poverty line. The per capita annual income is US$180. There is widespread illiteracy, especially among women (72 per cent). Communicable diseases and unemployment are rampant, while the rural economy is generally deteriorating.

In Nepal, women are marginalised from birth by socio-cultural pressures. Rural families, especially women and girls, experience great difficulty in sustaining themselves, because of a limited resource-base and the social constraints that women face in household decision-making about existing resources. Deteriorating conditions and soaring inflation affect everyone. However, it is the women who, in the final analysis, suffer most from these socio-structural problems. And the vulnerability of families to the trafficking of their female members is a symptom of the desperation they experience in trying to survive through whatever means possible. But in Nepal, once a woman has been wittingly or unwittingly forced into prostitution, there is no going home. Once she has been trafficked, a family's moral code means that even a daughter or a wife is rejected.

In June 1995, WATCH (Women Acting Together for Change) organised a national public hearing, so that women's voices could be heard on these issues. Violated women offered testimonies about their experiences. Their stories highlighted the prevalence of violence against women. They revealed how women's human rights are systematically neglected in Nepal. The objectives of the hearing were:

- to enable women's groups in Nepal to reflect more deeply on the problems of the trafficking of women;
- to provide feminist and national perspectives on the issue of trafficking;
- to get feedback on potential strategies and/or actions for protecting, defending, and promoting the human rights of Nepalese women;
- to contribute to women's global efforts to campaign for women's rights as human rights, by highlighting the increasing phenomenon of violence against women in the form of trafficking in women;
- to promote the views of violated women to the UN Women's Conference in Beijing, September 1995;
- to strengthen the advocacy of Asian women's groups for stopping the trafficking of women through greater networking, more extensive analysis of the problem, and creating opportunities to share strategies;
- to generate national and international public support for victims and survivors;
- to serve as a venue for developing an action plan, with participation by survivors and women's support groups;
- to focus the attention of governments, political groups, NGOs, donors, and the international community on the increasing violence against women, by gathering specific data and case studies of trafficked Nepalese women;
- to call on governments, political groups, NGOs, donors, and the international community to take up recommendations by women, human-rights activists, and development NGOs to redress human-rights violations and end violence against women.

The public hearing: sex trade and survival

The sex trade is a very profitable enterprise. Its profitability, combined with local conditions of extreme poverty and few employment opportunities, creates perverse incentives for families and their female members. There are some villages in the middle hills of Nepal from where parents willingly send their young daughters, saying, 'We've already sent one of our daughters and a sister to India to earn money'. Some of these women do return 10 or 15 years later with a little money, new clothes, and some domestic materials. But material possessions do not change the reality of the social position of these women; they continue to be abroad and discarded when no longer of use.

Extreme poverty and patriarchal definitions of development force innocent, poor rural women to become victims of the sex trade. In some communities, women are forced into this through social pressure, and because society imposes a patriarchal view that women are born only for the sexual pleasure of men.

Voices of the victims and voices of the State

In the hearing, eleven women and one man shared their feelings. They described their pain at being forced into prostitution or otherwise affected by such crimes. They told their own stories of the brothel, the ineffectiveness of the legal code or government representatives, and the social rejection they experienced upon their return.

> I was sold by my neighbours to Bombay before I was 15 years old. When I came back after eleven years of trafficking, I tried to get support from police and the local authority to punish the trafficker. But I never got support. Yet my husband, who rescued me and married me, was arrested just because he filed the case. We have been threatened by local political leaders many times.

> Now I have three children from three men, but I do not know who are they and where are they. I am doing this work unwillingly, because society is imposing this tradition. As women we have to keep continually silent.

> When I was twelve I was sold by a man to India. After working for two years in a brothel, I got HIV from clients. Then I was rejected by the brothel owner and came back to my home. But I am also rejected by my stepfather. After that I used to sleep in the public toilet, and I suffered from many sicknesses. Now I'm taking treatment for tuberculosis and getting support from WATCH.

The hearing was designed to balance the voices of the victims and their defenders against the positions taken by representatives of the State. Each side assumed a 'bench', described as the 'solidarity bench' and the 'listening bench'.

The 'solidarity bench' consisted of people working in the field of women's trafficking, legal-rights awareness, HIV/AIDS issues, and the international women's movement. After listening to the women's own stories, this bench responded critically, asking: 'Is there any government in this country for sexually abused women?' They also questioned the definition of the legal framework for human rights, and decided that the existing law is more of a handicap than a help, without the commitment of the nation. Objecting strongly to problems of social rejection of affected or infected women, this bench concluded that there is a strong need to link the voices and experiences of these violated women with regional and international women's initiatives, in order to strengthen the movement by getting solidarity from outside Nepal.

The 'listening bench' consisted of government representatives — policemen, government lawyers, Social Welfare Council members. The establishment of a 'listening bench' was a new idea in the area of such public hearings organised by women's groups. WATCH used the forum to initiate interactions with people at various levels, including government officials, in order to involve them in the campaign and make them more aware of the issue. However, after hearing the testimonies of twelve women, this bench responded defensively. They argued that there is a strong law in Nepal with regard to trafficking and related issues, but that 'this type of women and their families' are unwilling to use it. Representatives of the police noted that they are forming a women's cell to address social crimes against women. The bench unanimously agreed that the government should take strong action to prevent the trafficking of women, that there should be political commitment to this goal, and that the government should mobilise its bureaucracy to punish traffickers and their agents.

Both benches emphasised that there is an urgent need to start coordinated actions on this issue.

Round-table discussions on the hearing

Following the public hearing was a day of round-table discussion with concerned people: advocacy NGOs, police representatives, official lawyers, representatives of women's organisations, political parties, and those who had testified. Participants reflected deeply and decided that some attempt at coordination or networking should be made among activists, NGOs, and other concerned groups. They agreed that the issue is complex, requiring a collective and coordinated response. NGOs shared their experiences and discussed the challenges. The main question was: how to proceed?

Participants decided that it is vital to initiate practical co-ordination through building a nationwide alliance against trafficking in women, the objectives of which are:

- to support affected and infected women who have been forced into the sex trade;
- to link local campaigns against trafficking with regional and global campaigns through solidarity and experience-sharing, and to create pressure for taking action against traffickers;
- to support the government in implementing the existing law, by initiating discussions about how to make it work in reality.

The alliance consists of 17 people including NGOs, testifiers, lawyers, representatives of the National Planning Commission, and women's organisations.

Reflections

The flesh trade, sex industry, and trafficking are all part of a business that today contributes to most national economies, particularly in Asia. Like other forms of trade, the sex trade has expanded into newer markets outside national boundaries, providing a profitable environment for pimps, agents, and illegal networks. This business is sustained and supported not only by the Mafia and the networks of brothel owners and managers, pimps and agents, and families who feed this trade, but also by the State, either directly or indirectly.

Nepal's economic policies are geared towards privatisation and the liberalisation of the market economy. These policies have contributed to the paralysing poverty facing rural Nepal. They have forced people to migrate in search of a means of survival. Often, these individuals are absorbed by a growing national and international market that seeks to exploit women's sexual labour.

Article 20 of the Nepali constitution, adopted in 1990, prohibits trafficking in human beings, slavery, and forced labour in any form. Any contravention is punishable. However, manipulation of this law by politicians and other powerful people creates a positive environment for pimps and sex-trade agents. Testimonies at the public hearing showed that enforcement of this part of the Constitution is lacking, providing evidence that criminals are, in fact, being protected by politicians. The testimonies also questioned the professional ethics of the police, with evidence that accused persons are routinely released from custody, and that lower-ranking police officers become common clients who take their sexual pleasure free of charge. Such voices clearly indicate that there is no real sense in making laws, if there is no commitment on the part of those responsible for ensuring their enforcement.

Prevailing patriarchal law and those customary norms which negate women's perspectives will never offer justice to the victimised female members of our society. Officials at various levels of national government show mixed responses. One minister argued that trafficking in women is not an important national issue, because it 'affects just one part of society' — namely, women. The Prime Minister suggested that there is need to address this issue 'holistically', with the government developing a practical strategy. He also mentioned in his inaugural speech that women should have equal rights to property. Listening to these different views, it is difficult to discern the government's real position. However, it is clear that the problems of trafficking in women must be identified as a national problem by political parties, decision-makers, planners, and legislators, before any real commitment to protecting women as victimised and violated members of our society can be realised.

■ **Meena Poudel** *is a Public Health Nurse and founder and Chairperson of WATCH, with ten years' involvement in issues concerning the trafficking of women, and HIV/AIDS.*

■ **Anita Shrestha** *is an economist who has worked with WATCH for two years, producing materials for rural women, activists, and NGOs, on HIV/AIDS, trafficking, and gender issues.* *This article was first published in* Development in Practice, *Volume 6, number 4, in 1996.*

Power, institutions and gender relations: can gender training alter the equations?

Ranjani K. Murthy

Since the mid-1980s gender training has become an important strategy for the women's movement, NGOs, government, and funding agencies in addressing the subordinate status of women in India. This paper is concerned with gender training in NGOs that work at the grassroots. Three distinct objectives underpin such efforts:

1. Gender-aware institutional change—to make NGOs more gender-sensitive through creating spaces to reflect upon objectives, programmes, and internal functioning from a gender perspective.

2. Empowering women in NGOs—in the context of their personal lives, and interactions within the NGOs and with the community.

3. Re-defining the power of men in NGOs—motivating male staff to re-define their relations within their families, the NGOs, and the community from a gender perspective.

Central to these is the issue of power: re-negotiating power relations within NGOs, enabling women staff to discover the power within themselves, and raising awareness among male staff of the injustice and disadvantages of their retaining overt or covert power over women through institutions. This paper examines the strengths and weaknesses of gender training as a strategy in altering the equations of power, both within oneself and in institutions; and identify ways to strengthen gender-training efforts. Beforehand, it may be useful to clarify the meaning of power and institutions, and review gender issues in the context of NGOs in India.

Power and institutions

Understanding power and institutions

Power is an element of social relationships and is difficult to separate from related concepts such as authority, control, influence, and domination. Kabeer (1994a) identifies three kinds of power: power to, power over, and power within. Some see power as the ability of an individual to influence decisions in the direction s/he desires even against resistance. Bacharan and Baratz argue against this restricted definition as the 'power to' decide at an interpersonal level on conflicting issues (cited in Kabeer, 1994a; Stacey and Price, undated). Power, they maintain, is exercised not only in the process of deciding. Some groups are prevented from raising issues that are inimical to the interests of the power-holders, and these topics are kept off the decision-making agenda by the dominant groups. This 'power over' setting agendas is rooted in the institutional rules and practices which, by demarcating issues over which decisions may or may not be taken, systematically benefits certain individuals and groups at the expense of others. Gender division of labour, rights to property, control over fertility and sexuality, are thus routinely kept off the agenda for decision-making whether at the level of the household or of the state — and within NGOs.

A third dimension of power is seen when conflicts of interests are not just suppressed from decision-making, but also from the consciousness of the various parties involved. Conflicts may not be seen, simply because both subordinate and dominant groups are unaware of their oppressive implications, or incapable of imagining alternative ways of being and doing. Kabeer (1994a) perceives a considerable overlap between this and what feminists call 'power within'. Institutions in which gender relations are played out conceal the reality and pervasiveness of male dominance through their official ideology, and rules and practices. Four major institutions that impinge upon men and women, and often in an interlocking manner, are households, communities (inclusive of religion), markets, and states. Multilateral aid agencies have also become important institutions. All institutions have an official ideology (Kabeer 1994b) namely that:

- households are sites of altruism and co-operation;
- markets are neutral (to gender and other social relations) and are about efficient allocation of resources;

- state is about the national interest and welfare of citizens, including women;
- community is about service provision and promotion of a moral society;
- global institutions act in the interest and welfare of men and women in developing countries.

However, these institutions all embody *relations of power* that operate through ideologies far removed from the official doctrine, *people* who have internalised these ideologies, *resource distribution* in favour of the powerful, *structures* of hierarchy headed by the powerful, and *rules and practices* to reinforce these aspects at a policy and day-to-day level. Power within these institutions may be exercised on the basis of gender, caste, class, religion, or ethnicity.

NGOs as gendered and gendering institutions

NGOs are institutions that constitute communities, but are distinct from traditional institutions such as caste, Panchayats, or Gram Sabhas. Most male-headed NGOs (though not all) are also governed by relations of gender power, with ideologies, people, structures, resource distribution patterns, and rules and practices acting overtly and (more often) covertly in the interest of men within the NGO and in the community with which it works. As NGOs reflect power relations in society, they can be seen as 'gendered' (term used by Goetz, 1992) institutions.

However, NGOs have a degree of autonomy from the patriarchal structures, and some have played an important role in re-negotiating gender relations within the households, markets and community, through struggles around property rights, equal wages, and violence against women. Thus, some NGOs play an active role in the process of what Goetz (1992) calls 'gendering'. However, this role is not always positive. Quite often, NGOs reinforce the gender division of labour and resources, and hierarchies of power both through their programmes and in their internal functioning.

Gendered and gendering ideologies, objectives, and programme policies

The gendered and gendering dimensions of NGOs are reflected in their objectives, which in turn reflect their underlying ideology. With growing pressure from the women's movement and from funding agencies, the terms 'women' or 'gender' (often thought to be synonymous) entered the objectives of several NGOs from the mid-1980s. But the manner of this entry, especially in male-headed organisations, reflects or perpetuates gender hierarchies in society. Some NGOs seek to improve the conditions of women, not because women occupy a subordinate status, but because they are seen as instruments for developing other family members and the larger community. To quote one NGO in Maharashtra: 'the lack of education in women limits their awareness of the benefits of learning for their children... (further) women's awareness on health will lead to improved health status of their children and family'. Such NGOs tend to adopt *gender neutral policies* (Kabeer 1994a, b) — policies neutral to existing divisions of labour and responsibilitie s— and indeed use these as the basis for allocating activities to improve family welfare. In the process, it perpetuates these socially-constructed divisions. Typical examples of such activities are preventive health education, childcare, and family planning, which are more or less exclusively targeted at women. These perpetuate the myth that it is 'natural' for women to cook, bring up the children, and take care of the health of the family.

Other NGOs seek to work with women not in an instrumentalist fashion, but because they believe that women occupy a secondary status in society. However, they perceive that women themselves and their poverty are the main barriers to their development. Women's illiteracy and lack of motivation, unity, and skills, combined with their lack of access to (rather than control over) resources are seen as hindrances. Such NGOs tend to adopt gender-specific policies — which are targeted at women and seek to address their practical gender needs — but leave their strategic gender interests unarticulated, and the position of men intact. Water, fuel, credit, skills-training, and income-generation programmes (IGPs) tend to promote such policies. Often these are built upon and perpetuate the belief that women are primarily responsible for domestic work and childcare. Programmes that recognise women's productive role often perceive women as supplementary earners, and do not challenge the gendered division of public and private spaces. It is not uncommon in IGPs to find women involved in home-based or village-based activities (extended private domain), and men mediating on their behalf in public domains like markets, government officials, and NGO offices.

Very few NGOs see women's subordination as arising from the distribution of gender-based power that is reflected in social institutions, or seek through their programmes to alter such power relations. To do so would entail adoption of gender-transformatory or gender-redistributive (Kabeer, 1994a, b) policies, to provide spaces for women to articulate their strategic gender interests and mobilise around them, organising for example around male violence, property rights, equal wages, or the sharing of domestic work.

Gendered and gendering structures and staff policies

NGOs also reflect and perpetuate existing gender hierarchies through their structures and rules (Initiatives: Women in Development ((IWID)), 1991). In male-headed NGOs, the hierarchy is reflected in the fact that few women are able to set agendas (power over) or take decisions (power to). The allocation of tasks within NGOs is also gendered with women staff in charge of health and education programmes and home-based cottage industries, while men co-ordinate agriculture and environment programmes. Within the bureaucracy, women are more involved in secretarial work, public relations, cleaning, and making refreshments, while the finances are managed by men. Women staff in NGOs also have less access to training and career promotion opportunities or to facilities like childcare and toilets. Few provisions are made, such as flexible working hours or space, to take into account women's double burden. While most NGOs offer maternity leave (though not always for three months), few provide paternity leave — and those which do allow only a few days. Sexual harassment also takes place within NGOs.

Such divisions in decision-making, allocation of tasks, staff policies, and norms of behaviour give indirect messages to men and women with whom the NGO works about their appropriate roles and responsibilities.

Gendered and gendering people

In all-women and women-headed organisations, the gendered hierarchy of power is often less explicit. Women do have the power to set agendas and take decisions. The gender division of labour on the basis of tasks, or sexual harassment, does not arise. Most of the NGOs which have adopted gender-transformatory policies are headed and chiefly constituted by women: autonomous women's groups (which prefer not to call themselves NGOs), grassroots women's organisations like SEWA, Women's Voice, and Mehila Samakhya (a society registered by the government). In fact the gender-transformatory nature of the last two categories of NGO is reflected not so much in programme content as in the process and strategy adopted to address self-identified needs.

However, the fact that an organisation is headed or constituted by women does not make it automatically gender-sensitive. Not all women are conscious of the exact mechanisms of their own subordination and that of other women, nor can they identify and move towards their strategic gender interests. This is not surprising, as men and women are products of various patriarchal social institutions — households, community (including religion), media and the state — and are 'gendered' human beings. At the same time, women and men can exercise some individual agency *vis-à-vis* these institutions, and some do challenge ideologies, structures, resource allocation, and rules and practices. Men have less interest in doing so, as the costs involved (in terms of power, resources, and additional responsibilities) far outweigh, and are more tangible than, the benefits (access to the experience of child-rearing, self-reliance, and 'humanness'). While the benefits of challenging institutions are more tangible for women, such gains are not assured. In fact, their efforts can lead to the loss of 'bargains' (see Kandiyoti 1988) which women have struck within patriarchal institutions such as marriage, households, and community, to address practical needs for housing and water, but also to exercise some control over their bodies and sexuality, which may not be possible if they remain single.

Gendered distribution of resources

Finally, the distribution of resources within NGOs is also gendered. Gender-neutral and gender-specific policies often entail unequal distribution of resources. In the former case, economic programmes and the resources tied to them often by-pass women. In the latter, economic resources are targeted at women but are often much smaller than those targeted at men. For example, loans for irrigation are directed at men, and loans for petty business and home-based activities at women. Men often hold better paid jobs in the NGO than women: for instance, Agricultural Extension Officers may be paid more than Health Officers, accountants more than secretaries. Apart from salaries, women staff may have less access than men to office resources like vehicles and administrative services.

Can training change the equations?

Gender training is acknowledged to be an important strategy for changing the 'gendered' nature of NGOs and their staff, and ensuring that their 'gendering' influence challenges the social construction of gender and alters the equation of power within the NGO and with respect to other institutions.

What is gender training?

Despite its popularity, gender training means different things to different people (Murthy 1993). For some, it is a strategy for understanding the different roles which men and women play in society in order to increase the efficiency of development projects. This is reflected in the objectives of a gender-training programme for NGOs and government officials, organised by the Indian government and a bilateral aid agency:

> (To) increase understanding of how to conceptualise the activities of women ...and how these need to be incorporated in project design and implementation.
>
> (To) develop analytical skills to systematically categorise information on women in development and translate these into the project framework. (Department of Women and Child Development 1988: 4)

Most gender-training programmes have moved beyond a concern with efficiency. However, some see gender training as a vehicle for transferring management skills, so that a gender relations perspective is routinely incorporated in programme work. Such training tends to emphasise a package of 'planning tools' for integrating a gender perspective: Moser method, Harvard Case Study method, Gender Analysis Matrix, and so on. As observed by feminists in an Initiatives gender-training workshop 'Women in Development', while these frameworks do link up feminist theories and analysis with development planning, the process of doing so is often depoliticising, since they are not preceded by a grounding in gender relations and an analysis of institutions within which such relations operate (Subrahmanian, 1992).

What kind of gender training can, then, have an impact on power, social institutions, and gender relations? Gender trainers in India with a socialist—feminist perspective believe that it can have such an impact only if it is political in nature: if it questions the gendered nature of development, clarifies the concept of patriarchy, perceives gender relations as social relations of power, and links these concepts with a reflection on the individual, and on NGOs as institutions. For us, 'gender training' refers to training programmes with such a perspective.

Limits and potential of gender training

As we have already said, gender training in the NGO context often has one or a combination of three explicit or implicit objectives, with the issue of power lying at the core of each.

Gender training, patriarchal bargains, and power within

There are generally two kinds of women participants in gender-training programmes: the converted who need conceptual clarity in which to root their understanding, and those who have not yet started the process of questioning. Reflecting on the gender-training programmes that I have facilitated, I feel that most of them helped strengthen the converted, but did not have enough impact on those who had internalised patriarchal norms.

Part of the problem was with the methodology. For example, in a training of gender trainers (TOGT) workshop, spaces were created for discussions on the concepts of gender, patriarchy, feminism, and how to integrate these into development programmes. The concepts were primarily dealt with through lectures along with group discussions to link these concepts with the experiences of the participants. The participants (especially those who had already started the process of questioning) found the workshop extremely useful, and I also felt empowered through it. But then I visited the NGO in which two of the participants worked (one male and female staff at middle level) for an intra-NGO organisational development process, I could observe no visible impact of the programme. Further, though I had hoped to draw upon these staff as co-facilitators, I soon realised that deep down they too believed that women's subordination partly arises out of their biology: less physical strength, a physical body that makes rape possible, and ability to give birth and breastfeed.

I then reversed the methodology, starting with personal experiences and developing the concept of gender out of this sharing. Participants were asked whether if they were born again and could choose their sex they would prefer to be born male or female. This was followed by a discussion on differences between men and women in terms of their roles and responsibilities, qualities and behaviour; and the reasons for these. This led to the understanding that the female body was not a problem. Rather, the problem lies with the social reality of male violence. The ability to give birth was not a problem, but problems arose from the social belief that nature dictates that only women can bring up children. Thus, the difference between socially-constructed gender and biological sex was clarified. At the end of the workshop, a woman participant walked up to me and said, 'Didi, I can now understand what we mean by gender'.

If a feminist consciousness could be raised simply through appropriate methodologies, the problem would be simple. Often, women NGO staff, like other women, have struck bargains with patriarchal structures: they have evolved different games to maximise security and optimise life options. For example, one older woman participant was known to harass her daughter-in-law. On probing, we realised that as a young bride she had faced deprivation and humiliation at the hands of her own mother-in-law and husband, and she had internalised these patriarchal norms. Her only source of security was through her married son; and the only way she could exercise authority was through dominating her daughter-in-law and controlling her labour. Her inner consciousness would not change just through a workshop. Young women also strike bargains. For example, in a workshop with women on gender and development, of whom three participants were soon to marry, we discussed the importance of, and strategies for, negotiating conjugal contracts before marriage, and division of parenting responsibilities (not because marriage and motherhood are the only options for women, but because of the reality of their lives). One participant said 'What can I do? I do not have a choice. If I object to an alliance because he does not agree to my working, my brother and parents will throw me out. Where will I go?'. Another suggested that she move in with her family, thus compensating for the loss of security which patriarchal structures offer.

Thus gender training, while necessary, may not be enough to enable women staff of NGOs to realise and act upon the power within themselves. Structures such as women's fora within NGOs may be required, and also among NGOs at a district or state level, in order to create spaces for women to share their experiences, gain strength from each other, and reinforce and deepen learning from workshops. Nari Shakti in Orissa, which emerged through the process of reflection initiated by Association for World Solidarity, is an example of an inter-NGO forum.

Gender training and male power

There are generally two kinds of men who attend gender-training programmes: those who are aware of gender hierarchies in society and wish to change these, and those who do not wish to question institutional power as the costs involved are high (in terms of loss of control over resources, and over women's labour, mobility, and bodies). Looking back at the gender-training programmes I have organised or facilitated, they have had a positive impact on the men who are sympathetic to change, but who are still unclear about the underlying reasons or strategies for empowerment. For such men, workshops on gender and development (with appropriate methodologies) help them to understand that it is not female biology which is the problem, but socially-constructed power relations between men and women. Further, such workshops often help them to place the issue of domination of women by women in the larger context of patriarchal structures. These workshops also enable them to understand the non-material gains they could secure through re-negotiating gender relations: the joy of nurturing, bringing up children, letting go of emotions, and the lack of pressure to be the family breadwinner.

Nevertheless, back in the workplace, the NGO's culture can negate these experiences. This is especially true among participants who do not occupy decision-making posts. The issue of translating what they have learnt within their families is even more complex. One participant, whom I met six months later, expressed that he was, to an extent, able to incorporate a gender perspective within development programmes, but not within his family. His wife, he said, objected to his entering the kitchen; and continued to insist that his daughter help in housework. While this could be seen as an excuse for not giving up power, it also reveals the importance of sensitising not only the staff (men and women) but also their partners. Adithi, an NGO in Bihar, organised a workshop for couples in which one or both partners were involved in development; and at least two couples felt strengthened through this.

While gender training may strengthen those men who have come with an open mind, in my experience, it has remained inadequate in changing those who do not want to lose the material benefits of the present distribution of power ('power to' and 'power over'). Often such men adopt different forms of resistance (Kannabiran and Bhasin 1992). The first is to deny women's subordinate status. One such participant said, 'How can women be subordinate, when we men worship them as goddesses?'. Another asked, 'What is wrong with the division of labour? Women and men complement each other and it is based on comparative advantage...'. Another common response is to generalise from personal experience: 'In my extended family, we give equal amounts of food, health care and education to girls and boys. Things have changed in society'.

Others accept women's subordinate status but see it as arising out of female biology or lack of interest amongst women in taking advantage of 'equal' opportunities in society. A few admit that individual men may oppress individual women, but do not accept the existence of patriarchal structures. In fact, they argue, it is more common for women to oppress other women than for men to oppress women. The ultimate form of resistance is to deny the insights of the resource-persons, by labelling them as urban, 'western', and middle-class feminists with no belief in religion. Women trainers who are unmarried have even more serious charges levelled against them.

The concern here is that if gender training cannot lead to (insensitive) men giving up their power to control different aspects of women's lives within various institutions, what other strategies can be adopted? Where an individual is not the head of the NGO, and the head is sensitive, the problems are less severe. It may be possible to challenge gender hierarchies within the organisation and biases within programmes, by enforcing a hierarchy based on authority. (This tactic may not work so effectively in challenging gender hierarchies within the family.) Some NGOs have tried to enforce a gender-sensitive code of conduct for staff—for example, prohibiting staff to give or take dowry, beat their wives, or sanction child marriages. Where the head of the NGO is himself insensitive to gender issues, funding agencies have at times intervened, both in the programmes and in the NGO's internal functioning. Women's groups have played an important role in taking action against sexual harassment within NGOs. They have brought such instances to the attention of Board Members, and where the Board has not taken action, they have exerted pressure through the donors and the media. Thus, when gender training fails to challenge gender-based power, power based on authority and women's collective strength may need to be used.

Gender training and institutional bending

Inter-NGO gender-training programmes which seek to provoke institutional change often assume that if you change the thinking, beliefs, and skills of a few staff through intensive periods of reflection on experiences, institutions will automatically change. This is seldom so, even where the individual participants are open-minded. As noted by participants in the 'Gender Training for Women and Men in NGOs: Issues and Strategies' workshop organised by IWID, when participants go back to their old set-up, the institutional culture and ethos may not be conducive for critical reflection on objectives, policies, programmes, structures, and resource distribution from a gender perspective. This 'translation' gap is more acute when leaders do not themselves attend gender-training programmes, but send staff from middle and field level. This often happens when the pressure to attend comes from donors rather than out of perceived needs.

Intra-NGO gender-training programmes have had a better impact on changing institutions. But conventional gender training per se is inadequate to bring about institutional change. Other inputs are needed. In one case, gender training was followed by a process of reflection on what work participants were doing with women, and why? This helped gain clarity on the objectives of the NGO's overall work. It resulted in a shift in its underlying objective from working with women to 'promote family welfare and communal harmony' to working with women so that they have 'greater awareness and control over resources and their lives' through which the secondary objectives of development of families and community would also be achieved. The programme policies were also critically reviewed and action plans were formulated to shift from gender-specific to gender-transformatory policies. A follow-up workshop reviewed the action plans, and another is planned to review the internal functioning (structure, organisational culture, division of labour, etc.) from a gender perspective. Women staff also demanded training in writing proposals, budgeting, project planning, monitoring, and evaluation so that they would be better equipped to assume leadership positions.

Conclusions

This paper has sought to examine the strengths and weaknesses of gender training in empowering women within NGOs, motivating men to move to a higher order of power as 'power within', and bringing about gender-sensitive institutional change. It is suggested that the extent to which gender-training programmes succeed in achieving these objectives depends, firstly, on their underlying perspective. An emphasis on gender relations (as relations of power), rather than gender roles is more likely to be effective.

However, even such training programmes may not, by themselves, be enough to empower women staff, especially those who have struck bargains with patriarchal structures to ensure their day-to-day survival. Women's fora within and among NGOs, and other measures to provide alternative forms of security, may be essential. Further, a gender-training programme can strengthen the efforts of men who are open or partially converted to move towards a more egalitarian distribution of power. However, it is likely to be ineffectual in altering the consciousness of those who do not want to give up the material gains of exercising power based on gender hierarchies ('power to' and 'power over') in different institutional contexts. To counter this, power based on authority, financial resources, and collective strength may need to be used.

To change the gendered and gendering nature of NGOs as institutions, it is not enough to sensitise a few staff, especially if they are not in decision-making roles. Intra-NGO gender training followed up by gender-aware institutional development, may be more appropriate. To assume leadership, women also require training to strengthen their management skills.

Acknowledgement

I would like to acknowledge the contribution of participants in different gender-training programmes, experience gained with IWID, and interactions with Naila Kabeer, in shaping my thoughts. However, they bear no responsibility for the arguments presented here. An earlier version of this paper appeared in the Indian NGO journal *Madhyam*, Volume X, Number 1, 1995.

References

Department of Women and Child Development (1988) 'Workshop on Gender Analysis in Project Planning for Policy Makers and Project Managers', National Institute of Public Co-operation and Child Development, New Delhi.

Goetz, A. M. (1992) 'Gender and administration', *IDS Bulletin* 23/4.

Initiatives: Women in Development (1991) 'Tamil Nadu Inter NGO Workshop on Women and Development', IWID, Madras.

Kabeer, N. (1994a) *Reversed Realities: Gender Hierarchies in Development Thought*, London: Verso.

Kabeer, N. (1994b) *Gender Planning: Some Key Issues*, Brighton: Institute of Development Studies.

Kandiyoti, D. (1988) *'Bargaining with patriarchy', Gender and Society* 2/3.

Kannabiran, V. and K. Bhasin (1992) 'A dialogue on feminism: a workshop with men in NGOs on women's issues', in *Link*, Madras: Achan, Vol. 11.

Murthy, R. K. (1993) *Issues and Strategies in Gender Training of Men and Women in NGOs,* Madras: IWIS.

Stacey, M. and M. Price (undated) *Women, Power and Politics,* London: Tavistock Publications.

Subrahmanian, R. (1992) 'Report on the Workshop on Gender Training for Men and Women in NGOs: Issues and Strategies', IWID.

■ **Ranjani K. Murthy** *is a consultant on gender and development, focusing on poverty, environment, and human rights concerns. Her professional interest is to mainstream gender within development organisations; and her personal struggle is to put this into practice in her own life. She is presently editing a book, in collaboration with ICCO entitled* Opening Windows to the World Capacity Building for Women's Empowerment. *This article was first published in* Development in Practice, *Volume 8, Number 2, in 1998.*

Soup kitchens, women and social policy: studies from Peru

Luiba Kogan

The worsening situation in Peru has profoundly affected the daily lives of poor women. State spending cuts coincided with the worst recession this century, and with the outbreak of terrorism. Soup kitchens, organized by women's groups, emerged from the early 1980s to address food shortages.[1]

In 1996, a multi-disciplinary team from the Peruvian non-governmental organizations (NGOs) ALTERNATIVA, FOVIDA and INCAFAM, examined the challenges facing these kitchens, from the perspective of the women. Information was drawn from interviews with leaders and members of 12 soup kitchens in Lima; from the 21 women who took part in a workshop on soup kitchens; and interviews with leaders of the Federation of Organizations of Self-Managed Soup kitchens of Lima and Callao.

Soup kitchens

There are two types of soup kitchen: the self-managed variety that make decisions autonomously and negotiate agreements with various donors; and those that started as mothers' clubs, are recognized by the state, and depend on government programmes. Initially, the former merely prepared food, while the latter also engaged in such activities as day-care services and minor business enterprises (mainly involving sewing and knitting). Now many more soup kitchens are acting as bases for 'connected activities' — income-generation or social services aimed at cutting family expenses.[2]

Soup kitchens operate on communal premises that may be rented, borrowed, or owned. Working conditions depend on the space, infrastructure, equipment, and utensils. Membership also varies.

Self-managed soup kitchens average 35 members, though some have as many as 100. Mothers' clubs average 60 members. In both cases, active members work cooking shifts and receive a set amount of meals in return; while ordinary members buy food and take part in assemblies. Soup kitchens prepare between 100 and 560 daily meals and charge a unit price of less than one new sol,[3] which does not cover the actual cost. Law 25307 (yet to be fully enacted) will require the state to subsidise at least 65 per cent of the food costs of social organizations that provide meals.

Soup kitchens start at about 5.30 a.m. when some women go to market while the others start on cooking. By mid-day everything is ready. The women serve meals in receptacles the members bring, and clean the kitchen before going home to eat. Meals are cooked in daily shifts by two to four women, who usually cook once a week. However, if someone cannot work her shift, she can pay a substitute — the amount and method of payment is worked out between them.

All soup kitchens belong to a central body either at zone or district level.[4] Most have statutes and regulations, but not all are legally incorporated. Organizational structures usually comprise a governing board (chair, secretary, treasurer, social worker, and auditor) and a decision-making assembly. Most hold monthly meetings, but some meet more often. Issues concern the functioning of the soup kitchen (accounts, receipts, cooking shifts, food supply, and meal standards) and organization (training, new members, selection of welfare cases, reports to the central body, and relations with outside agents)[5] Soup kitchens that engage in connected activities also report on these.

Soup kitchen assemblies seldom deal with women's specific problems, such as family conflicts and domestic abuse. However, the governing board may exonerate members from payment for meals, or take other action, for instance in cases of extreme physical abuse.

Connected activities

These have arisen in response to demands from members and to offers from agencies such as development NGOs or the state. The involvement of soup kitchen members in running 'connected activities' is geared largely to their ages and the number and age of their children, as this determines the time they can dedicate. Women become involved for various reasons, but the main one is the desire to help their children or partners: personal aspirations do not enter into it. The more personal reasons given for taking part, like awareness-raising, self-esteem, and the possibility of learning new skills, stem from a deeper desire to help their families. However, women have developed expectations that were not previously voiced through belonging to the soup kitchens — such as their interest in earning cash, coupled with the wish to serve their families and community.

The desire for an income as well as for services was clear in the interviews. However, no soup kitchen we saw has yet run these services with enough collective organization to satisfy members' needs. However, the emergence of connected activities enabled us to analyse new processes within these organizations, together with the rise of new tensions, such as solidarity versus market economics, or individual versus collective gain.

Among the studies were soup kitchens that had not embarked on connected activities, others that had started running medicine dispensaries or early education programmes (PRONEI), and others that run activities like guinea-pig breeding, bakeries, communal shops, and yoghurt and jam-making. We found only one that engaged both in economic and social services. These activities are not formally incorporated in the organizational structure of the soup kitchen. Those in charge report on progress to the assemblies: as often as not, they are themselves also the soup kitchen leaders.

We found situations where connected services were recognized both by the community and soup kitchen members. However, we also saw problems. In the case of dispensaries, these included finding people to replace those in charge (because they are the only ones qualified to provide the services), observing regular opening times, lack of clients, and so on. As regards PRONEI, the main problem is the low wage that supervisors or teachers receive for this work.

We found some successful income-generation activities in the sense that they were managing to turn a profit, with the proceeds ploughed back into the soup kitchens. Most activities are not complex, have low output levels, and produce limited gains. If they do generate any profit, this is because the workers are unpaid. However, the women's perception of connected activities is a sense of stability or permanence in their daily operations, with little thought for whether they are efficient or effective in economic or social terms. Members have identified significant accomplishments as well as limitations. They suggest that the continuity of connected activities depends on their commitment, though this may be changing since some hope to improve the way activities function in order to obtain real economic gain. Thus, tensions have developed between some members over the need to obtain individual income to supplement family earnings and to create jobs both for them and family members.

> Well, I volunteered to take charge of the dispensary, but they don't pay me a wage, you see? So I need to work. I'm wasting my time here helping the doctor and not getting paid for my trouble.

> The years go by and I'm permanently stuck in the soup kitchen. I give of my all to help others, but what's in it for me? That's why I'm thinking of leaving the soup kitchen for a while... All the women here have got jobs on the side. I've got to think about myself, my old age. I need a job too.

These tensions stem mainly from the fact that the women involved are unremunerated. Several women said that by leaving the soup kitchen they could earn more money. However, staying guarantees a secure supply of decent food. Further, the hours they spend cooking and taking part in connected activities are not overly demanding, and they work in their own neighbourhood near their children. However, we found that several women were suffering a conflict of ideals, where the desire to serve the community was tempered by the question of whether it was worthwhile to continue investing their own time and effort for no pay. For many leaders who are also in charge of connected activities, the conflict is intensified by the excessive workload.

> I had too much on my plate having to find time for the soup kitchen and the dispensary as well. I had a double schedule because I was the zone co-ordinator. At that time we had 84 soup kitchens on the go... I'd have to shut the dispensary to go to the assembly. Someone would come round for their medicine but the doña wasn't there because she'd gone to the assembly.

However, other leaders do not feel the added strain, either because the extra work is not too demanding, because they see this as an investment rewarded by learning a new skill, or because the service benefits their families.

Benefits and sacrifices

Personal benefits and sacrifices

Women who get involved in connected activities, or those who work only on the food service side, can expect both personal and family benefits and sacrifices. However, in the soup kitchen, all the activities blend into a single daily experience, making it hard to pinpoint the area in which the learning or capacity-building process occurs.

In the case of simple soup kitchens, the chief benefit is access to cheap meals. There is also a sense of security in knowing that one can count on the emotional support provided through working in a friendly environment. This helped women to learn to communicate better and to speak with greater confidence both inside and away from the soup kitchen. They said this had shown them how to function in a group and to get along better with others. They also appreciated the training they received and what they have learnt about management, organization, and women's rights.

However, there are frustrations and sacrifices. Many women are increasingly convinced that soup kitchens do not satisfy their economic needs because they do not undertake activities to supplement their incomes, while their organizational or cooking efforts are unpaid. Additionally, many soup kitchen leaders are so over-burdened that their personal and family lives suffer. And the soup kitchens are often the scene of fierce and difficult disputes between members.

Soup kitchens with connected activities also have their share of benefits and sacrifices. Benefits include learning new skills (e.g. guinea-pig breeding, bread-making, pharmaceuticals management) or acquiring knowledge that can quickly be of use in the home (e.g. administering injections, treating illness, early child education), or that could serve in the future to set up a small business or workshop. Membership in a soup kitchen also provides access to certain 'perks', like medical attention, extra food, or medicines. Some women benefit from the possibility of earning a part-time income by working in dispensaries administering injections or standing in for others unable to work their shifts.

One drawback to participating in connected activities is that women receive little financial incentive to do so. Another is that it can be difficult to replace those in charge because only they have the administrative or productive skills. These women are under pressure not to give up their work, in spite of the added burden and the conflict with their family responsibilities.

> I don't let on about my problems, at home at least. I've spent years... 11 years... in the soup kitchen. My kids were small back then. I've neglected them a lot. They're older now. There'd be no point leaving them breakfast served on the table or taking them their lunch: 'Here's your lunch. Eat.' I've treated them like objects. Now time has passed and they say to me: 'Mum, you spend loads of time at the soup kitchen and hardly any with us.' They're right.

Personal changes

Involvement in connected activities has changed the way women perceive themselves. Although these changes are not radical or profound, they are important. When they first started managing soup kitchens, they were silent, submissive, unskilled and unsure of themselves. Now they have acquired confidence, self- assurance, knowledge, and self-esteem.

> Before I was stuck in the house and never went out. I looked after my kids and did the housework. Going out was good because I learnt to become a leader, to talk to people. I trained myself and became aware of reality: how we should be; how we should work. This has helped me to change. It's given me a different outlook on life. Now I feel more sure of myself, no longer worrying that someone's going to pull the wool over my eyes...

It is difficult to separate the impact of connected activities from that of the soup kitchen. Women's involvement in economic or social projects affects their personal development, teaching them to communicate and overcome the shyness and humility that had prevented them from expressing their views; the soup kitchen has given them the means to develop self-assurance and awareness of women's rights, and provided a space for leisure, emotional stability, and social contact.

Skills and capacity building

Women value the capacities and skills acquired through participating in a soup kitchen and connected activities. Access to information and capacity-building gives a boost to the self-assurance, feelings of power, and recognition from applying this knowledge, both at the soup kitchen, and in other spheres.

The basic skills acquired are to be able to cook low-cost quality meals for the community, and a considerable capacity for organization. Women who become involved in connected activities also develop the skills needed for a particular type of social service or productive enterprise. For example, the women who help run dispensaries learn about basic medicines, how to treat common complaints, administration, and first aid. The leaders who promote PRONEI learn how to negotiate with state education bodies, and have a greater capacity for organization and communicating information on children's rights. Productive activities teach women skills in areas such as business management, marketing, business administration, loan negotiation, and customer service.

Social recognition

The women feel that their work in soup kitchens is socially recognized by the community and/or by their organization, though the connected activities often suffer from the lack of interest from members and others who are not directly involved. However, these are accepted as making a social contribution at least by service-users if not by community groups and institutions.

Gender relations

Women's participation affects the relationships between couples and how the home is run. The main issue is women's need to find time for the activities and assemblies, which involves restructuring work and responsibilities, especially with respect to household chores and childcare.

> He would say, 'now you're working in the soup kitchen you forget about the children', but that's not true. I still do all the things I normally do, washing clothes and cleaning. It was only at first that he'd get a bit annoyed because I'd be called to an emergency meeting and I'd have to go, leaving the laundry half done, say, when I was supposed to wash that day. Then he'd say, 'You see. You couldn't do the laundry because of the soup kitchen'.

A woman's participation may not produce positive changes in her relationship with her partner, although the 'old-timers' have usually managed to get their partners to accept it, especially since the men cannot earn the family's keep.

> While he had a job he'd say that because of the soup kitchen you don't get anything done in the home, because of the soup kitchen you don't look after the kids as you used to, that what got him. He didn't know how to deal with his problems away from home, so he'd take it out on me... I'd wonder if he wasn't right, but then decided not to take any notice. I'd only be leaving

the soup kitchen for his sake so I decided to stand firm and that why I'm still here... I don't get bored with it. I've got to stay here because that's how I help. Even if its only a plate of food, it's still something. That shuts him up and he doesn't bother much any more. He's slowly coming to terms with my job.

Overall, however, women's involvement in soup kitchens has led to domestic tension and conflict. Sometimes the husband manages to forget his insecurity and distrust, while the women gain independence and confidence. However, it is rare for a husband to do his share of the housework: even when he is unemployed he is reluctant to help at home because he sees this as 'women's work'. It is usually the children — the daughters — who take on the household chores when their mothers are out. So, while men's initial rejection and hostility may have changed to resignation, appreciation, or even collaboration, there are no substantial or widespread changes towards gender equality and a fairer distribution of domestic labour.

Older children provide support by doing the housework and helping at the soup kitchen when they collect the day's meals. Children seem to recognize and value their mothers' contribution, but some are fiercely critical of the fact that they make no money, and imply that 'they are wasting their time.' Of course, each family situation influences how the children see things; but children tend to be more understanding and supportive than husbands.

Outlook for soup kitchen organizations

Soup kitchen and connected activities

Soup kitchen members know that they satisfy the food needs of the poor by providing low-cost and even free meals (for so-called 'welfare cases'). But they see the service merely as a palliative: if the kitchens were to disappear, there would be no solution to food shortages. However, many women probably feel the real solution lies within the family.

At the same time, women are also looking beyond the soup kitchen to ways to earn money for themselves and to secure employment. They do not see the connected activities as an effective means of solving their needs, nor as fulfilling their earlier expectations. On the face of it, women get involved in order to learn useful new skills.

Overall, the soup kitchens are the clearest and most solid example the members have of satisfying basic needs. The kitchens that also undertake social service activities are seen as benefiting the community, while those that only operate a meals service or income-generation activities are seen as benefiting only the members and their families. Some feel that the soup kitchens should stick to providing a meal service, while others believe they should address women's need for childcare, literacy, self-esteem training, and income-generation activities. Some, however, consider that the soup kitchen is not a suitable environment for addressing women-specific problems, arguing that women's problems — like domestic abuse — are private matters, or that women-specific problems should be dealt with by the state.

Leaders who are considering whether to start up connected activities are well aware of critical issues that must be resolved beforehand. Apart from the problems inherent in a any business activity, they understand the need for sound and efficient administration, which calls for dedication, time, and skills; care over the technical aspects of production; and machinery and equipment that are technologically competitive. External aspects mentioned were the importance of market research, publicity, and a marketing strategy to ensure the venture's profitability.

When embarking on social services, members emphasized the need for good co-ordination with state bodies like the Ministries of Health or Education, in order to optimize quality and gain support so that the activity can be properly structured and managed.

The soup kitchen women proposed three main courses of action:

1. *To improve the connected activity in progress:* Soup kitchens propose to continue and improve their existing activities. In income-generation activities this involves adapting administration and management, raising output and productivity, and improving product quality. The relationship with the soup kitchen would be unchanged, and the gains from the enterprise would benefit the collective. In social service activities, improvements would take the form of strengthening and expanding into other fields.

2. *To turn the activity into a small business:* This would involve volunteer work by members with the necessary skills and knowledge. Benefits would be individual, that is only for the members involved.

3. *To implement income-generation activities in those soup kitchens that currently offer only a meals service:* There is a strong desire for

productive activities, especially garment-making, since many soup kitchens have received donated machinery of this sort.

In summary, soup kitchens are much valued for their contributions to the living standards of members and their families. Connected activities are less appreciated because of the problems they entail. Paradoxically, however, the latter continue to generate high hopes in terms of the possibility of generating an income, whether collective or individual.

Relations with external bodies

Women do feel that soup kitchens should become less dependent on the government. Hence, there is a strong belief in the need to complete the enactment of Law 25307, since it will commit the state to providing consistent and substantial support that will meet the needs of soup kitchen organizations while moving away from a charity focus. According to the soup kitchen members, private agents compete with each other over delivery and type of food donated, and even insist on being the sole private supplier.

The women's main demands centre on basic community services such as water, electricity, and sewage; good quality food; infrastructure and equipment; financial incentives; and access to credit. Most grassroots organizations are relatively unaware of the changes taking place in the role of the state; changes which will do little to encourage the further consolidation of the soup kitchen organizations, or address anything other than short-term needs.

The women feel that government agencies and NGOs should help in developing co-ordinated platforms of action with other grassroots organizations, in order to make concrete plans and engage on a wider scale. The Federation of Organizations of Self-Managed Soup Kitchens of Lima and Callao has attempted to negotiate with the state. However, difficulties have arisen owing to the government's policy of non-negotiation with grassroots organizations, and to its disregard of the Federation by going directly to the grassroots with its support. The PRONAA (National Food Assistance Programme) is a prime example.

In spite of the apparent reluctance of private or state bodies to negotiate, there are areas such as health, food and income-generation where there is an opportunity for joint work and where the Federation could boost the state's poverty-focused efforts. The key to this lies in its organizational capacity, its knowledge, and its ability to develop criteria for focusing help on the poorest sectors.

In conclusion, our interviews suggest a need for a social strategy that takes women's demands into account, particularly their economic demands, while strengthening the soup kitchen movement as a civil organization.

Acknowledgement

INCAFAM, ALTERNATIVA and FOVIDA are grateful for support from the Andean Office of Oxfam-GB, particularly Gabriela Byron and Richard Hartill.

Notes

1 There are several types of grassroots women's food organizations: Mothers' clubs, soup kitchens and Glass of Milk Committees. In 1994, Lima had some 15,000 such organizations. According to 1991 figures, 570,000 meals were distributed in Metropolitan Lima daily, benefiting 13 per cent of poor families and 8.5 per cent of families overall (Ministry of Labour, 1992 Metropolitan Lima Households Survey, in National Report on Women, Fourth World Conference on Women, Ministry of Justice, 1995).

2 Henceforth, *soup kitchen* refers to both types of project.

3 One new sol equals approximately US$0.42.

4 Each type of organization has its own form of centralized, representative organ at metropolitan, provincial or departmental level. There is no body uniting them all, however.

5 'Welfare cases' are individuals or families unable to meet the cost of meals. Soup kitchens assume this cost until their circumstances improve.

■ **Luiba Kogan** *is Professor of Sociology and Research Methodology in the University of Lima and the Pacific University. She is also an independent consultant on gender and development, and a researcher on issues such as women and micro-enterprise. Other members of the research team included Carmen Javier, Leonor Espinoza, and Adela Rivera Santander (INCAFAM), Doris Mantilla and Josefina Huamán (ALTERNATIVA), and María del Carmen Bastos and Roelfien Haak (FOVIDA). This article was first published in* Development in Practice, *Volume 8, number 4, November 1998.*

Annotated Bibliography

Most cultures could draw on a long, if fragmented, tradition of scholars, writers, and political activists who have sought to understand and challenge the basis for women's oppression and social exclusion. Yet while contemporary women's studies, and specifically the 'women in development' (WID) and 'gender and development' (GAD) approaches have generated a vast amount of literature in the past 25 years, this work is still widely regarded as a specialised branch of development studies, rather than a necessary and integral component of mainstream thinking and practice. This Annotated Bibliography offers only a glimpse of the wealth of material now available in English. For reasons of space, we have not been able to include works by many seminal authors who have shaped Western analytical traditions, from the economist Esther Boserup to the political philosopher Simone de Beauvoir, the anthropologist Margaret Mead, the author Virginia Woolf, or the sociologist Ann Oakley, who first articulated the distinction between biological sex and social gender. Still less have we been able to include the many historical accounts of women's struggles to obtain and defend their basic rights, works not available in English, or polemical works by writers such as Germaine Greer, Kate Millett, or Dale Spender. We deeply regret that this has necessarily resulted in a somewhat Eurocentric collection, though we have sought where possible to include edited compilations that reflect a far wider authorship. We trust, however, that something of the varied legacies of leading women writers on development is reflected in this bibliography, which was compiled by Fenella Porter, an independent consultant on gender and development, with Deborah Eade, Editor of Development in Practice.

Books

Haleh Afshar (ed.): *Women and Empowerment: Illustrations from the Third World,* London: Macmillan Press, 1998.
With case studies from Latin America, Southeast Asia, and the Middle East, this volume explores the different experiences and roles played by agencies, donors, and recipients, and the way in which isolated groups who are engaged in political negotiations with the state can use links with the international empowerment agenda to strengthen their own position. Afshar is particularly renowned for her work on women and Islam. Recent books include *Women and Politics in the Third World*, Routledge, 1996; and (with Fatima Alikhan), *Empowering Women for Development: Experiences from some third world countries,* Booklinks Corporation, 1997.

Asoka Bandarage: *Women, Population and Global Crisis: A Political-economic Analysis,* London: Zed Books, 1996.
Offering a broad theoretical perspective of the debate on population, poverty, the environment, and security, this book brings out the dialectics of gender, race, and class on a global scale. The author shows how population control serves the interests of capitalism, industrialism, and patriarchy, and explores global visions of and efforts towards peace, justice, and ecology, all based upon partnership.

Maruja Barrig and Andy Wehrkamp (eds.): *Engendering Development: Experiences in Gender and Development Planning,* The Hague: NOVIB, 1994.
Covering issues from conceptual aspects of gender and women's autonomy to planning strategies and evaluation methodology, this book gathers the experiences of Latin American and Dutch development consultants in bringing a gender perspective to their work with local NGOs and international donors. A collection of personal reflections, the contributions offer perspectives on the usefulness of concepts and theoretical frameworks, both for individuals and for institutions. (Also available in Spanish.)

Olivia Bennett, Jo Bexley and Kitty Warnock (eds.): *Arms to Fight, Arms to Protect: Women Speak Out About Conflict,* London: Panos, 1995.
A collection of women's testimonies the psychological and physical damage of war, the battle for economic survival, and their efforts to rebuild their lives and those of their families and communities.

The Boston Women's Health Book Collective: ***Our Bodies Ourselves for the New Century,*** Boston: Touchstone, rev. 1998.
Written and researched by a feminist health education NGO, this handbook (originally published in 1973 and since translated into many languages) discusses a range of issues concerning women's health and includes sections on violence against women, abortion, the politics of women's health, sexual health, birth control, and sexually transmitted diseases.

Rosi Braidotti, Ewa Charkiewicz, Sabine Häusler, Saskia Wieringa: *Women, Environment and Sustainable Development: Towards a Theoretical Synthesis*, London: Zed Books, 1994.
This book clarifies the major political and theoretical issues at stake in debates on women, the environment, and sustainable development. The authors review feminist analysis of science and the power relations inherent in the production of knowledge, and examine ideas of alternative development, social ecology, and ecofeminism, based on such values as holism, mutuality, justice, autonomy, self-reliance, sustainability, and peace.

A. August Burns, Ronnie Lovich, Jane Maxwell and Katherine Shapiro: *Where Women Have No Doctor: A Health Guide for Women*, Basingstoke: Macmillan, 1998 (published by Hesperian in the USA).
An illustrated volume that combines self-help medical information with an understanding of the ways in which poverty, discrimination, and cultural beliefs affect women's health and limit their access to care. The volume covers information on women's sexual health, HIV/AIDS, pregnancy, birth, breastfeeding, mental health, rape, and violence as well as the health concerns of women with disabilities, girls, older women, and refugees.

Mayra Buvinic, Catherine Gwin and Lisa M. Bates: *Investing in Women: Progress and Prospects for the World Bank*, Washington DC: Johns Hopkins University Press, 1996.
This study examines World Bank lending intended to benefit women, and the way in which this influential financial institution has addressed the needs of half of the world's population. The authors examine the concepts of gender, mainstreaming, and participation, and discuss successful projects from which wider lessons can be drawn.

A. Chhachhi and R. Pittin: *Confronting State, Capital and Patriarchy: Women Organising the Process of Industrialisation*, London: Macmillan, 1996.
Based on the work of activists and researchers of women's and labour issues, with contributions mainly from Asia, Africa, and Latin America, this volume looks at the linkages between North and South, at the global nature of industrialisation, and at organising to confront economic structural adjustment policies.

Sylvia Chant: *Female Headed Households: Diversity and Dynamics in the Developing World*, Basingstoke: Macmillan, 1997.
The author explores the reasons for the phenomenon of women-headed households, their increased numbers worldwide, and their capacity for survival. Case studies from Mexico, Costa Rica, and the Philippines illustrate the varied routes by which low-income women become heads of household, and the outcomes for them and for other household members.

Nickie Charles and Helen Hintjens (eds.): *Gender Ethnicity and Political Ideologies*, London: Routledge, 1998.

Drawing on studies from Eastern Europe, France, Israel, and Chile, the volume is framed by concerns about how ethnicity and nationalism affect women, given the reality of political violence based on religion and ethnicity. Although not directly addressing questions of development, it provides a good analysis of complexities which gender and development practitioners all face.

Sarah Cummings, Henk van Dam and Minke Valk (eds.): *Gender Training: The Source Book*, Oxford: Oxfam GB and Amsterdam: KIT Press, Critical Reviews and Annotated Bibliographies Series, 1998.
While gender training theory and practice have been largely dominated by academic and development institutions in the North, training has also been undertaken and developed by gender specialists and practitioners in the South. Contributions are drawn from different regions and diverse fields, and an annotated bibliography includes journal articles, books, directories, and unpublished material from the South.

Nawal El Saadawi: *A Daughter of Isis*, London: Zed Books 1999.
The autobiography of a leading activist against women's oppression, particularly in the Middle East, and author of *The Hidden Face of Eve: Women in the Arab World* (Zed Books, 1980), and *Woman at Point Zero* (Zed Books,1983). El Saadawi addresses issues such as sexual aggression against girls, FGM, prostitution, sexual relations, marriage, and divorce, relating women's position in the Middle East to political struggles within Islam.

Diane Elson (ed.): *Male Bias in the Development Process*, Manchester: Manchester University Press, 1991.
In this compilation of the arguments underpinning feminist economic critiques of development, six authors analyse the forms of male bias in the development process, its foundations, the way in which it changes over time, and the possibilities of overcoming it. Elson has written extensively on gender and economics.

Tovi Fenster: *Gender, Planning and Human Rights*, London: Routledge, 1999.
Based on detailed case studies in various multicultural societies, the author examines ways to integrate gender and human rights issues into planning, development, and policy making.

Nancy Folbre: *Who Pays for the Kids? Gender and the Structures of Constraint*, London: Routledge, 1994.
The author focuses on how and why people form overlapping groups that influence and limit what they want, how they behave, and what they get. The book takes a detailed look at feminist theory and political economy, and at collective action and patriarchal power. A section on how structures of constraint have shaped histories of social reproduction in Europe, the USA, Latin America, and the Caribbean illustrates the relationship between different forms of patriarchal power and the expansion of wage employment.

Anne-Marie Goetz (ed.): *Getting Institutions Right for Women in Development*, London: Zed Books, 1997.
This book argues that strategies to 'institutionalise' gender equality must involve fundamental change and institutional transformation. Contributions look into the structures, rules, and cultures of a range of development organisations from NGOs (including women's organisations) to multilateral agencies. A conceptual framework for exploring the gendered politics and procedures within institutions is applied to the empirical case-study material.

Irene Guijt and Meera Kaul Shah (eds.): *The Myth of Community: Gender Issues in Participatory Development*, London: IT Publications, 1998.
'Participatory approaches' have been widely adopted by NGOs, community-based organisations, and academic institutions. This volume takes a critical look at whether this work is benefiting women and men equally and argues that if community differences are simplified, power relationships poorly understood or misinterpreted, and conflicts avoided, women are the likely losers. Authors present experiences from Asia, Africa, Latin America, and the Caribbean, and analyse how women can be equitably and appropriately involved in participatory processes, and how gender issues can be tackled more meaningfully within communities.

Wendy Harcourt (ed.): *Feminist Perspectives on Sustainable Development*, London: Zed Books, 1994; and *Power, Reproduction and Gender: The Intergenerational Transfer of Knowledge*, London: Zed Books, 1997.
Harcourt has written widely on gender and development and her most recent work *Women@ Internet* (London: Zed Books, 1999) deals with the way in which Southern women relate to information technology. Power, Reproduction and Gender explores issues of health, empowerment, sexuality and reproductive rights, while Feminist Perspectives brings together diverse contributions on issues such as resource management, power and knowledge, culture, health, and economics.

Betsy Hartmann: *Reproductive Rights and Wrongs: The Global Politics of Population Control and Contraceptive Choice*, New York: Harper and Row, 1987.
Hartmann shows the link between the population 'problem' and the position of women in society, women's poverty, and the quality of healthcare available to them. She calls for a fundamental shift in population policy towards the expansion rather than the restriction of reproductive choice, and places the emphasis on women's control of their own bodies and their right to choose whether or not to give birth. A controversial book in its time, it set the scene for the reproductive rights movement and exposed the political motivation behind the 'population problem'.

Cecile Jackson and Ruth Pearson (eds.): *Feminist Visions of Development: Gender Analysis and Policy*, London: Routledge, 1998.

This volume includes contributions from leading gender and development scholars, reviewing 20 years of work in this area. Addressing issues such as environment, education, population, reproductive rights, industrialisation, macroeconomic policy, and poverty, the authors re-examine previous structural analysis, asking whether feminist perspectives can further our understanding of development.

Rounaq Jahan: *The Elusive Agenda: Mainstreaming Women in Development,* London: Zed Books, 1995.
This book examines the response of international donors to the challenge of the international women's movement and its vision of fundamental social transformation. The author examines the contradictions between the movement's high-profile advocacy and the overall growth in women's poverty. Comparing donor priorities with those of their various funding partners, she argues that despite significant achievements, the vision of transformation has not informed this progress.

Patricia Jeffery and Amrita Basu (eds.): *Appropriating Gender: Women's Activism and Politicised Religion in South Asia*, London: Routledge, 1998.
Many women respond to religious and nationalist appeals, but they have also asserted their gender, class, caste, and regional identities and often challenged state policies and practices. Focusing on women in South Asia, this volume includes chapters on secularity and sexuality, class, sovereignty and citizenship, legal reform and the Muslim community, Hindu identity politics, and women's everyday experience of and responses to gender and religious identity.

Naila Kabeer: *Reversed Realities: Gender Hierarchies in Development Thought,* London: Verso, 1994.
Kabeer uncovers the deep biases which underpin mainstream economic development theory and account for the marginal status given to women's needs. in development policy. Criticising the usefulness of the 'poverty line', she examines alternative frameworks for analysing gender hierarchies, puts forward an analysis of the role of social relations embedded in the family, community, market, and state, and sets out the 'social relations framework' for understanding gender inequalities in the development process.

Mandy Macdonald, Ellen Sprenger, and Ireen Dubel: *Gender and Organisational Change: Bridging the Gap between Policy and Practice,* Amsterdam: KIT Press, 1997.
This book examines the need for donor and development agencies to practise the same ideals of gender equality as they ask of their 'partner' organisations, seeing this as 'clearly two sides of the same coin'. The authors look at the process of organisational change, at why organisations need to change, and how they resist doing so.

Maria Mies: *Patriarchy and Accumulation on a World Scale: Women in the International Division of Labour* (2nd edition), London: Zed Books, 1999.
Mies explores the history of the related processes of colonialism, the witch hunt and 'housewifisation', as well as issues such as women's work in the new international division of labour, increasing violence against women, the relationship between women's liberation and national liberation struggles, and why patriarchal coercion so often (re)asserts itself. First published in 1986, this book is a classic gender and development text.

Carol Miller and Shahra Razavi (eds.): *Missionaries and Mandarins: Feminist Engagements with Development Institutions*, London: IT Publications, 1998.
This volume examines the various strategies employed by women working to transform the bureaucratic structures of state organisations, multilateral institutions, and NGOs, in order to make them more gender-equitable. Authors examine these strategies in terms of institutional rules and procedures, and resource allocation, as well as at the more discursive level of constructing and contesting women's needs. While acknowledging the gendered nature of bureaucracies, institutions are shown not to be monolithic and impermeable.

V. M. Moghadam: *Women, Work and Economic Reform in the Middle East and North Africa*, Boulder CO: Lynne Rienner, 1998.
Moghadam has written extensively on women and identity, and other recent titles include *Gender and National Identity: Women and Politics in Muslim Societies* (Zed Books, 1994) and, with Nabil F. Dhoury, *Gender and Development in the Arab World* (Zed Books, 1995). *Identity Politics and Women: Cultural Reassertions and Feminisms in International Perspective* (Westview Press, 1994) addresses discourses on and movements based on religious, ethnic, and national identity. Gender and Development and Women, Work, and Economic Reform look at women's economic role in the Middle East and North Africa and, in the context of globalisation and the changing political economies of the Arab world, make connections between gender relations and economic reform.

Caroline O. N. Moser: *Gender Planning and Development: Theory, Practice and Training*, London: Routledge, 1993.
This book explores the relationship between gender and development, and presents the conceptual rationale for what is now a widely used tool commonly referred to as the 'Moser framework' of strategic and practical gender needs. Drawing on Maxine Molyneaux's earlier work on gender roles and interests, Moser identifies methodological procedures, tools, and techniques to integrate gender into planning processes and emphasises the role of gender training.

Martha Nussbaum and Jonathan Glover (eds.): *Women, Culture and Development: A Study of Human Capabilities*, Oxford: Clarendon Press, 1995 (Study for WIDER).
This volume explores the issues of women's quality of life, confronting charges of Western imperialism and criticising cultural relativism. Offering accounts of

gender justice and women's equality, contributors include Amartya Sen and Martha Chen, and are based on experiences in Asia, Latin America, and Africa.

Helen O'Connell: *Equality Postponed: Gender, Rights and Development,* Oxford: WorldView, and London: One World Action, 1996.
The author examines how women's struggles for equal rights are undermined by the economic policies of the international financial institutions and donor governments, in direct contradiction of their avowed support for women's rights and gender equality. Examples drawn from Asia, Africa, and Latin America show how economic policies depend on the existing and unequal division of rights and responsibilities between men and women, serving to perpetuate gender inequality.

Rosalind P. Petchetsky and Karen Judd (eds.): *Negotiating Reproductive Rights: Women's Perspectives Across Countries and Cultures,* London: Zed Books/IHRRAG, 1998.
This book grows out of four years of collaborative research and analysis by the International Reproductive Rights Research Action Group (IRRRAG) in Brazil, Egypt, Malaysia, Mexico, Nigeria, Philippines, and the USA. Based on individual and group interviews, the book asks whether and how ordinary women express a sense of self-determination in decisions about child-bearing, work, marriage, fertility control, and sexual relations. It examines the strategies employed with husbands, health providers, and the larger community over reproductive and sexual matters; and the role of economic constraints, religion, tradition, and motherhood.

V. Spike Peterson and Anne Sisson Runyan: *Global Gender Issues,* Boulder CO: Westview Press, 1993.
A textbook which offers a gender analysis of world politics, including women's access to political power and economic resources, and a gender-sensitive re-interpretation of international relations, political legitimacy, state security, and globalisation. Violence, security, labour, economics, and resources (equity and ecology issues) are also examined, and the politics of resistance is surveyed by analysing gender as a dimension of non-state, anti-state, and trans-state movements. A distinction is made between practical and strategic interests, and various movements (from revolutionary to sustainable ecology) are described.

J. J. Pettman: *Worlding Women: A Feminist International Politics,* London: Routledge, 1996.
The author argues that international relations is male gendered, although women are also (largely invisible) players in the world that international relations seeks to explain. Drawing on the work of Southern feminist thinkers such as Mohanty, Afshar, Kandiyoti, and Moghadam, and highlighting the growing visibility of women and feminist transnational organising, Pettman puts forward a 'feminist international politics' and discusses 'transnational feminisms'.

Sheila Rowbotham and Swasti Mitter (eds.): *Dignity and Daily Bread: New Forms of Economic Organising among the Poor Women in the Third World and the First*, London: Routledge, 1994.
Often employed in vulnerable positions in the informal sector, where their work remains invisible in economic calculations, and excluded from trade unions or job security, women workers have had to devise their own empowerment strategies. This book analyses how global economic change is affecting women internationally, and focuses on their responses to this. Contributors compare the lives of Third and First World women, and examine how women have resisted and reorganised existing forms of production in order to create alternative, more humane circumstances of work and daily life.

Carolyn Sachs: *Gendered Fields: Rural Women, Agriculture and Environment*, Boulder CO: Westview Press, 1996.
Focusing on land ownership and use, copping systems, and women's work with animals, the author uses a feminist and environmentalist approach in investigating how the changing global economy affects rural women. Women's multiple experiences are analysed in terms of their gender, class, and race. Examples from different countries show how environmental degradation is the result of economic and development practices that disadvantage women; and describe women's resistance and survival strategies in the face of these trends.

Krishna Sen and Maila Stiens (eds.): *Gender and Power in Affluent Asia*, London: Routledge, 1998.
Looking at femininities, public and private spheres, and the changing shapes of class and nation in Indonesia, Malaysia, Singapore, China, Vietnam, Thailand, and Philippines, contributors discuss the gendered nature of the processes of modernisation and globalisation. They demonstrate the importance of women's agency in transforming economics and ideologies, reveal the costs of authoritarianism and development that are borne by women, and describe the contradictory searches for new forms of autonomy.

Vandana Shiva and M. Shiva: *Women, Environment and Health: An Ecological and Feminist Perspective*, Penang: Third World Network, 1994. Also, Vandana Shiva: *Staying Alive: Women, Ecology and Development*, London: Zed Books, 1988, and *Ecofeminism*, London: Zed Books, 1993.
A writer and international activist on development, environment, and women, Shiva has come to exemplify the school of thought known as 'ecofeminism', which examines the position of women in relation to nature and links the violation of nature with the violation and marginalisation of women, particularly in the Third World.

Sinith Sittirak: *Daughters of Development: Women in a Changing Environment*, London: Zed Books, 1998.
Sittirak questions the meaning of 'development', asking what it means to development theorists, to the author's mother in Thailand, to feminists, and to

the author herself. An accessible read, it brings to light many questions regarding development of a Southern woman who refreshingly argues that while it is acceptable to quote the World Bank in academic work, it appears unacceptable to quote ordinary women and men from developing countries, such as her mother.

Edith Sizoo (ed.): *Women's LifeWorlds: Women's Narratives on Shaping their Realities*, London: Routledge, 1997.
This book presents personal narratives by 15 very different women who describe their own lives and those of their grandmothers, mothers, daughters, or other close female relatives. The collection represents the life-stories of women in Asia, Africa, Latin America, and Europe, spanning over a century, and challenges traditional assumptions about womanhood, life, society, culture, and religion.

Margaret C. Snyder: *Transforming Development: Women, Poverty and Politics*, London: IT Publications, 1995.
Snyder, the founding director of UNIFEM, describes its beginnings, examines its work, and looks at the long-term effects of projects that have come to an end. She locates UNIFEM as a UN organisation, and describes the struggle to integrate its priorities and work with women into the development 'mainstream', viewing it within the wider context of women transforming development.

Kathleen Staudt: *Policy, Politics and Gender: Women Gaining Ground*, West Hartford CT: Kumarian, 1998.
The author underlines the need to analyse institutions in their political context, in order to understand why gender inequities persist and how they can be addressed. She shows how feminists have engaged with development policy in the last 30 years, logging both successes and failures, and setting out to inspire new generations to take informed and strategic activism in pursuit of gender justice. Staudt is also the author of *Women, International Development and Politics: The Bureaucratic Mire* (updated), Temple University Press, Philadelphia, 1997.

Jane Stein: *Empowerment and Women's Health: Theory, Methods, and Practice*, London: Zed Books, 1997.
A book that links development, women's empowerment, and women's health, and puts forward a new approach to researching, evaluating, and caring for women's health. The study locates women's circumstances and their health in the context of international development policies and offers an analysis of the interwoven factors. It also examines connections that escape narrower attempts to isolate remediable causes, and makes a powerful case for an international feminist health agenda.

Lynne Stephen: *Women and Social Movements in Latin America*, London: Latin America Bureau, 1998.
The author looks at women's grassroots activism in Latin America, particularly its combined commitment to basic survival and challenging women's

subordination to men. Women activists insist that issues such as rape, abuse, and reproductive control cannot be divorced from women's concerns about housing, food, land, and healthcare. The book includes interviews with activists, detailed histories of organisations and movements, and a theoretical discussion of gender, collective identity, and feminist anthropology and methods.

Irene Tinker (ed.): *Persistent Inequalities: Women and World Development,* Oxford: Oxford University Press, 1990.
Synthesising research done in the 1970s and 1980s on the roles of women in economic development, this anthology provides a historical and political overview of the field. Contributors include Esther Boserup, whose work established the theoretical foundation for the study of women's roles in economic development. A standard resource in women's studies, political science, sociology, development economics, and gender and development.

Nalini Visvanathan, Lynn Duggan, Laurie Nisonoff and Nan Wiegersma (eds.): *Gender and Development Reader,* London: Zed Books, 1998.
A comprehensive reader, with contributions that are essential reading for anyone involved in gender and development, including 'classics' which have not been published in earlier anthologies (e.g. Kandiyoti's 'Bargaining with Patriarchy' and Mohanty's 'Under Western Eyes'). It includes an introduction to the field, sections on households and families, women in the global economy, social transformation, and women organising. The main questions facing gender and development activists, practitioners, and researchers are addressed, and theoretical debates are illustrated by case studies drawn from all world regions.

Georgina Waylen: *Gender in Third World Politics,* Buckingham: Open University Press, 1996.
Politics in this book covers both 'high politics' and political activity at the grassroots, with a focus on women's organisations. The author examines the impact of policy and politics on gender relations and on different groups of women, developing the analysis through a study of different political formations: colonialism, revolution, authoritarianism, and democracy and democratisation.

Sarah White: *Arguing with the Crocodile: Gender and Class in Rural Bangladesh,* Dhaka: University Press Ltd, 1992.
This book raises key issues about the relationship between class, culture and gender, women's power, and feminist research. Criticising the 'women and development' (WAD) approach, White argues that power and power relations are central to gender relations, and that the key lies in examining the relationships within which productive and reproductive work is carried out. Although based on fieldwork in Bangladesh, this book is significant in international gender and development debates.

Saskia Wieringa (ed.): *Subversive Women: Women's Movements in Africa, Asia, Latin America and the Caribbean*, London: Zed Books, 1996.
An anthology of feminist writings from Africa, Asia, Latin America, and the Caribbean, which demonstrates the complexity, diversity, and courage of Southern women's movements and organisations. Contributors look at their own countries and the forms of resistance to colonial policy and patriarchy, and explore both Northern and Southern definitions of 'feminism'. Throughout, a historical perspective shows that women have always subverted the codes that determine the spaces in which they move, and have empowered themselves as well as actively resisting the prevailing power relations.

Women in World Development Series, London: Zed Books, prepared by the Joint UN NGO Group on *Women and Development.*
Each title outlines issues and debates on a given theme and includes an introduction to resources and guidance on how to use the books for training and discussion purposes. Titles include: *Women and Literacy* (Marcela Ballara), *Women and Disability* (Esther R. Boylan), *Refugee Women* (Susan Forbes Martin), *Women and Empowerment* (Marilee Karl), *Women at Work* (Susan Leather), *Women and the Family* (Helen O'Connell), *Women and the Environment* (Annabel Rodda), *Women and Health* (Patricia Smyke), *Women and Human Rights* (Katarina Tomasevski), *Women and War* (Jeanne Vickers), *Women and the World Economic Crisis* (Jeanne Vickers).

Kate Young, Carol Wolkowitz, Roslyn McCullagh (eds.): *Of Marriage and the Market: Women's Subordination Internationally and its Lessons* (2nd edition), London: Routledge, 1984.
A compilation of influential feminist thinkers including Olivia Harris, Maxine Molyneux, and Ann Whitehead, which addresses the question of universal gender inequality. Representing a critique of both traditional Marxist theory and of contemporary socialist practice, this volume marks the international feminist challenge of the 1980s to the orthodox interpretations of women's position in society. Kate Young is also the author of *Planning Development with Women: Making a World of Difference*, The Macmillan Press, London 1993 (reprinted 1994), and the founder of Womankind Worldwide.

Nira Yuval-Davis: *Gender and Nation*, London: Sage, 1997.
Yuval-Davis provides an authoritative overview and critique of writings on gender and nationhood, presenting an analysis of the ways in which gender relations affect and are affected by national projects and processes. Arguing that the construction of nationhood involves specific notions of 'manhood' and 'womanhood', she examines the contribution of gender relations to nationalist projects (the reproduction of culture and citizenship), as well as to national conflicts and wars, and explores the relations between feminism and nationalism.

Zed Books has an extensive list on gender and development, many of which are included in this bibliography. Other books published in 1998-9 include Saskia Everts: *Gender and Technology;* Christine Heward and Sheila Bunwaree (eds.): *Gender, Education and Development;* Pnina Werbner and Nira Yuval Davis (eds.): *Women, Citizenship and Difference;* and Marylin Porter and Ellen Judd (eds.): *Feminists Doing Development.*

Journals

Development in Practice published five times a year by Carfax on behalf of Oxfam GB. ISSN: 0961-4524. Editor: Deborah Eade.
A forum for practitioners, policy makers, and academics to exchange information and analysis concerning the social dimensions of development and humanitarian work. As a multidisciplinary journal of policy and practice, it reflects a wide range of institutional and cultural backgrounds and of professional experience. Other relevant titles in the Development in Practice Readers series include *Development and Social Diversity* (also published in Spanish), *Development and Rights*, and *Development and Social Action.*

Gender and Development (previously Focus on Gender) published three times a year by Oxfam GB. ISSN: 1355-2074. Editor: Caroline Sweetman.
A thematic forum for development practitioners, policy-makers, and activists on contemporary issues of gender and development. Recent topics include organisational culture, men and masculinity, education and training, violence against women, and religion and spirituality. Each issue of the journal is also published separately in book form.

Signs: Journal of Women and Culture in Society published quarterly by University of Chicago Press. ISSN: 0097-9740. Editors: Carolyn Allen and Judith A. Howard
A feminist scholarly journal, with recent articles on issues such as women in the Vietnamese revolution, FGM, prostitution, and women in science and engineering. The broad themes, which are also of interest to activists and feminist development practitioners and researchers, are also brought together in a series of occasional readers.

Feminist Review published three times a year by Routledge. ISSN: 0141-7789. Editors: Feminist Review Collective.
Offers a combination of academic and activist papers on feminist theory, race and ethnicity, class and sexuality, black and Third World feminism, cultural studies, and includes photographs, poems, and cartoons. Feminist Review is much used in women's studies courses and within the women's movement.

Feminist Economics published three times a year by Routledge. ISSN: 1354-5701. Editor: Diana Strassman.
A forum for dialogue and debate about feminist economic perspectives, the journal aims to enlarge and enrich economic discourse in order to contribute to improving the living conditions of all children, women, and men.

Reproductive Health Matters published twice-yearly by Blackwell Science Ltd. ISSN: 0968-8080. Editor: Marge Berer.
Offers in-depth analysis of women's reproductive health, from a woman-centred perspective, and is an authoritative and broad source of information on the central issues of reproductive health and rights.

Aviva, 41 Royal Crescent, London W11 4SN, UK. Website: www.aviva.org
An International Women's Listings Magazine ('webzine') which provides news, extensive free listings on women's groups (both non-government and inter-government), courses, and events around the world on a wide range of themes. With many leads and 'links', this is an excellent starting point for web-based research on international women's activism.

Networks and organisations

Association of Women In Development (AWID), 1511 K Street, NW, Suite 825, Washington DC 20005, USA. E-mail: awid@awid.org
An international membership organisation of practitioners, scholars, and policy-makers who are committed to gender equality and a just and sustainable development process.

CHANGE, 106 Hatton Square, 16-16a Baldwin Gardens, London EC1N 7RJ, UK. E-mail: CHANGE_CIC@compuserve.com:
CHANGE mainly carries out advocacy on women's human rights. It offers training courses at the UN Commission for Human Rights and has a range of publications including Georgina Ashworth (ed.) *A Diplomacy of the Oppressed: New Directions in International Feminism*, London: Zed Books, 1995; Georgina Ashworth; *Changing the Discourse: A Guide to Women and Human Rights, 1993;* and *Of Violence and Violation: Women and Human Rights*, 1996.

Center for Women's Global Leadership (Global Center), Douglass College, Rutgers University, 160 Ryders Lane, New Brunswick, New Jersey 08901-8555, USA. E-mail: cwgl@igc.org Website: www.rci.rutgers.edu/~cwgl
The Global Center develops and facilitates women's leadership for women's human rights and social justice worldwide, placing the emphasis on violence against women, sexual and reproductive health, and socio-economic well-being through its twin programmes in advocacy and global education.

DAWN, c/o Claire Slatter (current president). E-mail: dawn@is.com.fj
A network of Southern scholars and activists concerned with the impact of current development models on women and on the nature of poverty. A comprehensive presentation of DAWN's vision and agenda is Gita Sen and Caren Grown, *Development Crises and Alternative Visions: Third World Women's Perspectives*, New York: Monthly Review Press, 1987. In the lead-up to the 1994 International Conference on Population and Development (ICPD), DAWN representative Sonia Corréa (with Rebecca Reichmann) produced *Population and Reproductive Rights: Feminist Perspectives from the South*, London: Zed Books (in association with DAWN). The rotating secretariat is presently based in Fiji.

Feminist.com, Website: www.feminist.com
An internet page, with information on activism, resources, women-owned businesses, women's health, a 'query service' on feminism, and an online 'bookstore'.

IIAV, Obiplein 4, 1094 RB Amsterdam, The Netherlands. E-mail: info@iiav.nl Website: www.iiav.nl
An international information centre and archives for the women's movement, including an extensive library on women and women's studies, and a database search facility.

INSTRAW (UN International Research and Training Institute for the Advancement of Women), EPS-A314, Box 52-4121, Miami, Florida 33152, USA. E-mail: instraw.hq.sd@codetel.net.do
A UN body to promote and undertake policy-oriented research and training programmes, to contribute to the advancement of women worldwide, and to contribute to a global agenda of gender equality and sustainable development. INSTRAW focuses on the gender impact of globalisation.

Inter-Africa Committee on Traditional Practices Affecting the Health of Women and Children, c/o Economic Commission for Africa, PO Box 3001, Addis Ababa, Ethiopia (Liaison Office: 147 rue de Lausanne, CH-1202 Geneva).
A pan-African network that works for the health of women and children by fighting harmful and promoting beneficial traditional practices through training programmes, information campaigns, research, and educational and non-formal materials.

International Women's Tribune Center (IWTC), 777 UN Plaza, New York, NY 10017, USA. E-mail: iwtc@igc.apc.org
IWTC is a major information, education, communication, networking, technical assistance, and training resource for women, and produces a range of regular and occasional publications.

Women's International Information and Communication Service (ISIS)
Originally one organisation, ISIS published Women in Development: A resource guide for organisation and action (London: IT Publications, 1983), a guide for WID activists. Now three separate organisations:
Isis International, which has an English-language publication: PO Box 1837, Quezon City Main, Quezon City 1100, Philippines. E-mail: isis@mnl.sequal.net. Website: www.sequel.net/~isis
Isis-WICCE, PO Box 4934, Kampala, Uganda. E-mail: isis@starcom.co.ug, a women's international resource and information centre with regular publications.
Isis Internacional, Casilla 2067, Correo Central, Santiago, Chile. E-mail: isis@reuna.cl, which holds an extensive resource and documentation centre, and runs programmes on violence against women and women's health, as well as a publishing programme.

Kali for Women, B1/8 Hauz Khas, New Delhi 110 016, India. Fax: +91 (0)11 686 4497.
A feminist publishing house in India run by Urvashi Butalia who, with Rita Menon, is author of *Making a Difference: Feminist Publishing in the South* (Oxford: Bellagio Studies in Publishing, 1996). Kali for Women publishes a wide range of materials, books as well as monographs, including papers by leading activists such as Kamla Bhasin (author of *What is Feminism?* and *What is Patriarchy?*).

Match International Centre, 1102-200 Elgin Street, Ottawa, Ontario, Canada. E-mail: matchint@web.apc.org.
A feminist development organisation committed to a vision of development that requires the eradication of all forms of injustice.

Oxfam GB, 274 Banbury Road, Oxford, OX2 7DZ, UK. Website: www.oxfam.org
Oxfam's progressive gender policy is reflected across its publishing programme. Recent titles include: Fenella Porter et al. (eds.): *Gender Works: Oxfam Experience in Policy and Practice*, 1999; Candida March and Ines Smyth: *A Guide to Gender-Analysis Frameworks,* 1999; Jo Rowlands: *Questioning Empowerment: Working with Women in Honduras,* 1997; Deborah Eade and Suzanne Williams: *The Oxfam Handbook of Development and Relief,* 1995; and Suzanne Williams, with Jan Seed and Adelina Mwau: *The Oxfam Gender Training Manual*, 1994 (also available in Spanish and Portuguese).

Vrouvenberaad Ontwikkelingssamenwerking, PO Box 77, 2340 AB Oegstgeest, The Netherlands. E-mail: vboswide@antenna.nl Website: www.vrouwen.net/vboswide/
A network of gender experts on international development aid with a quarterly publication, Connections: gender perspectives on international cooperation.

UNIFEM, 304 East 45th Street, 15th floor, New York, NY 10017, USA. Website: www.unifem.undp.org; website for the UN system for women: www.un.org/womenwatch/
UNIFEM promotes the participation of women in all levels of development planning and practice, and acts as a catalyst within the UN system, supporting efforts that link the needs and concerns of women to critical issues at every level. Publications include Ana Maria Brasileiro (ed.): *Gender and Sustainable Development: A New Paradigm — Reflecting on Experience in Latin American and the Caribbean*, New York: UNIFEM, 1996; Noeleen Heyzer et al.: *A Commitment to the World's Women: Perspectives on Development for Beijing and Beyond*, 1995; UNIFEM (with UN-NGLS): *Putting Gender on the Agenda: A Guide to Participating in UN World Conferences*, 1995; and Mary B. Anderson: *Focussing on Women: UNIFEM's Experience in Mainstreaming*, 1993.

Women's International Network (WIN), 187 Grant Street, Lexington, MA 02173-2140, USA. E-mail: winnews@igc.org
WIN runs a technical assistance and consulting service for women's development. Its publication WIN News is an open communication system by, for, and about women of all backgrounds, beliefs, nationalities, and age groups.

Women's Global Network for Reproductive Rights, NZ Voorburgwal 32, 1012 RZ Amsterdam, The Netherlands. E-mail: office@wgnrr.nl
Publication: WGNRR Newsletter. The Network is an autonomous network of groups and individuals in every continent who support reproductive rights for women. Building links and exchanges between women worldwide, WGNRR organises and participates in international campaigns and actions, particularly for the prevention of maternal mortality and morbidity.

Women, Environment and Development Organisation (WEDO), 355 Lexinton Ave, 3rd floor, New York, NY 10017, USA. Website: www.wedo.org
An international advocacy network that seeks to transform society through the empowerment of women, and focuses on lobbying at the UN level and monitoring UN agreements.

Women, Law and Development International, 1350 Connecticut Ave, NW, Suite 407, Washington DC 20036, USA. E-mail: wld@wld.org Website: www.wld.org
This NGO promotes women's full and equal participation in all nations by advancing universal respect for human rights, expanding rights education and legal literacy among women, and challenging discriminatory socio-economic barriers. It has inspired similar regional networks, for example Women in Law and Development in Africa (WiLDAF) and Asia Pacific Forum on Law and Development (APWLD). In Latin America, CLADEM is a key network of organisations that work to defend women's legal and human rights.

Publishers addresses

Blackwell Publishers, 108 Cowley Road, Oxford OX4 1JF, UK. Fax: +44 (0)1865 791 347.

Carfax Publishing Company, PO Box 25, Abingdon OX14 3UE, UK. Fax: +44 (0)1235 401 550.

The Clarendon Press, Walton Street, Oxford OX2 6DP, UK.

Harper and Row Publishers, 10 East 53rd Street, New York, NY 10022, USA.

The Hesperian Foundation, 1919 Addison St #304, Berkeley CA 94704, USA. E-mail: hesperian@igc.apc.org

Intermediate Technology Publications, 103-105 Southampton Row, London WC1B 4HH, UK. Fax: +44 (0)171 436 2013. E-mail: itpubs@itpubs.org.uk

Johns Hopkins University Press, Journals Publishing Division, 2715 North Charles Street, Baltimore MD 21218-4363, USA. Fax: +1 (410) 516 6968.

Kali for Women, B1/8 Hauz Khas, New Delhi 110 016, India. Fax: +91 (0)11 686 4497.

KIT Press (Royal Tropical Institute), PO Box 95001, 1090 HA Amsterdam, The Netherlands. Fax: +31 (0)20 5688 286.

Latin America Bureau, 1 Amwell Street, London EC1R 1UL, UK. Fax: +44 (0)171 278 0165.

Macmillan Press Ltd, Houndmills, Basingstoke RG21 6XS, UK. Fax: +44 (0)1256 842084.

Manchester University Press, Oxford Road, Manchester M13 9NR, UK. Fax: (0) 161 274 3346.

Novib, Mauritskade 9, 2514 HD The Hague, The Netherlands. Fax: +31 70 361 4461.

The Open University Press, Celtic Court, 22 Ballmoor, Buckingham MK18 1XW, UK.

Oxfam Publishing, Oxfam, 274 Banbury Road, Oxford OX2 7DZ, UK. Fax: +44 (0)1865 313790.

Oxford University Press, Walton Street, Oxford OX2 6DP, UK. Fax: +44 (0)1865 556 646.

Panos Publications, 9 White Lion Street, London N1 9PD, UK. Fax: +44 (0)171 278 0345. E-mail: panoslondon@gn.apc.org

Lynne Rienner Publishers, 1800 30th St, Boulder, Colorado 80301, USA. Fax: +1 (303) 444 0824.

Routledge, 11 New Fetter Lane, London EC4P 4EE, UK. Fax: +44 (0)171 842 2302.

Sage Publications Limited, 6 Bonhill Street, London EC2A 4PU, UK. Fax: +44 (0)171 374 8741.

University of Chicago Press, 5801 Ellis Avenue, 4th Floor, Chicago IL 60637, USA.
Fax: +1 (773) 202 9756.

University of Pennsylvania Press, 418 Service Drive, Philadelphia PA 19104-6097, USA.

The University Press Ltd, Red Crescent Building, 114 Motijheel C/A, GPO BOx 2611, Dhaka 1000, Bangladesh.

Verso, 6 Meard Street, London W1V 3HR, UK. Fax: +4 (0)171 734 0059.

Westview Press, 5500 Central Avenue, Boulder, Colorado 80301-2877, USA. Fax: +1 (303) 449 3356.

Worldview Publications, PO Box 595, Oxford OX2 6YH, UK.

Zed Books, 7 Cynthia Street, London N1 9JF, UK. Fax: +44 (0)171 833 3960.